The Lost Library

THE LOST LIBRARY

The Autobiography of a Culture

WALTER MEHRING

Translated by Richard and Clara Winston

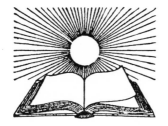

WESTHOLME
Yardley

Originally published in 1950 by the Bobbs-Merrill Company, Inc.

Westholme Publishing, LLC
904 Edgewood Road
Yardley, Pennsylvania 19067

Visit our Web site at www.westholmepublishing.com

First Printing: September 2010
10 9 8 7 6 5 4 3 2 1

ISBN: 978-1-59416-121-6

Printed in the United States of America.

To my wife

Whom I love as I once loved
France and Europe

Contents

Contents

PART I

My Father's Library

Chapter I

*The Regiments of Progress—The Battle of the
Books in St. James's Library and the First
World War—So Many Dead Bodies and No
Souls—Death and the Enlightened Man.*

THE LAST PLACE where I felt at home was Vienna. This
was before Vienna fell and I was still surrounded by all
the books of my father's library. I cannot remember how
often since then the view outside my window has changed
—a view more than once obstructed by bars. But in
Vienna I still had my legacy of books; they had been
salvaged thanks to the Czech Embassy in Berlin, and
especially to the efforts of the Embassy attaché, Camill
Hoffmann, who was a lyric poet of the Prague caba-
listic-minded group, which numbered among its members
Werfel, Meyrink, Kafka and Čapek. Hoffmann was later
burned alive in a crematorium.

In former times, when I was on a jaunt and not on the
run, I always took a few books with me for bedside reading.

Hans Christian Andersen's tales went with me to
Odense, Denmark, to the street where everyone's name
was Andersen, and to his provincial gabled house. Here
everything smelled like a museum. In the author's spotless
and moldering study lay the bereaved top hat, the worn-
out galoshes of fortune and a battered suitcase that would
fly up the chimney with you if you pressed the latch. And

everywhere in the house the articles which were his characters still waited around, as though Hans Christian, in a lace cap and apron, his favorite costume, were just around the corner, gossiping with the old women of the neighborhood.

I took with me on my first sea voyage the works of Captain Marryat and Defoe's *Robinson Crusoe* (just in case), for I sailed from Hamburg through a heavy gale on a coal freighter bound for Newcastle.

Louis Sébastien Mercier's prerevolutionary panorama of French life, *Tableau de Paris,* and Balzac's *La Comédie Humaine,* I took with me on my long-planned move to Paris. They were still as useful as when they were written as guidebooks to French bureaucracy, French justice and French newspapers.

Ovid's *Metamorphoses* went with me to the Mediterranean, where the phenomena described there still occur in the noon hush, the witching hour in the olive groves which is known as the hour of Pan.

Cervantes I took with me everywhere I went; no matter what folly I committed, I always felt better for reading *Don Quixote* afterward. It also served as a textbook for studying the travesty of freedom in the Spanish Republic, whose end was to be as ignoble as the *tragedia soldades* of orphaned Sancho Panza and the masterless steed Rosinante.

Just for a whim, I took *Peer Gynt,* the Norwegian Faustus-Don Quixote, to the village of Lofthus on the Hardanger Fiord. I stayed at the very hotel where Ibsen labored on the play. And beside me at table, where salmon was served for every meal including breakfast, sat a silver-maned, female mountain troll who puffed clouds of smoke from fat cigars. She was the widow of the composer of the *Peer Gynt Suite,* Edvard Grieg—beloved Solveig, now eighty years old.

The Book of Exodus accompanied me to the Saharan pyramid city of Ghardaïa, in the Algerian Mzab, where the Abadites live in their Islamic *golus.* Among them dwell the last authentic Israelites, who call themselves Ishuruni—the Upright.

So everywhere I went I had at least a few of my father's books at hand, a bit of home. And when I left the library in the lurch, when I fled headlong from Vienna, hearing the Sodomite yowls from every lane and alley, when I dodged through the raging mob and zigzagged through the darkness of the park to the railroad station, passing by the open casement window of my room—I suddenly understood the angel's advice to Lot not to look back upon Sodom and Gomorrah.

And I kept my eyes fixed ahead, lest I be changed into a pillar of salt.

I left behind me the protecting wall that my father had once built up out of thousands of volumes—each one a product of the white magic of Enlightenment. By their combined exorcisms my father, serene atheist and believer in progress that he was, thought himself well defended against relapses into superstition, against howling with the werewolves.

Now the books had been taken prisoner. But even so they were not silenced. They still stood intransigent, shoulder to shoulder, always ready to offer resistance—though among themselves they still disagreed about God and the world.

"God exists because my reason must assume him in

the world order as the geometricians assume their diagrams . . ." the Cartesians said.

"God has arisen, as it were, by a process of distillation from many gods," Friedrich Engels, the materialist, broke in, without even noticing the weak spot in the chain of their argument.

"God is a gaseous vertebrate," the Darwinist professor, Ernst Haeckel stated. On the lecture platform he would throw a challenging look around to see whether any layman dared to argue.

His right to speak unacknowledged, the most impudent of the literati—Heinrich Heine—seized the floor: "The interminable hushaby-lullaby of Heaven . . ." But my father would forgive *him* any amount of impertinence.

Henri Beyle (Stendhal) could close argument by declaring: "The sole excuse for God is that he does not exist."

But the voice of Baudelaire resounded: "Even if God did not exist, religion would still be holy and divine. . . ."

This loosed a tumult from all sides: Snob! Renegade! Reactionary! To soothe all the ruffled temperaments, my father could always infuriate Baudelaire by quoting Voltaire: " 'Only a mole could have created all this glory,' said the mole. 'Nonsense, a June bug,' said the June bug."

"*Sic!*" my father had written on the margin. And since he had a blind religious faith in the enlightenment of the human species, he had cheerfully accepted six months' imprisonment as a Dreyfusard so that he might be eligible for the Order of the Irreligiosi.

"All the books will be yours when I am dead," my father used to say whenever I came to borrow a volume from him. This, then, was to be my legacy. Included was the ample central bookcase, more than half filled with difficult Greeks and Latins—Plutarch, Thucydides, Tacitus, Suetonius—who were nothing to me but exasperating subjects for school themes, for calisthenic exercises in grammar and syntax, further complicated by all the torments of Greek aorists. How could I ever imagine that I myself would one day meet with storm troopers like the red-shirted cryptia of Sparta, with Nero's incendiaries and other such legendary horrors? Where was it written that the educated sons of the upper-middle-class intellectual élite who made pilgrimages to Bayreuth festivals and to Maeterlinckian dream temples, who went overboard for the Pre-Raphaelites, Debussy and the socialist oratory of Jean Jaurès, who peppered their discussions with maxims from Nietzsche, paradoxes from Oscar Wilde and sarcasms from Anatole France—where was it written that the schoolmates who sat beside me in the Gymnasium would start believing in witches, would take part in pogroms and would generally run amuck?

At the time I would normally have thought that classics existed only for penitential purposes, to provide a chance for tough schoolmasters to cane us. I would have thought the classics consisted only of such maxims as *dulce et decorum est pro patria mori,* if I had not come across "unexpurgated" editions in my father's library. Even then I feared that Amor and Psyche were purely legendary phenomena, that such divine nakedness, such firm marble curves existed only in torsos dug out of the rubble of the Acropolis, or on the frescoes exhumed from the lava of Pompeii; that lush courtesans, lustful nuns and complaisant shepherdesses could be found only in Boccaccio's spicy

15

anecdotes, in the *Heptameron* of Marguerite de Navarre
or in Balzac's *Droll Stories*. My firm belief was that even
the *midinettes* and painters' models were only fictional
characters and showed so much froufrou and lace under-
clothing only in Maupassant studios. For the ladies that
I had any opportunity to observe were always wrapped
up in trailing, sacklike garments buttoned right up to the
chin.

I had no preparation whatsoever for a martyr's life,
although that was the kind of life I had to take up in order
to keep my integrity as my father had taught me I must—
though he had not the faintest inkling of what was to
come. As Horace has it:

> *Justum et tenacem propositi virum*
> *Non civium ardor prave iubetium*
> *Non vultus tyranni*
> *Mente quatit solida . . .*

My earliest glimpse of the ugly future came when I sat
in my father's library and listened to the stories of a colleague of his, a Russian writer who was telling about the
hardships and tortures he had endured in Siberian prisons.
Shortly before that, my father had given me Dostoevsky's
The House of the Dead to read, and *Siberia* by Kennan,
the heroic American journalist. This was the first unbiased
report from a Siberian prison camp. Kennan had obtained
forged deportation papers and had let himself be transported. Later on he escaped, managed to steal secret orders from the Czar's desk, and by publicizing these had
aroused public opinion in all free countries.

The last visitor my father received in his library was
Ernst Toller, at that time a student who had enlisted in

the army as a volunteer. On his way to the trenches of the First World War, Toller stopped off to show my father a few timid beginner's poems.

An hour later my father was reading aloud to me. In the middle of a sentence from Kant's *Critique of Pure Reason,* he started up from his desk and collapsed into my arms.

"Hold me up" were his last words.

And then I had to take over my legacy.

In the twenty-three years which followed that day, I used it less and less.

Most of the books seemed to me stripped of magic and power in the same way that the totems and talismans, the spears and clubs of some savage lose all value after his tropical paradise has been remodeled into a commonwealth, after slavery has been abolished and a proletariat created, after all the blessings of progress have been showered on him: planned economy, trade unions, barrack settlements, compulsory vaccination and compulsory military service. But with me the process was reversed. I had been living in an advanced culture, in an enlightened kingdom of the intellect. And suddenly I was driven out by highly cultivated barbarians, by technically trained primitives, by uniformed cannibals. . . .

The idols of the new savages were the lowest sort of petty spirits, the sort of men my father would have laughed at and the nineteenth century despised. The principles of humanism and humanity lay shattered and buried in the sands of the desert they had created; they had flung down and trampled on all principles of truth.

So I left Germany and went into exile. I went up and

down over Europe. Then one day I grew tired of my aimless wanderings and settled down in the gay and slowly parching oasis of Vienna. By devious means I managed to have my legacy of books sent after me. In going to so much trouble I was flouting the basic rule of exile, which prohibits such pleasures as settling down where you like to be or reading whatever you enjoy.

In the secondhand bookshops along the Graben in Vienna could be found everything an infidel's heart desired, and in the cafés the authors, believers and unbelievers both, sat unanimously on the scoffers' bench. No censor could have cut them off from the banned literature because they had it in their heads. But I was not so much interested in individual books as in the unique historical, aesthetic and philosophical configurations in my father's library. Together they formed his particular horoscope of the nineteenth century. And I wanted to examine that horoscope once more and to see its pattern, no matter how fantastic or catastrophic the prediction.

The books had been delivered at dawn by several grumpy truck drivers whose Viennese imaginations undoubtedly stocked the many crates with thoroughly tangible luxury items. All that first morning I read madly.

A man can become as addicted to reading as to any other intoxicant. That is especially true for Europeans, who from long heritage are as dangerously given to books as they are to alcohol. You reach for a book as you do for a drink, to escape the depressing banality of newspaper headlines, to wash away the disgusting aftertaste of the medicines served up in the hospital known as Contemporary Civilization. And there's nothing so good as a potent brew of well-aged pathos, preferably distilled in verse. At once you feel cleansed and ennobled. The trouble is that you don't stick to the select vintages very long. And in reading as in drinking you incline to mix the cocktail stiffer and stiffer; you are looking for self-assurance and for a general absolution.

And you find it. Suppose you have had outlandish desires of which you were ashamed, as you might be of a hidden deformity or a pathological disposition. Then, in the posthumous works of some genius whom you worship you find that he, made reckless by the euphoria of creation, has told secrets as shameful as your own. Mortal sins, hatred, spite, acts of malice which we would never stoop to, are unabashedly celebrated in the oldest texts. They are even to be found—no, they are especially to be found—in the epics of national heroes, in *Beowulf,* the *Song of Roland* and the *Nibelungenlied.* We drank in their blood-thirstiness with the mother's milk of our education. The sad fact is that even the reformers, the revolutionaries, the born Führers, the very literature-hating people who censor, ban and burn all contemporary writing, are poisoned through and through by reading. They have all imbibed their fanaticism from elsewhere—they are hardened drinkers of the rotgut manufactured by Draco, Jean Bodin, Hobbes and others, and they have committed their murderous reformist acts while in a state of hangover.

My father, who as I have said was a model pupil of critical reason, would never have suspected that the germs of "spiritualistic" epidemics lurked among the volumes of his library. He no more suspected this than the other cultured persons of his generation, all of whom were as solemn about compulsory education as their forefathers had been about attending church. Unaware of the possible evil effects of printed matter, they handled it with as much assurance as the thaumaturges in the experimental sciences handled plague cultures. They took no precautions even when dealing with the most dangerous components of the soul—genius and madness.

My father never realized—unless some sudden illumination came to him in the moment of death—that his study was a *fin-de-siecle* replica of an alchemist's chamber. That was what it was, for all its dated luxury, its Persian divan flanked by the white bearskin rug, its walls hung with political caricatures and with agnostic lithographs, its gasmantel lamp on the Empire bureau which was littered with review copies and fat scrolls of proof sheets. He never realized that all his life he had been a necromancer amid the martyrologies of natural selection and the abracadabra of positivism. It never occurred to him that he, one of the early battlers for freedom of thought, was still in Faust's "high-arched Gothic room":

> *Weh im Kerker noch . . .*
> *Beschraenkt mit diesem Buecherhauf*
> *Den Wuerme nagen, Staub bedeckt,*
> *Den bis ans hohe Gewoelb hinauf*
> *Ein angeraucht Papier umsteckt . . .*
> *Urvaeter-Hausrat drein gestopft . . .*

—that he, too, freethinker that he was, was still only a Faust marionette dangling above the stage of the mechanistic universe and put through the gestures of progress by the German Mephistopheles who made him travel round and round the circle of investigable reality. For all along he imagined that he and his fellow men were masters of their motions, were heading onward and upward on a straight course, and acting out of pure knowledge.

He was convinced that at the stroke of midnight on the New Year's Eve that marked the transition from the nineteenth to the twentieth century, the hour of intellectual liberation for the world had also struck. He was schooled in the magic formulas of objective research, armed with chemical compounds against the evil spirits of the air, the bacteria. Theoretical physics had immunized him against the "invisible rays" of the universe. His pact with socialism protected him against the underground powers, against eruptions from the lower depths of society. Thus armed, he was sure he was at one with "the starry sky above him and the moral law within him." He thought Faust's conjuring book was safe in his hands. And then the deviltry of uniforms and technology broke loose: the First World War.

My father was at the time in a medically approved resort for sufferers from heart disease. The regimen forbade writing and all other excitement. No sooner had he read the news of the assassination at Sarajevo of the Austrian crown prince than he rose from his reclining chair and, in the prophetic tones of a seasoned newspaperman, declared to the moribund invalids around him: "This means world war."

He took the next train back to his books. Past his train streamed the troop trains, filled with humanistic young men, the children of a working class imbued with the ideals of international socialism. Each conscript carried his iron rations, his handbook of military regulations, his army prayer book and—my father comforted himself with the German propaganda story—Goethe's *Faust* and Nietzsche's *Zarathustra*. Each was obeying the mobilization order, but the Kantian categorical imperative as well. Each was joining Prussian Potsdam's assault upon the world, but was also defending the city of geniuses, Weimar. For as long as the library stood, everything in the books was still valid. My father's trust in his books was unshaken. Monstrous and horrible as this war seemed, there was nothing mysterious about it. Three schools of prophets had predicted the great war of the twentieth century.

The Darwinists had predicted the war. All life was a struggle for existence; nature would pick the fittest to survive. Regrettable, perhaps, if a few generations or whole peoples were destroyed in the process. Nevertheless, the trend was for the good, for it insured the higher development of the select survivors.

The Nietzscheans had predicted the war. They had heralded the coming of the last judgment by the superman—"rectangular in soul and body."

And the anabaptists of the poor in spirit, the Marxists, had predicted it. They had threatened that the Messiah would come, the World Spirit of Hegel turned upside down, and His coming would be marked by merciless class struggles.

The books still stood upright on their shelves, firm as the walls of Troy around Helen's kidnaped beauty. The cannon of the Rights of Man still pointed as straight as the cannon of the French Revolution against the Holy Alliance. Humanism still held on all fronts; its forces were drawn up according to disciplines, as they had been for the Battle of the Books in St. James's Library: anno 1697–

the battle between the authors of classical antiquity and the Moderns (of that day) which had been described for us by the greatest of English satirists, "the Honourable Jonathan Swift (written for the Universal Improvement of Mankind, published by John Nutt, MDCCIV)."
Wrote the militant Dean of St. Patrick's:

> In these books is wonderfully instilled and preserved the spirit of each warrior while he is alive, and after his death his soul transmigrates there to inform them. . . . So we may say a restless spirit haunts every book till dust and worms have seized upon it, which to some may happen in a few days, but to others later; and therefore, books of controversy . . . have always been confined to a separate lodge from the rest, and for fear of mutual violence against each other it was thought prudent by our ancestors to bind them to the peace with strong iron chains.

My enlightened father would stand for no mystical incoherencies in his literary sphere. The only place where he allowed the overstepping of the limits of the senses and the transcending of the boundaries of logic was in the arts —in pure poetry, in the sheer association of sounds, which was governed by laws he understood (he had written a book on prosody). He also accepted Impressionistic and Pre-Raphaelite painting, which seemed to have a scientific basis in Helmholtz's optical experiments, and music. He did not take naturally to music and was rather confused by it. (But music was my mother's native soil.) He explained all other emotional phenomena as disturbances —presumably electrical—of the central nervous system.

Accordingly he considered ghosts as nothing but figures of speech, vehicles of jokes, melodramatic foolishness. He tried to inure me against my childhood fear of darkness by shutting me in a darkened bedroom into which not a ray of light could penetrate.

I had been vaccinated (unsuccessfully) against smallpox for the second time before a pretty housemaid told me something about a dear God in Heaven who saw everything, even in the dark. Then came the day when my earliest sorrows in love so befuddled me that I was left back at school. When I came home, I saw lying on my patented orthopedic reading desk two books: Dr. Thesing's *Elementary Textbook of Reproduction and Heredity,* and a pamphlet by the Genevan entomologist, Auguste Forel: *The Dangers of Masturbation.* The books were intended to bring me to my senses.

My father was a man of letters who took care that his integrity should not be corrupted by emotions. To his way of thinking, integrity required solidarity with the insulted and injured against the obscurantist powers-that-be—the clergy and the military clique, heavy industry and the large landowners. Toward his family, his colleagues and himself he was inflexible; he insisted on absolute abstinence from theological spirits, on total continence with regard to intercourse with phantoms. He put an interdict on unauthorized astrological claptrap in his universe. He would not have anything in nature that was not susceptible of microscopic or chemical verification.

He was a stern and righteous judge who looked at the man and not at the halo. He would never have turned the Son of Man over to a grand inquisitor—as Dostoevsky's Ivan Karamazov did. But he would have issued a summons for the Anointed Miracle Worker to appear before an "investigating commission of impartial scientists" (such as Ernest Renan had proposed) and would politely have requested Him to "repeat His experiments under careful scientific scrutiny."

Nevertheless, when my father called the roll of his books every morning he could not help noticing an alien presence in the line-up of realism. He could see stirrings of dead delusions which he had thought long since buried in the graveyard of the Middle Ages. He could see sphinxes, griffons and other such mongrels perching on the shelves —"psychotic geniuses." Each morning anew, he was uneasily aware of nocturnal excesses, committed in an incomprehensible region of impulses, in a sphere beyond good and evil. For example, the preoccupation with *le beau crime*—murder considered as one of the fine arts. Did not Lombroso, Griesinger and F. del Greco hold that all prophets, philosophers, artists and illuminati were pathological cases, potential criminals? There were schizoids like Leo Tolstoy; epileptics like (probably) Buddha, Mohammed, Napoleon, Dostoevsky; manic depressives like Dante; paranoids like Newton or Blake; neurasthenics like Molière; victims of dementia praecox like the poet Hölderlin, the archetype of German romantic melancholy. There were Dionysiac progressive paralytics, Zarathustran St. Vitus dancers. . . . These were the deformed spawn of romanticism, ghostly atavisms living on in ordinary life.

Then there were the phenomena of mesmerism or hypnosis. Formerly cases of this sort had been classed as mere hallucinations, smuggled into literature by such writers as E. T. A. Hoffmann or Edgar Allan Poe, or as something out of a magician's act. But now hypnosis was being demonstrated in the lecture halls of the Sorbonne under the auspices of a serious practitioner of medicine, Jean Martin

25

Charcot. The interpretation of dreams, a business for gypsies and silly servant girls, was being undertaken in dead earnest by Charcot's pupil, a Viennese doctor. Even in America, the New World of Edison's practical inventions and P. T. Barnum's colossal humbugging, the pragmatist William James claimed to have detected a "subliminal self" which existed below the threshold of consciousness and stored up "forgotten memories" which might at any time break through into the daylight world. And the Russian Bekhterev spoke of outbreaks of mass suggestion which were transmitted from mind to mind like bacterial epidemics.

It was true that all these mystical mutinies were taking place in the contested no man's land of the psyche. My father could still fall back on the aphorism of Rudolf Virchow, the shining light of German anatomy:

"I have dissected many cadavers and never found a soul."

Sometimes I would ply my father with questions: "Did Moses make it all up?" "Where was I before I was here?" And often in the evening Father would take me walking under the chestnut trees along Landwehr Canal in Berlin. And as an answer to my questions he would point to a single light burning in the dormer window of a tenement and say to me, "Virchow is working there."

When we came home and I was sent to bed, he would shut himself up in his library to interrogate his books. For it was necessary to maintain a strong guard along the frontier between knowledge and the deceptions of religion. There was no one whom you could completely trust. Even the great Charles Darwin, the discoverer of Creation's plan, was said to have gone to church on Sundays. Cesare

Lombroso, the originator of the genius-madness theory, and Camille Flammarion, the popular astronomer, had been converted to spiritualism. Huysmans, though an adherent of the naturalist school, defended the miracle cures of Lourdes against his master Zola. Maurice Maeterlinck, the symbolist, dabbled in theosophy. August Strindberg, the former realist, went in for occultism and alchemy.

My father's church was a church militant of the all-highest universal morality. It had its own breviary: Swinburne's praises of Venus; it had its own mass: Offenbach and Hector Crémieux's *Orpheus in Hell*. It had its own Golden Legend: the revolt of Anatole France's anarchist angels. It had its hagiographers, such as Sienkiewicz (*In Hoc Signo*) and Flaubert (*The Temptation of St. Anthony*). It had its inspired missionaries of freedom, like Harriet Beecher Stowe (*Uncle Tom's Cabin*). It had its dove of peace, Bertha von Suttner (*Die Waffen Nieder*). And it had its martyrs, its "victims of class justice," such as the Barcelona nihilist, Ferrer; the leaders of the Haymarket Riots; the paraders who had followed Gapon, the people's priest, and had been massacred in front of the Winter Palace at Petersburg.

My father endorsed "propaganda by action," especially in the form conceived by Aristide Briand: the general strike. He even gave reluctant approval to bomb-throwing terrorism. But he thought such actions must be undertaken for the sake of the individual against the state. In this he agreed with Herbert Spencer, with Louise Michel and with the Russian nihilist, Prince Kropotkin. He rejected Count Leo Tolstoy's program of reform as not only aristocratic in bias, but also totally inadequate, since it was directed solely against the large landholdings of Tolstoy's pan-Russian peers, instead of against the Czar and despotic rule in general.

Secretly, my father would have preferred to sleep away a hundred years like Julian West, the hero of Edward Bellamy's utopian Communist novel, and to awaken in the arms of Dr. Leete, the first "socialized" physician. Father would have felt most at ease "looking backward," carefree and unprejudiced, from the year 2000 A.D., after the successful operation on the economic cancer of society was all over. His real image of the revolution was an artistic one—the full-bosomed romantic abandon of Delacroix's women—and he longed for it to take place under the tricolor of France.

He would have liked Saint-Simonism—"to each according to his abilities and services"—had it not been for Saint-Simon's ecclesiastical trimmings.

For my father believed in general in a hierarchy of the intellect, both in the world of books and the world of nature. Man, as the most intelligent mammal, was on top. He also held that some nations were more highly developed than others, like France. There were evolving nations, like the United States (as proved by Walt Whitman's hymn: "O to die advancing on . . . Pioneers! O pioneers!"), degenerate nations like Imperial Germany; and fossilized mammoths like Czarist Russia.

However, it would be a "retrogression to the darkest Middle Ages" to infer from this that there existed zoological "inequalities among the races of men" (the title of a pseudoscientific potboiler by the Comte de Gobineau— a French diplomat and author of the splendid epic drama, *The Renaissance,* who became a propagandist of pan-

Germanism and a trumpeter of Wagnerian anti-Semitism).

"The soul of a nation is expressed in its literature," my father used to say.

And accordingly he was wounded to the quick when demonstrations of bad taste and poor sense cropped up among the French—who were out of reach of the Czar's knout, the Black Hundred and the reactionary Rasputins. That such things could happen in broad daylight, on the front lines of *raison!* And happen they did; processions went to Lourdes, and there were ugly clashes on the very boulevards of Paris during the Dreyfus affair.

"The power of darkness," my father used to call such manifestations, using Tolstoy's phrase. I imagined the power of darkness as a Berlin cop, martial, mustachioed, steel-helmeted, saber-rattling. For my earliest conceptions of any higher power had been formed in my childhood when two policemen came into my father's library and took him away. They also removed a large number of "writers dangerous to the state" from his bookshelves. He was being arrested for lese majesty. Young as I was at the time, I shall never forget Father's proud bearing. He was the image of the cosmopolitan patriot, the militant pacifist.

Often, later, when I eavesdropped at his door or surreptitiously opened it a crack, I would see Father jump to his feet in the midst of reading a review copy, and break out with: "Nonsense, utter rot, old wives' tales!" He would rush to his shelves, pull out a volume by that indefatigable progressive, Herbert Spencer, or by the monists, Haeckel and Ostwald, and begin a muttered, imaginary duel between himself and the absent author.

The Lost Library

"There, I've caught you. Defend yourself in black and white. Without speculative evasions. On the basis of facts . . ."

For he believed with all his being that words were equivalent to deeds, that his books were weapons and that Truth was on the march—*rien ne l'arrêtera!* He was convinced that the strategy of "force and matter," the barren battlefield of causality, guaranteed him ultimate victory. All the achievements of technology were on his side: the telegraph, the telephone, Count von Zeppelin's dirigible balloon, the Wright brothers' flying machine (uniting all nations in the ether, he was convinced), and Nobel's dynamite, nihilism's ideal stuff of peace. Backing it all was the god of technological improvement which would automatically benefit the cause of the exploited, the oppressed, the persecuted, the proletarians, the colonial slaves. World fraternity and the individual's right of self-determination would be won by the machine—*deus ex machina.*

And when my father fell dying into my arms, when Kant's *Critique of Pure Reason* dropped from his hands, he left his library to me lined up in model nineteenth-century battle order, all ready for the "final conflict" heralded by the Internationale. Loyal disciple of the Enlightenment, he would never have guessed the condition in which I was to find the books again—crazily packed into crates, smuggled out at the risk of many lives. Never would he have guessed that I would be taking the volumes one by one out of their crates while all around culture came crashing down and the West rolled headlong toward the finale of Götterdämmerung.

Chapter II

*Fairy-tale Witches and Witch Trials—From the
House of David to Rougon-Macquart—Satanic
Genesis of Divine Inspiration—From Artificial
Paradises to the Hundred and Twenty Days of
Sodom.*

MY FATHER arranged his books according to his private
classification. As I set about restoring order in the chaotic
pile, it was as though I were painfully trying to recon-
struct from the ruins of memory a landscape out of my
childhood—setting up first the eccentric gables of horror
stories and going on to the towering mountain ranges of
the world sages with their glaciers of dead languages,
their eternal snow of frosty truths and dizzying crevasses
of dialectics—on all the way to the far horizon of my own
ideas.

My childhood books and the Greek or Latin texts had
been packed on top of each crate to convince the border
guards of the dictatorship that the books were worthless
trash. Elves and nymphs, Aristotle and Plato, had withstood all papal bulls against paganism; frog kings and
sleeping beauties had survived the guillotining of the aristocrats; Eros and Thanatos had resisted all vaccination.
So, too, this library had escaped the book burnings, the
race persecutions. And it only reached me thanks to those
ancient creatures of myth and fable whom I too had loved.
For—to my father's regret—I too had roamed through

enchanted forests and into the caves of dragons before I began the long climb through higher education to Enlightenment. . . .

I began arranging the top books first.

Modern parents worry whether children ought to be given access to all the hocus-pocus of primitive sorcery and wicked fairies. They might as well debate whether or not the Eskimos ought to be allowed to keep their amulets and angekoks.

From a literary point of view, little objection could be raised to fairy tales like *Sleeping Beauty, Little Red Ridinghood, Puss in Boots* and so on. After all, their authors, Charles Perrault (of the Académie Française) and the Comtesse d'Aulnoy had introduced them into the salons of Louis XIV's aristocracy. And the tales were presented in so elegant and courtly a form—like the contemporary works of Boileau and La Fontaine—that they were everywhere received as the legitimate inventions of their royalist editors. The plebeian, in fact the Asiatic and even Negro pedigrees of these stories, were not discovered until the nineteenth century when German and Russian philologists began looking into their ancestry. Then the brothers Grimm copied the stories down without embellishments, as they heard them from the people—in order, so they said, "to save them for the poor and simple people from whom they have been stolen."

But the material the Grimms were unearthing got out of their control, as so often happens in the sciences. The good philologists had intended to preserve the treasures of legend and myth stored in the minds of simple peasants and venerable nurses. But they stumbled on caverns where flocks of obscene succubi fluttered into their faces. A brood of vipers and basilisks crawled toward them and the bloody stench of a witches' cauldron rose to their nostrils.

At the same time, and again unwittingly, the brothers Grimm promoted a conspiracy which is permanently seething throughout the human race—the conspiracy of the children. For children, with the malice of underprivileged dwarfs, are always sabotaging the absurd realm of the giants, the grownups.

Meeting the enemy squarely, my father presented me with *Grimm's Fairy Tales* in a reproduction of the original 1832 edition. And on the long winter evenings when I was apt to get out of hand, he would reward me for eating my supper like a good boy by reading me the stories. To counter-balance the horrors, the cannibalistic giants and the witches burned in ovens, he read the tales metrically, like poetry. He familiarized me with the art forms of folklore, and in doing this he taught me how to defend myself against the goblins in the chimney, the imps in the cupboards and the nightmares in the billowing curtains; he put all my terrors neatly back in their compartments before bedtime. For he read everything to me and concealed nothing—neither the wiles of stepmother queens who mixed deadly poisons, nor the misdeeds of robber chieftains who beguiled foolish maidens with three kinds of wine, cut up their bodies and sprinkled salt on the pieces. He recited the mad chant of the goosemaids and their changelings—and he even read me the folk jest about the dishonest Jew whom the peasant lad with the magic fiddle forced to dance in the thornbush.

For my father refused to practice any censorship in the arts. When he took me to the museum he showed me the caricatures of Jews on Gothic plaques, and he dealt as frankly with the fairy tales. After all, the Grimm brothers had belonged to the "Goettingen Seven"—a group of liberal university professors who were banished for conspiring against the almighty Prince Metternich and the King of Hanover, in the dark days of absolutism and reaction.

My father saw to it that the fare for my intellectual suppers was of the choicest quality. I was plied with the finest translations. And at the time no other European literature had so rich a store of good translations as the German. In the eighteenth century the Germans had shown every indication of becoming the encyclopedists of the heart—as the French were the encyclopedists of the mind. They were well on their way to being aesthetic mediators between the Latins and the Slavs. It had all begun with the reformer of taste who taught the Germans to appreciate "folk" poetry—Johann Gottfried von Herder, the Protestant pastor and humanist. Herder translated and adapted from all the world's *Naturpoesie*. He provided the Germans with a psalter of Hebrew, Persian, Scotch, Lapp, Estonian and Greenlandic folk songs, and with translations of the *Cid* and *Ossian*. He wrote for them a "gospel of singing nature" and preached the equality of all nations in the realm of aesthetics.

Thus the religious instruction I received at home was strictly literary. It followed the catechism of ethical beauty and encouraged the worship of artistic perfection, in which everything had its place: minerals, plants, animals and men. I believed in the Olympian gods, in satyrs and sirens, in Amor and Psyche, as firmly as I believed in an Allah, in the seventy-four houris, in jinns and the roc, that great bird. I believed in Homer, Scheherazade and

Wilhelm Hauff, the Satanic romanticist of German adolescents. I believed in the pantheism of Hans Christian Andersen, who endowed swallows, snowflakes, bootjacks and shirt collars with human characteristics, and who had the gift of all tongues—a Danish Francis of Assisi conversing with domestic utensils. And I believed in the divine order of La Fontaine's animal world; I respected the animals more than the appended human moral.

The autumnal whispers of the erlking's daughter stirred me more than the jubilation of angels plucking their harps on the steps of the throne of Eternal Justice. I was more interested in the mandrake than in the Sacred Rose. The sufferings of Tantalus from hunger and thirst were grimmer and more real to me than the torments of Job. I felt the plight of a shade in Hades more keenly than that of a soul in the fires of purgatory. I had more admiration for the twelve labors of Hercules, for his struggle with the centaurs and his success in taming Cerberus, than for Samson's suicidal revenge upon the Philistines.

This went so far that when I entered school I felt like a foreigner among my new classmates whose preschool education had been in the figurative language of the Old and New Testaments and in patriotic mythology.

However, as I now saw, there had been no lack of Bibles in my father's library. About a dozen folio volumes lay, because of their size and weight, at the bottom of the biggest crate, underneath the encyclopedias, with which they had formerly shared one of the taller middle shelves. They had leather or shiny cloth bindings, stamped with Hebrew letters or the curlicued Gothic letters of the Lutheran Wittenberg folios. Many of them were critical revisions of

the Word of God, edited by progressive theologians along
modern lines to prove that "the revelations and the miracles are not to be rejected as mere deceptions of the priests,
but should rather be interpreted as fundamental source
material for the historical science of religion."

In sorting out all the Bibles I found a number of separate volumes containing parts of the Scriptures, which my
father had scattered among thoroughly profane bookshelves. Their environment seemed to have worked a total
change in their pious character—as though they had been
removed from the anonymity of the One and Only whose
name cannot be named with impunity, and handed over to
the collective responsibility of secular authors.

This regrouping was not just a bibliophilic crotchet of
my father's. It went much farther back, to Reason's dec-
laration of independence from faith. That break had been
as revolutionary as the revolt of the sciences against theology and Aristotelian scholasticism. Natural science had
declared: "We want to learn the naked truth." And aesthetics had proclaimed: "We want to strip Beauty naked."
Just as Descartes had announced the autonomy of the
thinking self, Kant the autonomy of the moral self, so
Lessing, Winckelmann, Schiller, Coleridge and Wordsworth had asserted the independence of the imaginative
self. Thereby they had founded republics of criticism—
those of Sainte-Beuve in France, of Carlyle and Ruskin
in England, of Fontane, Fritz Mauthner and Harden in
Germany, of Brandes in Scandinavia and of Belinsky in
Russia.

After Hegel, the philosopher of the *raison d'état,* after
Taine, the philosopher of artistic reason, it had become
standard practice to assess all cultural works as products

of *race, milieu et moment*. In the re-examination of all printed matter, the Book of Books had lost its right to transcendental extraterritoriality: it was no longer inviolable. In its fight for existence it had to appeal to all the control commissions of literary and textual criticism, and it was constantly being reassigned to new categories.

All this was a consequence of the above-mentioned Great European Battle of the Books, which Swift described. It ended with the victory of the Moderns over the Ancients. Charles Perrault, the writer of fairy tales, had started the battle with his panegyric upon the Sun King (*Siècle de Louis le Grand*) and Swift had carried it on in St. James's Library.

Perrault, who was attacking Homer, argued that contemporary writers were superior to the Ancients if only because they had come later, quite aside from their more precise psychology, their improved methods of logic, their possession of printing, etc. Their advantages, in other words, lay in their belonging to a superior progressive era. Implicitly, this derogation of the classics involved the Bible.

The damage was already done. The logical next step came from the farsighted naturalist and sensitive court author, Georges Louis Leclerc de Buffon—director of the Jardin du Roi. Ordered by Louis XV to draw up a catalogue of the imperial collection of curiosities, Buffon overturned the whole story of the Creation. His reservation that the account in Genesis should not be taken literally—and that the "seven epochs" into which he had divided the Creation corresponded, after all, to the "seven days"—was of no avail. He had destroyed the basis of belief.

37

"Man," he admitted, "trembled on an earth that trembled under his feet. . . ."

The scandal was aggravated when Pastor Herder tried to save the Bible for literature by urging that it be "read humanly" and not as the Word of God. "God does not speak," he preached; consequently there could not exist in any language an authorized edition of His works.

"Natural religion" was taken up by the Protestant Church as a means of keeping up with the spirit of the Enlightenment, and Herder pushed this tendency to an extreme when he dared to claim that the New Testament was derived from "an undiscovered Oriental source." He praised the Song of Songs as "the oldest and sweetest love story of the East"; he recast the Psalms of David into odes in the meters of the pagan classics, and rewrote the laments of Jeremiah as a Lydian elegy. The result of his labors was that the church authorities condemned him as a freethinker, and he also ran afoul of his fellow poets of Weimar. For he was meddling in both their trades. Goethe was particularly wary of him and "carefully concealed from him my mystical, cabalistic experiments in chemistry, and especially my interest in subjects which could gradually be shaped into poetic figures—my interest in Faust."

Goethe sensed what was going to happen to the Bible. He predicted, in *Dichtung und Wahrheit,* "A peculiar and inevitable destiny awaits this book, as well as all the profane scribblers." How right he was, my father's library demonstrated.

My father owned a de luxe anthology adorned with vivid water colors and borders imitating the motifs of Oriental erotic miniatures. It was entitled *An Aphro-*

dite's Garden of World Lyrics and contained FitzGerald's
Victorian travesty of the *Rubáiyát of Omar Khayyám;*
Anacreontic epigrams on hetaerae and minions translated
by a classical philologist into German university jargon;
the Renaissance sonnets of Louise Labé, la Belle Cordière
of Lyons, to her aristocratic lover (recast into German by
Rainer Maria Rilke with Mallarméan preciosity). But the
pride of the anthology was "The Song of Songs," pur-
porting to be "originally an ancient Persian marriage
duet, of undisguised lewdness, between Sulamit and Shu-
lamo," who celebrated their nuptials without concern for
possible symbolic interpretations of their ambiguous en-
dearments, or for the ultimate consequences of these in the
history of morals.

Looked at in this light, the Bible became less objectionable to me. I had read it previously only in my class in
religion—as I had read Goethe and Schiller only in my
grammar class.

When I had outgrown fairy tales and, with the beginning of sexual maturity, had lost the "innocence of childhood," I could no longer abandon myself so harmlessly
before falling asleep to stories of fairies and mermaids,
robber girls and Indian princesses. I sensed this for myself and deduced it from certain of my parents' and teachers' questions. But love as it figured in the Bible, where
it was meant only symbolically and with reference to God
the Father—this heavenly love was too lofty for me. Yet
parents and teachers always spoke about the operations of
earthly love in careful circumlocutions and as something
unappetizing which was committed only in secret. They
always added that before the time came for me to know
what this earthly love was like—"you will have to read and

learn a great deal." And so I searched everywhere for the apple of knowledge, in the streets, in encyclopedias and in novels of manners. Whenever I caught a glimpse of the other sex, whenever I found a mention of it, my pulse raced and my temperature rose. So that when I came across a collection of *The One Hundred Best Short Stories* in a "flexible pocket edition," I immediately took up the volume that contained the "finest women characters." And when in this volume I discovered the Moabite orphan, Ruth, I was enchanted. She had the bohemian charm of a Mimi Pinson of Montmartre and the radiant freshness of one of the Goncourt brothers' *garçonnières*. In this collection was also the Book of Esther, with its background of a Russian police state; it would have been quite at home beside a Russian protest novel (say, Alexander Herzen's *Who Is to Blame?*). And there was also Judith who kills the enemy general after sleeping with him—as daring a girl as Maupassant's *Boule de Suif,* the little Norman prostitute who goes to bed with a Prussian officer in order to save her virtuous compatriots.

Samuel was evidently included in the collection with the idea of showing that it was a direct forerunner of the many-layered physiological novel of the type written by Balzac and Zola. These *"scènes de la vie militaire et scènes de campagne,"* this *"histoire naturelle et sociale d'une famille,"* these Old Testament patrician chronicles of the rise and decline of a ruling house, of its blessings and its degeneration, of the tragedy of incest between two brothers and their sister, of political feuds, seers, madmen and glorious artists—in their crude force and succinctness, these stories surpassed all the long-winded exercises of the naturalists in the technique of the novel. And certainly Jehovah's reiterated threats of vengeance and of punishment to the third and fourth generation are more likely to make men doubt the existence of divine grace than data on social and hereditary taints. In the Old Testament the merciful mitigation of psychiatric or biological knowledge was lacking, and the characters were abandoned to the judgment of a suprahuman conscience.

The revolt of the servants of God and their defection from the doctrines of their forefathers seemed more monstrous than, say, the nihilistic blasphemies of the medical student Bazarov (in Turgenev's *Fathers and Sons*) who worshiped the Baal of materialism at German universities.

In the Book of Samuel the dire fate of the monarchy began with Saul, Israel's first nomad king by the will of God. The prophet Samuel forced this cunning, God-fearing military leader to abdicate in favor of the shepherd boy David, a military child prodigy whose like was to appear only once more in the history of war, in the person of the shepherdess Joan of Arc. David was also a baroque lyric poet, a political reformer, a pioneer statistician of his people (for which the Lord chastised him)—and a common adulterer who sinned with a woman from a racially inferior vassal tribe. But through her he became the forefather of the blessed stock, the line of descent reaching from his bastard, Solomon the Wise, all the way to the Son of Man, born of the immaculately conceived Virgin.

But this genealogy lures the mind away from the faults and implications of Samuel. It leads to the tangled maze of testamentary proceedings carried on by casuists, distorters of Scripture and natural philosophers. It leads us also to the Hundred Years' and Thirty Years' religious wars, to the night of St. Bartholomew, to massacres of heretics and aristocrats, to chaffering over the rights of man that goes back to the marital relationships of Adam and Eve—old issues for which inheritors and disinherited are to this day slaughtering one another by nations and by classes.

For these were three ways of reading Genesis: The naturalistic-zoological, the aesthetic-folkloristic and the socio-historical approaches. With all of them and with the spread of novel reading throughout all classes of the people, divine justice was more and more discredited.

In the nineteenth-century novel the West discovered itself. By then the West had colonized all the Golden Lands of Ophir, all of Sir Thomas More's utopias and Rousseau's new paradise, and had Europeanized their exoticism. The battles with dragons and the troubadour loves began to be located right at home within the family, in the factories and laboratories, in Balzac's boardinghouses and Maupassant's houses of ill fame. Incredibly savage tribes loafed around the London slums and the Parisian lower depths: Victor Hugo's poor wretches, Eugène Sue's asocial scum (*Mysteries of Paris*), bomb-throwing Russian terrorists. All around the big cities stretched the darkest quarter of the globe, "the Provinces—the land of idiocy, of all milieus the most stupid, the most prolific in absurdity, swarming with intolerant imbeciles"—the hunting preserve of Gustave Flaubert.

The novel is the nineteenth century as it lived and breathed. Here was the most detailed and treacherously revealing self-portrait of a society. That society's urge to speak its mind, to talk about itself and cause others to talk about it, has in fact been transmitted to us. It was an urge toward unrestrained histrionics which often led to the trashiest kind of falsehood, which was as overstimulated as one of the bluestockings created by the Amazon genius George Sand, which blurted out horrible truths like a defendant in a Dostoevskian interrogation. The rise of Napoleon or of capitalism was a story so improbable that it "could only have happened in a novel"; the miracles of technology were so fantastic that they seemed "possible only in novels by Jules Verne."

When both author and publisher went out of their way to emphasize that the work was "based on a true incident" and "taken from life," every reader became eager to live his own novel. The husband wanted a romance with his children's governess or a real live actress; the lady of the house wanted one with a "Frenchman," the unmarried girl with a tenor, the son with his father's mistress. The servant girl longed for a count out of a tenpenny romance; the adolescent boy yearned for the life of Cooper's trappers and Indians; the proletariat hoped for the moral execution of the champagne-guzzling, caviar-gorging bankers who took advantage of every innocent working girl.

But the true hero of the *jeunesse dorée* was the fortune hunter, the *rastaquouère,* who like Balzac's Rastignac looking down upon the city of Paris whispered to Fortune: *"A nous deux, maintenant!"*

Both the most vulgar and the most snobbish requirements were satisfied by the *littérature industrielle* (against which Sainte-Beuve launched his most profitable campaign), the serial novel administered in doses of increasing intensity, which was introduced by Docteur Véron in his *La Revue de Paris*. The experiment was adopted by the boulevard press, whose *romans feuilletons* could never pall, for every day the story could be broken off anywhere with an enticing "To be continued." These novels were completely in the spirit of the other contents of the newspapers; they were· like criminal trials, unsolved murder mysteries and political crises—in short, they resembled life itself. Whether disguised as historical romances, as in Bulwer Lytton's *The Last Days of Pompeii*, Flaubert's *Salammbô* and Sienkiewicz's *Quo Vadis*, or disguised as detective stories, as in Conan Doyle's Sherlock Holmes series, these novels always remained snugly within the moral world order as defined by the daily newspapers. For the public subscribed to the principles of the newspapers.

It was the golden age of prosperity for clever and inventive minds—in literature as in other realms. Subjects were cheap as dirt. Material for novels was as available as capital for new businesses.

The society novelists kept accounts like tradesmen of the income and marriage portions which enabled their characters to afford carriages, banquets and their emotional life. The novelists' own enterprises were also on a large scale, and their production broke all records. Alexandre Dumas *père* had to his credit 257 novels, plus twenty novelistic plays. To keep the presses running the writers employed a staff of *nègres* (ghost writers). Like European civilization the world of fiction was threatened by overpopulation.

The novel became the bourgeois family picture gallery—where hung oil paintings of Thackeray's snobs, Alphonse Daudet's financial nabobs, Oscar Wilde's Dorian Gray, George Sand's Consuelo and Gerard de Nerval's Sylvie. Especially prized were the pictures of the owners'

44

multitudinous kin—namely, the Third Estate. In place of the plebeian Jacobin slogan, "Be brothers to one another," they had hung up a gilded scroll with the motto: "Be brothers-in-law and uncles to one another."

These portraits were not required to be flattering so long as they were good likenesses (as in family albums). And a number of attempts to produce highly unflattering likenesses were made by a German Romantic novelist of the miraculous—the engraver, caricaturist, composer and diabolist, E. T. A. Hoffmann. Some time before the chemist Joseph Nicéphore Niepce developed his "heliography" and the painter Daguerre "photography" on a silver plate, Hoffmann had made a specialty of cutting silhouettes. His subjects were the shadow profiles of gnomic philistines. At his desk he was still obsessed by the mystery of physiognomy. He saw his characters as through a camera obscura of the kind to be found in his day at every country fair—ingenious devices with an eyepiece like a doorkeeper's peephole through which one saw, reflected on a prismatically illuminated screen and magically exaggerated and distorted, the most ordinary passers-by and the most trivial happenings.

Hoffmann was an eccentric, haunted by nightmares, his nervous system shattered by wine, debts and sexual excesses with the elfin schoolgirls under his tutelage. He was everywhere pursued by misfortune and failure. A teacher of music and drawing in Königsberg, he lost his job for making indecent caricatures. He was fired from a second teaching position in Posen for drunkenness. Director of the Opera in Warsaw, he had to flee when the "accursed

45

Frenchmen" invaded the city. In marriage he was equally unfortunate; his wife became a permanent invalid and they lost their only child. As director of the Bamberg theater, Hoffmann was forced into bankruptcy. His opera, *Undine,* was performed in the Berlin Royal Opera House —and the opera house burned down immediately after the première. At the age of forty-seven, when he held the position of a judge in Berlin, he was stricken with paralysis.

As the author of fairy tales and family novels he would have come to no good either, had he not amused a public with a weakness for magic stunts, "elemental spirits" (the title of one of his stories) and other such hocus-pocus. His trick was that of the drawing-room "magnetizers" who invite a member of the family to come up to the platform and "mesmerize" the victim in an affected pose. To the uproarious applause of the good Christians, out popped a Beelzebub from the tails of a dignified alderman, a vampire from the crinoline of a ponderous demoiselle—the concealed serpent from the false bosom of a faded cocotte. Hoffmann himself, in the trance of creation, suddenly became aware that "the imagination can be made fertile by very simple methods; horror often resides more in the idea than in the phenomenon."

To put his technique in terms of old-fashioned photography: he placed a character before the lens of his imagination, which turned reality upside down, and out of the impression the image made on him he developed an *idée fixe,* a black-and-white negative, by exposing it to the full light of day.

Or to put the matter in medical terms: he suffered from the paranoid's disease of the alter ego, to which German "original geniuses" of the time were particularly susceptible. He was continually meeting his mirror image, his double. Even the staid Goethe in his memoirs reports a youthful attack of this; he describes meeting his own self while crossing a bridge. But Hoffmann transposed the whole phenomenal world into the blacks and whites of a photographic negative.

Thereafter all the dualistic novelists set their cameras to catch similar effects. Charles Dickens snapped the light-shy fog silhouettes that could be seen by the glow of London street lamps. Edgar Allan Poe took pictures of spiritistic ectoplasms (*The Case of Mr. Waldemar*). Guy de Maupassant took candid-camera shots of the marital bed and flashbulb pictures of a ghost from the colonies, *Le Horla*. But the Russians above all went in for such "photography": Gogol (*Dead Souls*), Dostoevsky (*The Dream of a Ridiculous Man*), Chekhov (*The Black Monk*). The original patent for reproducing all such hallucinations must, however, be assigned to the hypochondriac, spiritualistic, Royal Prussian Judge of the Court of Appeals, Ernst Theodor Amadeus Hoffmann.

Perhaps the nineteenth century would never have perfected its novelistic technique had it not been for the military precision of an aide-de-camp in Napoleon's army of occupation in Prussia, Henri Beyle (Stendhal, to use the best known of his pseudonyms).

The son of a high official in the French judiciary, he received his education from priests whose teaching only deepened his scorn of religion and his materialism. As an army officer in the Italian campaign and later as a diplomat, he became well acquainted with the political and amorous intrigues at the courts of princes and among the clergy, supplementing his own experience with his readings of Renaissance tales. As quartermaster with the army in Prussia he studied the German romanticists (Hoffmann, Jean Paul Richter, Novalis) and acquired a knowledge of the enemy's psychology.

He was given to an exacting "correctness" in all his relations with the outside world, in all situations. He was extremely finicky about his dress, for example, and there is a story that during Napoleon's disastrous retreat from Moscow Stendhal reported to his general's tent in immaculate uniform and trimmed beard, in spite of the raging snowstorm. He was equally finicky and "correct" about his emotions when he was jilted by a mistress, and he clung to this attitude when, after the fall of the Bourbons, he quitted public life and devoted himself entirely to the rich indulgence of writing for himself. These same qualities mark his biographies of musicians (Mozart, Metastasio), his reflections on painting and love, and his analytic psychological novels.

His efforts to introduce his judicial precision, his psychometric measurements and his "sensualism" into French literature were rejected by the public. It was not until the eighteen eighties—forty years after his death—that he was accepted by "a public which was tired of romanticism," as Stendhal himself predicted in a letter to Balzac about his *Charterhouse of Parma* (which Balzac, almost alone among French critics, had praised).

"Alone, talking to myself, two steps from death: I am still a hypocrite. Oh, nineteenth century!"

This pious exclamation from the last monologue of Julien Sorel (*Le Rouge et le Noir*), who dramatized his attempted murder of his married mistress as an act of Napoleonic heroism, is typical of the strained pathos of

Stendhal's characters. They wish to be great, but since they were living—in Stendhal's words—"in an age of transition and therefore of mediocrity," they were forced to represent their wretched doings as "energetic actions" and their weakness of character as a "protest against the impotence of humanity."

Stendhal was so "contemporary" that I did not care to reread him. I shelved his books and turned away from him and back to Balzac.

Sensitive as E. T. A. Hoffmann in perceiving the ghostliness of everyday life, as great a criminologist of the soul as Stendhal, Honoré de Balzac had built a giant moving diorama of the epoch.

Balzac's starting point was the observation that every individual radiates an aura of the will peculiar to himself, and through it influences the atmosphere in his environment. Equipped by nature with an abnormally sensitive eye, he was able so to disguise his photographic novelistic technique that—not suspected by the public—he assembled a complete rogues' gallery of daguerreotypes of all his contemporaries.

It grew to immense size. For that reason my father did not quite know what to do with the few volumes of selections he had picked up here and there. Since he accepted Flaubert's verdict that Balzac was "second-rate," Zola's that Balzac was "too reactionary, too digressive," and Sainte-Beuve's that Balzac was a journalist, he placed the volumes among his *romans feuilletons* (journalistic novels)—an act which incidentally would have delighted Balzac.

Impressed by the experimental novel of heredity, my

father deplored Balzac's disregard for the theme. He refused to recognize the power, the grandeur and the uniqueness of Balzac—although no writer before or since has ruled over so densely populous a state; none has governed such vast expanses of milieus as this Rabelaisian bastard of the race of Gargantua and Gargamelle.

From his "foxhole" at Passy on the slopes of the Seine, laboring like Sisyphus under a crushing burden of debt, Balzac directed one of the most complicated maneuvers in literature—though often his style was inadequate to the task. At his headquarters he autocratically knighted murderers, swindlers, usurers and fools, and ennobled provincial misses, ballerinas and courtesans.

He decreed that the fate of a soap manufacturer, César Birotteau, was more important to society than the career of a Napoleon. No secret service of a Talleyrand was ever so well informed on the conspiracies of the desires, above all on the passion for gold and the vice of miserliness. He penetrated to the highest ruling circles and the remotest provinces of hypocrisy. Fouché's police were never so conscientious in amassing information on every movement of thousands of persons, from the motive to the act. His eyes sleeplessly kept an entire human race under surveillance.

None of his successors succeeded in maintaining an empire of such proportions. Gustave Flaubert, the judge of mediocrity, saw—like shorn Samson in Delilah's lap—the philistines upon him. Émile Zola attempted to duplicate Balzac's feat, armed with all the equipment of genetics. In answer to Zola's appeal to decency, there roared back the voice of the human beast, the *bête humaine*.

To investigate society, Zola went down into its pits and

catacombs. He was, he boasted, "one of the busy workers who inspect the structure to locate the rotting beams, the internal cracks, the loosened bricks, all the damage which is not seen from outside and which could yet bring down the entire structure."

When Balzac wrote, the whole interior of the social structure, and every human organism which inhabited it, was made transparent. Zola used a pickax and laid bare the framework. He had a poor memory as well as poor vision, and therefore had to take note of what he saw on the spot. He viewed everything through the glasses of an undeniably magnificent temperament. But he overestimated the tools of his methodology and underestimated the miracle-working temperament. Actually it was his temperament that made Zola the crusader of his century.

Not for anything would I have denied the author of *La Débâcle*—the champion of Impressionist painting, the accuser before the world of a gang of general staff officers who hid behind the skirts of *La Patrie*—his rightful place in my father's library. At any rate, not today, when I think of the literary minions of the social order who have burned incense against the stench of the death-camp crematoriums and who fell on their faces before every holy image of the overseer of world slavery.

Maximilian Harden, Bismarck's protégé and the most redoubtable critic of Imperial Germany, wrote an obituary on Zola that amounted to an epitaph on the entire *école de Médan:*

> Zola believed in the sciences with all the fervor of a fearful soul who has been deprived of his gods and who

hastily looks around on earth for supports. To listen to him was to be convinced that science had solved all the riddles of the universe: Virtue and vice are products like sugar and vitriol. The laws of heredity are as well known as the laws of gravity. Man does not act as he wants to, but as he must; and the factors behind this compulsion are no longer a mystery. Anyone who has staggered through a course with Auguste Comte and Claude Bernard, with Taine and the English geneticists, is familiar with everything, understands everything, and is immune to scruples and doubts.

When Zola died, an era seemed to die too. The circumstances surrounding Leo Tolstoy's last hours create the impression that a saint was ascending into heaven, amid fumes of brimstone and pitch. Even among the hardened rationalists who despised Tolstoy's quietism, the report circulated like the rumor of a miracle that the dying man had sprung out of bed with supernatural strength to eject the priest whom Czar Nicholas had sent to him.

Each of Tolstoy's angry epistles—against the poisonous products of chemistry and medicine, against Shakespeare's "unnaturalness," on the incompatibility of Christianity and conscription, on "unchastity" in marriage—stirred up Europe as though these were the theses of a new Reformation, a new heresy.

The three schismatics of the age were Zola—the Donatist, the social sectarian who opposed the secular supremacy of the church; Dostoevsky—the Manichean ("Humanity is Satan's creature"); and Count Leo Tolstoy, who proclaimed a City of God.

Tolstoy's congregation was very large, especially in Germany and Scandinavia, and his followers boasted that in his Iliad, *War and Peace,* Russia had produced the only contemporary epic in world literature—which neither France nor England had been able to do. The heroine of his *Anna Karenina* is Flaubert's "narrow-minded, hysterical victim of bourgeois marriage," Emma Bovary, transformed into a Mary Magdalene, even as the story of an adultery is transformed into a legend of sin and grace. *Anna Karenina* was, in the words of Dostoevsky, a "masterpiece with which nothing in contemporary European literature can compare—essentially Russian."

Like a God-inspired desert preacher, Tolstoy wandered through a technological modern world. Right after his death a blurry close-up of him was shown in a newsreel. He looked like a primal myth, a cross, straggly-bearded, barefoot anchorite.

Like a Renaissance altar painter he reveled in the hues of the flesh: "Anna Karenina's shoulders, bosom and rounded arms, gleaming like old ivory." "The white breasts of a peasant woman in the square-cut peasant blouse—so white that they maddened him." "The white, threshing bodies of the soldiers bathing in the green-speckled pond, with their brick-red hands, necks and faces." And everywhere—in the perfume and powder of an aristocratic woman with her scent of the boudoir, in the stable odor of a horseman, in the sweat of a peasant girl smelling of rotten straw and rape, in the stale smell of unaired garrets and unwashed mistresses which clung to the social revolutionary—everywhere he scented the nearness of the Tempter, of the "Power of Darkness." He saw Satan coming in Russia, fled from him all his life, gazed at him in amazement from afar. He sensed that Satan was incarnate in Dostoevsky.

For Dostoevsky declared, referring to his attacks of

epilepsy, that he would sacrifice for such "a moment of higher existence, not only the life of one man, but all humanity."

Not so Tolstoy, who was fanatically attached to life. He lamented over the rottenness of feminine as well as artistic beauty, over the spoilage of the "fruits of enlightenment," and over the spoiled fruits of a diseased tree, with the same voluptuous horror with which St. Augustine of Hippo cried out against the corruption of the Carthaginian theater and Christianity. Both were apparently obsessed by the same compulsive idea: *Inter faeces et urinam nascimur.* . . .

The full force of Tolstoy's primitive Christian ethics and of his passion for the rude labor of the peasant was channeled into a hostility against his wife in particular and against the "torture of the marital yoke" in general. His penitential piety originated—according to his own confession—in his frequent attacks of fear of death. He admired the muzhik principally for his indifference toward death. Though he embraced the peasant as his brother man, his closest associates—the Tolstoyans who swarmed around him in his world-famous hermitage—were highly intellectual terrorists from the most dandified St. Petersburg society. . . . The most terrifying aspect of the man was his relationship to God—"like two bears in a cave," Maxim Gorki reported after visiting Tolstoy.

My father kept a file in which he collected bits of data on Tolstoy's personality: Tolstoy the field worker who perfumed his peasant smock; Tolstoy the epicurean vegetarian; Tolstoy the denouncer of music who was privately delighted when Wanda Landowska played Bach for him on the harpsichord. My father had clipped the frequent newspaper items on Tolstoy's "religious mania," and the daily bulletins covering the old man's sudden disappearance from Yasnaya Polyana. Even the rumors of a family scandal were here: his own wife's insinuations which resulted in the eighty-two-year-old Tolstoy's being suspected of homosexual relationships.

This "Tolstoyana" and similar "novels written by life," literary borderline cases which might perhaps have been classified with psychopathology, were placed on the bottom shelves of a corner cupboard which was half concealed behind the walnut armoire where my father kept his private papers. Some of the most questionable material was locked in the armoire.

My father had isolated these things as CULTURAL CURIOSITIES—as one places in an insane asylum distinguished madmen who are, unfortunately, dangerous to society. There were books over which the courts and the psychiatrists, the theologians and the critics disputed. Were these books written by saints or imbeciles, by revolutionaries or asocial personalities, by original geniuses or degenerates, immoralists or pornographers? There were books which my father included in his library for their aesthetic or scientific qualities, but which on pedagogical grounds he wished to conceal from me.

Perhaps because there was something obscene about their bindings (or so it seemed to me, especially those that were in tattered tissue-paper wrappings), or perhaps because of the permanent semidarkness in that corner of the library, there hung over them an aura of paternal taboo which both frightened me off and irresistibly attracted me.

And in fact these moldy old volumes dealt solely with

55

the "night sides of the soul," as the phrase of the day went; with the rudiments of primitive man which—so it was said —inexplicably continued a vegetative existence in us, like the appendix and the spleen.

A special ceremony was necessary to blow the dust from the edges and out of the grooves of the lettering, and to brush it off the covers, before the disreputable titles appeared:

Hallucinative Pseudo-Epilepsy in Paul of Tarsus.

The Confessions of St. Augustine—The Story of a Bisexual Man.

The Penitential Exercises of St. Ignatius of Loyola— or, From Erotomaniac to Saint.

And, packed with historical information and source material on satanic eroticism:

History of the Devil, by the devil's most zealous biographer, Roskoff, a Catholic professor at the University of Vienna.

These were the sort of books which are peddled around water fronts, in the neighborhood of waxworks and houses of ill fame, by itinerant booksellers and junk dealers, or are pulled from under a counter, with a wink.

The Nun, by M. Denis Diderot (piquant inside stories of a French nunnery).

Manon Lescaut (a terrifying picture of the morals of the French aristocracy and of prostitution in Paris, of the Louisiana penal colony and the American underworld, by His Reverence, the Abbé Prévost d'Exiles).

There were also:

Diary of the Chief Eunuch of Sultan Abdul Hamid (erotic and political life of the Sublime Porte).

White Slaves of the Italian Mafia and Camorra.

56

And there was a variety of other anticapitalistic, anticlerical and anti-Semitic books—a veritable black market of unsavory printed matter. It took me very little time to discover them, and I set to plucking out all the obscenities like juicy raisins out of bits of stale cake.

Some of my raisins were from:

Corvin's *Pfaffenspiegel,* a *chronique scandaleuse* for the use of anticlericals.

The Seventh Book of Moses, a potpourri of quotations from the Talmud, the Book of Sohar and the *Schulchan Aruch.*

An anti-French, anti-Semitic pornographic novel, *Biarritz,* written by a down-at-heels journalist of the Revolution of 1848 and containing the Proclamation of World Power by the Wonder Rabbi Löw.

(All three of these books were afterward republished by General Erich Ludendorff and the Nazi "philosopher" Alfred Rosenberg "for private study and analysis of the world Catholic-Jewish conspiracy.")

In unpacking the crates I also found among this gruesome collection a bibliophilic rarity which I had never noticed before, an octavo volume bound in flexible polished leather, imprinted with the fleur de lys:

Les dialogues aux Enfers entre Montesquieu et Machiavel.

It was a splendid specimen of underground pamphletry by the Parisian feuilletonist Maurice Joly, written to attack the dictatorship of Napoleon III. It won the author fame for a day, as well as a year and a half in prison—and then a posthumous fame of a sort he had certainly never expected. For secret agents of the Russian Ochrana used his pamphlet to construct a fake corpus delicti of "Jewish

Machiavellianism." The pamphlet reappeared, "faithfully translated from the Hebrew original" into Russian by a St. Petersburg orientalist, Sergei Nilus. Allegedly it had been "discovered" in destroyed ghettoes by pillaging Cossacks, and it was used to justify the Kishinev pogroms.

Beneath the ashes of burned Jewish villages the fire continued to smolder. Like a carelessly discarded cigarette that starts a forest fire, the slap-dash jest of a writer ignited a world conflagration. The *Dialogues aux Enfers* became the *Protocols of Zion;* the plagiarism of Czarist anti-Semites was used by a half-educated paranoid to burn to ashes Germany and the rest of Europe.

With the stench of that conflagration in my nostrils and the knowledge that the next gust of wind might set all Vienna afire, I started in alarm at the mere sight of a book that had left an unhealed trauma on my mind. It was the *Malleus Maleficarum* by (this is from memory) Henricus-Institutoris Kraemer, Jacobus Sprenger and Jacobus Gremper, Pope Innocent VIII's encyclopedist. These three writers, with German thoroughness and a disconcerting knowledge of pornography—but always leaning on Socrates, Marcus Aurelius, Seneca, St. Augustine, Thomas Aquinas, *et al.*—described the diabolic lewdness practiced by witches and heretics and the succubine wiles of women. These writers developed torture into an applied science.

Each of these demonologies, confessions and voluptuous fantasies of flagellants and stigmatists was a skillful brew. Like eye of newt, toe of frog and liver of blaspheming Jew in a witches' broth, Satanism, scholarship and social enlightenment were boiled together so spicily that they would inflame the blood of every virtuous spinster, as well as every populist; they would provide every roué with erotic tidbits and satisfy every adolescent's appetite for knowledge of forbidden things. . . . My own appetite was satisfied too early; I became prematurely acquainted with the repulsive vices and diseases of the human imagination. And I regretted it.

My father called this section of his library his "poison cupboard." That was the word in university jargon for the special shelves for publications offensive to public order and morality, which were open only to students of the subject and to the judicial experts on public morals. (While at the same time in the reading rooms of the public libraries the libertines of power could sit with fevered brains and abstracted hearts and copy out of Savonarola, out of Clausewitz [the German philosopher of total war], out of Déroulède [the lyricist of French anti-Semitism], and out of Houston Stewart Chamberlain [the Anglo-Saxon propagandist of pan-Germanism], the tactics to be used for mass rape. What diabolic progeny of divine reason! Unimaginable, what demons, what degenerate descendants of Brahmas, Yogas, illuminati, dwelt in such iniquitous volumes; what changelings were born of intercourse with incubi!)

On shelves above these stood the collections of forensic belles-lettres, which I now came across in unpacking. There was the *Causes Célèbres* of François Gayot de Pitaval, one-time advocate at the court of King Louis XV, containing the proceedings of the trials of the heretic, Joan of Arc, of the "incestuous rebel," Don Carlos, and of the

59

poisoner, the Marquise de Brinvilliers. The book, which had been translated into German by the dramatist Friedrich Schiller, provided a wealth of source material for both classic and romantic writers, for the novel, the theater and the opera. My father had also a German sequel to it, *The New Pitaval,* written by the patriotic lending-library author, Alexis, in collaboration with a Prussian police commissioner, Hitzig.

For literature owes to criminology some of its finest inspirations. "A work of art is gestated in the mind like a crime," wrote Joséphin Péladan, one of the *fin-de-siècle* literati who won a reputation with the rabble more by notorious conduct than by his literary achievements. For although the newspapers of the day were full of his interviews with the Sphinx, of his rowdyish Wagnerian concerts, his scandalous Black Masses, and his recitations in Parisian brothels, literary criticism took no notice of him. Of his few readers, only Strindberg praised him as "the Juvenal of modern Paris—he began everything that goes by the name of Symbolism."

Péladan, like Strindberg, went in for the occult arts of the alchemists. He had a flair for the perfumes of fallen angels and, as he demonstrated in his novel *Ishtar,* an excellent ear for the language of infernal propaganda.

When many persons vigorously share the same feelings at the same time, there takes place a phenomenon which official science will continue to overlook for a long time to come. A new spirit arises, that is, the emanation of many wills condenses to form a mass which is powerful and militant. In such a mass the voice of the individual, no matter how strong or impassioned it may be, cannot withstand the voice of the collective.

But men of culture were far too occupied with Louis Pasteur's hydrophobia vaccine to pay any attention to Péladan's "collective spirit."

Like Huysmans, Péladan was also placed on naturalism's index, condemned as an obscene mystic. Consequently he was not tolerated in my father's library—which was reason enough for me to read him. My attention was called to him by a pamphlet full of invective entitled *Ce Monsieur Péladan.* Next to this pamphlet stood another indiscreet volume whose title fascinated me: *Wanda in Furs—Pathography of a Sexual Anomaly*—or something of the sort. But unfortunately it turned out to be a sober psychiatric dissertation on the morbid marital life of a drawing-room poet and member of the Austro-Hungarian aristocracy, Monsieur le Chevalier de la Légion d'Honneur Sacher-Masoch. Sacher-Masoch was known for his novel of manners set in ancient Rome, *Venus in Furs.* This was volume one of a cycle entitled *The Legacy of Cain* which he never finished; he was ambitious to surpass Balzac's *Comédie Humaine,* but he succeeded in immortalizing himself only in the realm of sexual anomalies—as the beaten husband; Wanda was his wife's name.

For me he was a horrible disappointment. The copy of *Venus in Furs,* printed on Japanese paper perfumed with musk and kept by my father in a cardboard case tied with string, reminded me so painfully of my Latin teacher's grammatical excesses that I wondered what in the world was so disgraceful about this masochism business.

I found the diametrically opposite vice no more attractive when I read *The Marquis de Sade and His Times.* The German biographer was Eugen Duehren, alias Dr. Ivan Bloch, gynecologist of Berlin's Bohemia. I later met him. He was a bookworm, a veritable Linnaeus of erotic flora, and the prize specimen in his "herbarium" was De Sade. Bloch spoke of De Sade with a fine enthusiasm: "Sexual pathology, social history, literature—marvelous, phenomenal!"

Rummaging through my father's books, all I could find of De Sade's own writings was a slender essay, *Idée sur le Roman*. In it I came across such observations as:

> My brush is said to be too strong; I am charged with painting vice in the ugliest colors. The reason for this is that I do not want to make vice attractive. . . . Woe to those who garland crime with roses.

That sounded more like a timid moralist.

The biographical data about him were no more illuminating to me. Why had the Bourbon monarchy incarcerated him in the Bastille, the Tribunal of the French Revolution in the Conciergerie, and First Consul Bonaparte in the insane asylum at Charenton? The charges against him seemed to come down to no more than that he had fed bonbons containing Spanish fly to some prostitutes of the Marseilles water front.

Once, when I pertly brought up the subject in order to get my father to tell me something more about the procedures of sadism, my father said, "The Marquis de Sade was an aristocratic libertine and, it is said, a descendant of Petrarch's Laura."

But I was not interested in that. For it is the fruit of universal education that every halfwit knows that Petrarch was a Renaissance poet who had a beloved named Laura. Just as everybody knows, thanks to Rostand, that Cyrano de Bergerac had a long nose, while Cyrano's magical novel

L'Autre Monde—that boldest and wildest of all the interplanetary voyages, that rocket flight into the sun—has been snubbed by posterity as Petrarch was by his Donna Laura. Every two-bit journalist and every reader of the tabloids, as well as every demagogue nowadays, throws the cliché "sadistic" at the enemy. And every historian of literature uses the word when no other adjective is convenient.

Yet the legitimate descendant of Laura, De Sade, has remained as immortally famous as Petrarch, or rather immortally infamous. For although the National Convention of the French Revolution, acting with the stern morality of ideological sex murderers, destroyed the Marquis de Sade's principal work, De Sade left his mark—not only in the sign of Cain that was afterward branded on the brow of all voluptuaries of violence, but in the legacy of atrociousness which he bequeathed to literature.

Everywhere in my father's library and in the nineteenth century I found his mark.

Baudelaire swore by him, quite literally (*"par l'âme du Marquis de Sade"*). The French pope of literature, Sainte-Beuve, apologetically ranked him alongside Byron. Rimbaud invoked him in *Une Saison en Enfer*. Isidore Ducasse (Comte de Lautréament) sang his praises in his *Chants de Maldoror*. Swinburne honored him as his forerunner and recited him—with transparent intentions—to the "muse of the Pre-Raphaelites," naïve Elizabeth Siddall. Stendhal in his analysis of the conventional idea of God, Dostoevsky in his dreams of a pan-Slav orthodox world church, Huysmans in his satanic Catholicism, were sadists in word and thought. But of the sadists in the deed, the least guilty of all was De Sade.

If we are to judge by the consequences which follow when any government, church, state, monarchy or democracy acts in the name of the law, justice appears as an unnatural perversity. If any man is truly the image of God, we must conclude that the original is a hideous monster, a Baal whose chief concern is to scourge mankind through murderous wars, revolutions and diseases, a universal sadist.

The bestialities practiced upon the human body in the world of De Sade were not "inventions of an unparalleled monster." They were no more unusual than the acts of revenge wreaked upon the ladies of the French aristocracy for the delectation of the sans-culottes; than the flaying, impaling and rending of infants and pregnant women by Napoleon's famous guard—whose triumphs Goya recorded with his etching needle in his *Desastros de la Guerra*. However, the Marquis de Sade's crime was that he conceived his brutalities only out of "purely artistic, aesthetic motives," out of sheer pleasure in *"l'écriture artistique,"* like the brothers Goncourt after him. He was lacking in the moral earnestness which visualizes political terror as a means to an end—the end being to frighten potential apostates and to toughen the faithful so that they will not succumb to sympathy when they hear the screams and whimpers of the tortured.

The Hundred and Twenty Days of Sodom was the only De Sade novel that my father bequeathed to me. But during his lifetime he kept it hidden from me in his private armoire. And now, in the present era of sadistic action and masochistic thinking, I asked myself where I should place the book. With masterpieces of world literature, or with cultural curiosities?

The Lost Library

According to my father's system of classification, the book belonged beside a nineteenth-century satirist whose writings even in his time were as much bibliophilic rarities as those of the Marquis de Sade. (Probably today, after the loss of my father's library, scarcely a copy can be found.) The satirist was Oscar Panizza, a Bavarian Catholic by birth, an alienist by profession, Hoffmann-esque-Sadistic novelist by vocation. His *Visions of Twilight* was confiscated immediately after publication. He was also a dramatist whose plays were never produced, and an *avant-garde* poet. His poems, entitled *Parisiana,* were brought out in a first edition of 300 copies, went unsold and were never reprinted.

After the publication of his "heavenly tragedy," *The Council of Love (Das Liebeskonzil)*, Panizza was indicted for blasphemy and the distribution of obscene literature. Sentenced to prison, he fled to Zurich and lived there by the sale of his booklets: *Christ in the Light of Psychopathology, Effeminateness in the Cult of the Messiah* and others. Suddenly he returned to Germany to serve his sentence; apparently he considered it his inescapable fate. An alleged fit of insanity resulted in his being sent to a private sanatorium. His Munich coffeehouse colleagues claimed he was sent there because his uncle, a Jesuit, intervened at the request of his family, as the Marquis de Sade's mother-in-law had done. He remained in the sanatorium for twenty years, shut off from the outside world and continuing to write until his death in 1922. Like the Marquis de Sade at Charenton, no one was permitted to visit him. (I tried in vain to do so.) A Munich cabaret proprietor obtained part of Panizza's manuscripts, but he himself subsequently went insane. Oscar Panizza's principal works vanished without a trace—like the Marquis de Sade's.

Biblical diabolists—*poètes damnés* of Artificial Paradises, historians of Sodom and Gomorrah—where did they all belong?

Among the poetry of all ages and peoples?

Among medical documents?

In the blazing pyres of the Inquisition, or in the bonfires heaped high with books by our modern terroristic dictatorships? Or in the inferno of thought?

"When someone thinks and can no longer impart his thoughts to others," says Panizza's devil in *The Council of Love,* "that is the cruelest of all tortures."

Chapter III

The Council of Love—To Damascus—Das Kapital.

PANIZZA'S PLAY, *The Council of Love,* was in fact shelved elsewhere, among the great contemporary dramatists, the chorus leaders of the Eleusinian mysteries in the Periclean nineteenth century: Ibsen, Björnson, Strindberg, Rostand, Maeterlinck, Wilde, Shaw, Chekhov. Though Panizza had never had a play performed, my father put him in a place of honor. The slender volume, with a lush Rubens nude on the shiny cover, had been given padded binding, so that it would not be crushed among all the imposing "collected works" whose shelf it shared.

The book had been secretly suppressed by the censors almost as soon as it appeared. But in spite of the short time it was before the public eye, it had evoked a storm of indignation. One wondered what devilish power this literary foundling possessed. How had it been able to set in motion the whole powerful administrative apparatus of the police and the department of justice? How had it been able to arouse such turmoil in the minds of blasé atheists who had been already hardened by Byron's *Cain,* Blake's *Ghost of Abel,* Flaubert's *Temptation of St. Anthony* and Huysmans' *Là-Bas?*

The answer is that pacts with the devil are operative only when the other party to the contract is a true believer,

a practicing Catholic. Panizza had portrayed the un-
healthiness of symbolic figures who still lived within him.
Churchgoers sensed, far more clearly than those who had
given up the Church, that this was what things were really
like in their Heaven. They did not dare acknowledge this
diabolic truth; they would do everything in their power to
prevent this council of love from taking place. For it was
a council in which their senile God-Father, their consump-
tive Saviour, their "immaculate demi-virgin" and the host
of accursed, neglected saints and martyrs, sat in judgment
upon them on earth.

It is no wonder that the judges of Imperial Germany
were outraged, for they felt personally attacked. They
knew that the words of the crucified Christ in the Prologue
to *The Council of Love* were actually directed at them,
although ostensibly He was speaking of the court of the
Borgia Popes: "Down there they first stuff themselves to
the bursting with sins, and then they eat of me and become
free of sin and fat and heavy, while we grow thin and
wretched."

The judges understood that more was at stake here than
an incident in the history of the Renaissance, more, in fact,
than the wrath of a God of Christendom. They had no
need to fear Him, for they could depend on Panizza's
saints to stop the old man with the white beard before he
hurled the footstool of his throne down on mankind—
thereby also destroying the terrestrial authorities on whose
willingness to believe the entire celestial realm depended.
For Heaven did depend on these authorities—on the authority of a Bismarck, say, the Iron Chancellor who had
warned Christ's deputies on earth: "We Germans fear

God, and nothing else in this world." The God meant was
the God of blood and iron.

Goethe's Mephisto:

> For in the end we depend
> On creatures we have made ourselves.

And Blake's Satan:

> The Elohim live on sacrifice
> Of Men; hence I am God of men! . . .

A deity whose symbols are losing their life has no choice
but to enter into a defensive alliance with the dictatorship
of hell against the menace of humanity. There is but one
hope—that Primal Evil is as stupid as it is cruel.

While the apparent subject of *The Council of Love* was
a Renaissance pope afflicted with venereal disease, its real
subject was the contamination of all earthly authority.
Panizza's Lord says to the Adversary, who has been ordered to appear at once before the throne: "We give you
divine permission to find a means for making men's bodies
rot while they live, but in such manner that their souls remain susceptible to redemption."

This last was the diabolic codicil of the pact. For the
devil limps away and begets syphilis, in order to infect the
church from head to limbs. To find the proper carrier for
his virulent germ, the devil passes in review the most redoubtable concubines out of the Bible and world history.
He examines each one naked, strips her down to the soul
and at last chooses Salomé. He questions her:

The Lost Library

"Why did you dance naked before Herod?" (She does not know.)
"With the head of John?" (She nods.)
"The blood dripped on your fingers?" (She nods.)
"Tell me, have you ever loved anyone? Herod? John? Your mother?"

She responds to each of his questions with a blissful, transfigured silence, with pure, uninhibited, diabolic innocence.

This Salomé is in no way similar to Oscar Wilde's sophistical, necrophilic prima ballerina. Neither is she the obedient little bourgeois daughter of her perverse mother Herodias, as Flaubert makes her out. She has been begot in another bed. One of her half brothers is the pious murderer of children, Gilles de Retz—the patron of Joan of Arc, the martyr of Huysmans' *Là-Bas,* "the saint in spite of himself," as the proselyte Claudel called him. Her other half brother is Richard Wagner's Parsifal, the racially pure fool:

"Do you acknowledge your great fault?"
"I did not know it" [Parsifal sings].
"Who sent you hither?"
"I do not know."

One of Salomé's little sisters was a young lady named Lulu, a stage whore created by the dramatist Frank Wedekind, who was Panizza's crony in the Munich coffeehouses. Lulu goes about the studios of Bohemia as a kind of elemental spirit. As cynical as Oscar Wilde and innocent as Parsifal, she helps to send a few conceited fops to the devil.

"Do you believe in a Creator?"
"I do not know."
"Then what do you believe in?"
"I do not know."
"Have you ever been in love?"
"I do not know."

Heaven and hell struggle in person for the two souls that, *Ach!* dwell in the breast of the Faustian German. Neither of the souls knows anything about the other, but as soon as one of them falls in love the Faustian German is betrayed, sold out. Eve, Gretchen, Lulu: Watch your step, you Germans, Old Nick himself is dealing the cards. There is always a crooked Alberich in a humanitarian disguise to snatch your winnings from under your nose; when you are about to take your tricks, there is always a Hagen, black as a Semite, to stab you in the back. . . . The blond hero Siegfried, the romantic visionary Tannhäuser, had to pay dearly for their idealism, before a germ-free Anointed One appeared who resisted the unGerman temptations of Klingsor's magic garden, who triumphed over the primal evil of the Eternal Feminine, the Venus-Kundry, as Richard Wagner triumphed over the opera.

"Music is a woman," Wagner cried at the age of thirtyeight. And Nietzsche, at that time his close friend, offered the advice: "When you go to woman, don't leave the whip behind."

The Wagnerian prohibition against love (*Liebesverbot*) had become the first rule of "masculine virtue." It was actuated by fear of the woman's power to infect blood and soul, by fear of venereal disease, the "French" sickness.

Syphilis, the God-endorsed malady of the heavenly Council of Love, could engender madness and ecstasy, genius and imbecility. Nietzsche had contracted the disease out of spite, in order to bring shame and humiliation on Christian morality. It was the punishment of the strong man who had not been strong enough and had succumbed to his pity for the weaker sex. It was the golden ulcer of the rich whose idol (as in Strindberg's occultist mystery play, *To Damascus*) was Mercury, the god of trade and also the alchemist's symbol for quicksilver. Quicksilver coated the mirrors of purchased Venuses and served as a remedy for syphilitics.

Syphilis was the paradisiac original sin in materialist literature; it was the killer hidden in the marrow of sensual pleasure. It was the substance from which Schopenhauer extracted the essence of his pessimism and his misogyny; from which Nietzsche drew his insane will to power. From it Maupassant derived the heroism in his love stories, Charles Louis Philippe the heroism of his pimp, Bubu of Montparnasse, and the Norwegian Hans Jaeger the heroism of the coffeehouse Viking in his *Kristiania Boheme*.

Syphilis was the whiplash of the sexual enlightenment.

No social redeemer was hailed as tempestuously as was Dr. Paul Ehrlich for his discovery of the antiluetic drug salvarsan (Ehrlich-Hata "606"). He would now save mankind from the disease that was an allegory of the fall of man. Now all that was needed was to get rid of the other aspect of Mercury—money—and mankind would be saved, freed from wage slavery to heaven. A little bacteriology and Marxism would clean up the whole mess; the stupid devil would be cheated of his due. Where there was nothing left for him to work with, what could the devil do?

As for HIM up there . . . After the liquidation of his comrade in arms, the Archenemy, HE could simply be denied out of existence. Nothing had been heard from HIM anyway since Biblical times; there was no longer any talk of a covenant with HIM. The contracts which had been signed were the ones with Satan, and Satan was done for. . . .

But was he really done for, really dead as a doornail? The trouble was, you never could be too sure, especially when you were an atheist, which meant a born doubter. And for that reason my father very often took *The Council of Love* off the shelves and read Panizza's slender volume again and again, with loving respect. You couldn't ever tell about Satan. And for that reason, too, fifty years after Marx and more than thirty years after Ehrlich's conquest of the spirochete, exorcisms and trials of heretics still went on in the paradise on earth from which God and Capitalism had both been "banished." Satan became incarnate in the bearded, cunning counterrevolutionary Trotsky, the seducer of the proletariat's soul. And even after that "pimp of the plutocrats" had been ambushed in his overseas hiding place and finally killed, you still could not be sure.

Chapter IV

The Three Unities—Either/Or: All or Nothing
—Salto Mortale—Dream Plays—The Constant.

THERE IS every reason to believe that the state prosecuting attorney would never have paid any attention to Panizza's divine tragedy if the work had not been a play. But as a play it constituted a threat to the stage, and the stage was an important social institution. Once a work was honored by being performed, the Germans took it for a pronouncement ex cathedra—they were extremely susceptible to anything spoken from a raised platform. Worshiping *Kultur* as they did, the Germans were the chosen people of the theater. Their critic, Gotthold Ephraim Lessing, had set forth what was to be their intellectual codex in his *Hamburg Dramaturgy*. It was their theaters rather than their universities that most actively took part in European cosmopolitanism.

Their foremost contribution to world literature, the one that ranked with the masterworks of Dante, Cervantes and Rabelais, was Goethe's untranslatable and unperformable puppet play about Doctor Faust. How fateful it was for Germany, and how unfortunate for Europe, that the music of Goethe's poetry could not be transposed to the scale of any other language! For in that poetry the inadequacy of life "becomes event."

74

The Lost Library

Alles Vergaengliche
Ist nur ein Gleichnis;
Das Unzulaengliche,
Hier wirds Ereignis.

Nobody so clearly formulated the essence of the German spirit as Goethe in *Faust;* yet in spite of the clarity of *Faust* the Germans delighted to build around it their gloomy philosophical speculations which Goethe called "their chief handicap, which gives their style an unsensuous, vague, twisted and twining character." All their musing and meditating, their storming and stressing, was directed in the drama toward the end that justifies the means, toward the message rather than the manner. They expended all their skill on the coldly calculated revenge in the fifth act; they were much better at that sort of thing than at the sprightliness and fresh air of comedy. Their dramatic genius, Christian Dietrich Grabbe, died of drink, forever denied recognition and fame, in spite of his great devil's comedy, *Jest, Satire, Irony and Deeper Significance,* in which he jeered at the dignity of scholars and dared to laugh at the honor of a young girl of the nobility.

The dramatic Germans took to the Swan of Avon with all the ardor of their romantic souls and realistic hearts. "Is not Shakespeare," they boasted, "more German in character than British? Are not our Wieland translation and our Schlegel-Tieck re-creation superior to the original?"

The Germans were drawn to the theater as the living incarnation of books, full of pomp and action. They were drawn to it as the convert is drawn to the Catholic Church with its multitude of saints and martyrs—or perhaps as the criminal is drawn to the scene of his crime. Disciplined even in their sensibilities, they looked up to stage productions, or rather to the director, far more submissively than did the Latins. Witness the power Richard Wagner wielded over them. They were captivated by his babbling, alliterative Valkyries (Wigalaweia—Hojotoho!), by the demagogy of his leitmotivs, by his instrumental führerdom, the brazen tyranny with which he directed both his sunken orchestra and the outbursts of applause in the pit—printing the instructions for applause in his programs for the Bayreuth ceremonials.

The Germans shared their passion for the theater (as for many other collective phenomena) with the Russians. They had the highest regard for the devotion and discipline of the Moscow Art Theater under the commanding generals Stanislavski and Nemirovich-Danchenko. They followed the pantomime with all the more delight because they did not understand a syllable of the spoken text. They loved the gesticulations that accompanied the insane roarings of Ivan in the play *The Death of Ivan the Terrible* (in which Alexey Tolstoy employed the style of the Shakespearian histories). They were enchanted by the Molièresque verve in Gogol's farce of bureaucracy, *The Inspector-General,* and by the study in gray of Gorki's *The Lower Depths.*

From the Russians they learned the social collective drama; from the French (Antoine and Lugné-Poë) they learned the *coup de théâtre.* And before long they surpassed all others, thanks to Otto Brahm's virtuosity in the chiaroscuros of the proletarian drama and thanks to their unsurpassed Austrian master of ceremonies, Max Reinhardt.

The Lost Library

Without the theater I would have been a lost soul—born as I was in an apartment house in the bleak Prussian capital of Berlin. I would have had not one sacred memory of youth. But when my parents took me to an opening at which Joseph Kainz read from the roles of the poet martyrs—Goethe's *Tasso* and Rostand's *Cyrano de Bergerac,* when in his Lessing Theater Otto Brahm introduced a Naturalist, when Max Reinhardt put on Sophocles' *Oedipus* as a monster spectacle in a circus arena—then I too celebrated my high holidays. Ibsen, Björnsen, Gerhart Hauptmann, Wedekind, Shaw and Strindberg—these were the composers of the agnostic's Masses.

Now, as I unpacked, the scores all lay about me. I asked myself whether and when I would hear them again, since now there were but two places where their cathedrals were still open to me: Vienna and Salzburg during the festivals. And at the same time the volumes took up too much room—in boxes heaped one on top of the other, since I did not have enough proper bookcases. The room was half as large as my father's had been, for his had been designed to hold the books garnered during a lifetime. Now I was merely in a waiting room on the exile's trek, and books signified excess baggage. And in Vienna the ground was already beginning to quake perceptibly.

What finally moved me to unpack them and set them out anyway was a lingering remnant of piety and the recollection of the stage magic of domestic dramas, with their openings as dry and meticulous as a police report:

An untidy living room upholstered in faded plush. In the background a window opening onto a gloomy street. On the left a secretary desk piled high with accounts, and above it the yellowed photograph of an upstanding young couple in wedding dress. On the dining table the remains of a frugal meal and an empty bottle of whisky. Right, a half-open door leading presumably to a bedroom. When the curtain rises . . .

But the curtain which in rising had married the two fragmentary worlds on either side of the footlights no longer rose. Naturalism had meanwhile been carried so far that no illusion, no trap door, no foreground remained for the exiled imagination, and the public found itself in an open gladiatorial arena. The watchword of the founders of the Volksbuehne, those hotheaded young stage reformers of the 1880's, had been: "Truth! Truth! Truth!" "Art for the people" had been realized. The ruling majority had taken over as collective directors and would put up with no more illusions; audiences were to be abolished and everyone became a participant.

Earlier, theatrical critics had written scornfully: Your pretense of verisimilitude is a sham as long as your millionaire's drawing rooms and your poor people's cottages lack the "fourth wall."

The directors tried everything imaginable as a substitute: steps down into the orchestra, revolving stages, cinematic projection, open-air performances. But it was all in vain. For the fourth wall had been the rising curtain, and that they had eliminated.

I have rarely been more moved than by my first communion with the theater: the curtain turning red, trembling and rising. To me it was the revelation of everything that takes place between the printed lines of a book. To this day, when the curtain rises and the musty odor of the sets wafts toward me from any open stage, I always feel the same sensual shuddering. This always moved me more than the performance itself. True to tradition, my parents took me first to Schiller's *Wilhelm Tell*. But the Alpine fashion show, and the iambics over which all my schoolmasters had mulled, only annoyed me.

But I was utterly entranced by the theater when I went to a performance of a modern drama and saw actors moving about in ordinary street clothes, heard them talking in the very tones of my parents at home—and nevertheless elevated into another dimension. It was a performance of Ibsen's *Ghosts;* the topical realism touched me so closely because the dramatist who had invoked these scenes had until recently been alive at the same time as I. Ibsen was my contemporary, although he was far away in Norway and cut off from the world by the mental derangement of senility. His death was within my memory; the entire world press had mourned him as if he had been a king, and had proclaimed that he was already a classic.

Before the performance my father had recommended that I pay close attention to the way the actor would speak the final sentence: "Mother, give me the sun!" For every time the play was performed the public would violently debate that last sentence. Was the son who had been hereditarily infected by the sins of his father allegorically asking for the bright sunlight of faith? Not at all, the materialist idealists insisted: he was announcing the social demands of youth who had been cheated of their share in life. Nonsense, averred the disciples of the infallible Danish critic, Georg Brandes; that cry was nothing but a pathological concomitant of paralysis. The sick boy, blinded

by the shock of daylight, stammers: "Give me . . . the
. . . sun," but he really wants to say: "Mother, give me
the poison."

Probably all I grasped of this was an obscure premonition that from the very beginning some repulsive truth was concealed behind the scenes, and that the moment it was to appear frankly, unadorned, the nemesis intervened and the curtain fell. Ibsen's philosophy was the curtain which always fell before the solution to the problem. With the arrogance of which only the personally modest great men are capable, he had declared, "It's up to me to ask questions. Answers I have none."

His doctrine was the "life lie." There were the hidden sins in a wife's early life. There were the technological dreams of a commonplace photographer who wrecks his precarious family fortunes on a speculation. There was the lie of the tame "wild duck," the pet which the little girl has been given by her rich natural father—who has also bequeathed her a hereditary eye disease, so that the child is going blind.

Everyone raises his own wild duck! His life lie. How true! everyone exclaims, with a stern glance at his neighbor. Away with it!

And in every Ibsen play there was one character who was fanatical about the truth—a clergyman, a youthful reformer from a well-to-do family, someone suffering from what one Ibsen doctor calls "integrity fever," someone who opens the eyes of the willfully blind, of those who refuse to see the future—and thereby starts the whole tragedy. Ibsen rang the changes on this theme with such tortuous monotony that he returned in principle to the

Aristotelian unities (of time, place and action). And he also reintroduced the Greek Nemesis, which he had flouted in his early works (at that time hardly ever performed): the Faustian dramas *Brand* and *Peer Gynt*.

Brand, a Norwegian country pastor and self-appointed savior of mankind from the life lie, does not rest until he has sacrificed everything, his mother, friends, wife, child and life, to his gospel of *all or nothing*. He sets out for the ends of the earth, and the end arrives with his arrival; he ends with himself alone in the dull grandeur of the ice fields of Norway.

Hence: "Be wholly yourself."

Find your way back to yourself as that rogue of truth, Peer Gynt, after he tired of traveling through the world, found his way back to his now-aged sweetheart, Solveig. Or else: Give yourself up entirely like that fool of a savior, Pastor Brand. In other words, be all or nothing—which is what Brand's Danish pragmatic colleague, Sören Kierkegaard, preached in his *Either/Or*. "Either/Or is the pass which leads to the Absolute, to God!"

All or nothing!

Stubborn in his dogma, Pastor Brand extorts from his mother the entire patrimony, from his wife and child the whole content of their lives, from the authorities the entire public welfare fund for his church. And when he has at last built the church, he throws the keys into the river rather than make compromises with the omnipotent authorities. And then, when his locked-out congregation threatens to stone him, he still holds to his mission and escapes to Nature's church on the glacier, where he is awaited by the once-scorned, rejected sinner. She shields him from the ghost of his dead wife, from the Falcon, the mythic carrion-eating bird—but not from the natural catastrophe of the avalanche.

For how should a proud Ibsen hero owe his life to another's act of will?

BRAND

(bowing under the falling avalanche and calling to Heaven)

Tell me, God, in the face of death,
Does not a single grain of will
Weigh with you—*quantum satis?*

(The avalanche buries him.)

A VOICE

God is *deus caritatis.*

Kierkegaard: "One who went out thinking to commit suicide—at that very moment a stone fell upon him and killed him, and he died with the words: 'Praised be God!' "

"I have read little Kierkegaard and understood still less," Henrik Ibsen wrote indignantly in a letter.

Ibsen wanted to be Ibsen: Either/Or.

But Brand was his Sören Kierkegaard.

Of the performances of the plays of Ibsen's son-in-law, his junior by four years, his rival and a Nobel prize winner, Björnstjerne Björnson, nothing has stuck in my mind but a feeble memory of the end of the third act of *Beyond Our Power* (Part II). The scene is a banquet in a capitalist's castle which a nihilistic Jesus blows up with an infernal machine. After the pyrotechnic display on the stage, the savior himself dies, whereupon a sister of his announces that out of this suffering, Faith and Hope will appear. At this cue these promptly step forth and promise a Manchester-industry paradise on earth.

It was highly significant for the future that such a hodgepodge of nitroglycerin and ideology was a hit on the German stage—hailed nightly by outcries among the élite audience and by ladies fainting; already they were trembling voluptuously at the prospect of the world's going to smash in a Teutonic Ragnarok, of which the two Scandinavian dramatists were the scalds.

It might seem today that the naturalistic theater blew up, leaving no mark on literature except for a little soot after the smoke of the stage thunder had cleared. To be sure, there was a good deal of hysterical excitement in the orchestra on opening nights. In Antoine's Théâtre Libre and in Otto Brahm's Lessing Theater in Berlin a few members of the theater group would appear unshaven on the stage and in carefully rehearsed dialogue and gestures would deliver inflammatory speeches against the existing order and the prevailing morality. The men in frock coats and gold-braided uniforms, the ladies in pearl necklaces and evening dresses with long, rustling trains, would cry out, "Police, police! Censor! Help!" But perhaps this nervous tension arose from the bad conscience and the evil premonitions of a gala opening-night audience who felt themselves unmasked like Hamlet's uncle watching the players.

And when such an audience asked, "What is the play called," they found the title in their programs: "The Mouse-trap." And perhaps because we in Vienna were already inside the mouse-trap, we found that we had lost our appetite for naturalistic dramas; we were no longer very curious to experience their social "catharsis" and their "tragic irony."

It was therefore with a good deal of suspicion that I examined the dramas of the leading German playwright, Gerhart Hauptmann, erstwhile poet laureate of German Social Democracy, then the bard of the Kaiser's *Deutschland über Alles* in the First World War, then the Olympian of the Weimar Republic, then the revered old man of the dictatorship of the Third Reich.

In my youth my father used to tell me about those "glorious days of the nineties" when young Hauptmann, "brilliant as a young Goethe and with the primitive power of a Silesian drover," stepped into the theatrical ring and defeated the European champion of the worn-out *coup de théâtre,* Hermann Sudermann. My father would describe how infuriated the reactionaries were, and he always cherished fond memories of that notable achievement—even after his darling horrified him by writing a jingoistic Prussian puppet play in doggerel verse: *1813.* My father buried his review copy of this book behind the *Collected Works,* thus hiding from sight this first example of apostasy in the ranks of progressive literature.

Nevertheless, in *The Weavers,* Gerhart Hauptmann had given the German theater its only revolutionary play based on recent German history. The Silesian weavers' revolt against starvation in 1844 became, like the English Luddite movement, a classic subject for recrimination in the drama of social struggle.

A scribe who once upon a time was highly esteemed in London, Brussels and Paris, among the Bohemian exiles of the revolutions of 1848, no other than Karl Marx, was very much concerned with the weavers. He had derived his unreadable and casuistic theory of surplus value, as had Engels, from the misery of the English weavers. He dedicated his main work, *Das Kapital,* to the historian of the uprising of the enslaved Silesian weavers, Wilhelm Wolff. And he conferred Marxist canonization on his friend Heinrich Heine, the exiled poet who wrote the magnificently powerful weavers' hymn. After Heine's death Marx excommunicated him, calling him an "archscoundrel" and a "hireling of reaction"; but he included Heine's tempestuous stanzas in his proletarian breviary:

> . . . *Wir weben hinein den ewigen Fluch,*
> *Deutschland, wir weben Dein Leichentuch.*
> *Wir weben, wir weben.*
> (We weave into our work our eternal curse,
> Germany, we are weaving your winding sheet.
> Weaving, weaving, weaving.)

Heine's eternal curse and Wolff's historical material were woven by Gerhart Hauptmann, the propertied grandson of a poor Silesian weaver, into one of the most profitable series of scenes in the entire German repertory.

The first performance of the play took place under police supervision, behind closed doors. It was given by the Verein Freie Buehne, a Berlin theater group founded by Otto Brahm and Maximilian Harden, which occupied itself with censored literature, deification of the proletariat and companionate marriage. That first performance was a sensation, and word went out that a new Sermon on the Mount from the Silesian Mountains had been delivered. Before long the drama was being given in every theater in all the large and middle-sized cities of Germany, because it proclaimed the gospel of the "oppressed opposition."

The new gospel, "Necessity knows no law," was the counterpart of the motto of Hohenzollern imperialism: Might over right.

Hauptmann's characters were farm hands and servant girls. They spoke the unadulterated clumsy jargon of the peasants of the Silesian Mountains, which gave a glamour to their platitudes and obscenities. And as long as Hauptmann himself shared their rude and vulgar aspirations, he was astonishingly genuine. But then, at the height of his success, he fell victim to the sin of arrogance. Profundity was his undoing. It fogged his brain—but that was not the worst of it. Henceforth, for all his fame, no matter what fairy-tale swathings he wrapped around his peasant girls, no matter whether he stuck his heroes in knight's armor or the garments of Aztec idols—his characters were frozen in the pattern of *The Weavers*. They never got any farther and simply went on reiterating what seemed to be the ultimate wisdom of poor Hauptmann's almanac:

"I've been a good man all my life . . . and what have I got out of it?"

"And things have got to change, I tell you, and do it right now. We won't put up with it any more . . . Come what may . . . you imps of Satan!"

Things had got to change—that was the solution to everything. And at once. Rise and be transformed! Arise, ye wretched of the earth! Since being good, being as tame as a corpse, had led to nothing, the next step was: All or nothing, Either/Or. Come what may. And what might, came, barely fifty years later. And came, in any case, at the right time for the author of *The Weavers* and for his interested audience from the orchestra to the fourth balcony—though not for the weavers. The weavers got as little out of it as they had got out of being good. When the great change came in Russia and in Germany, it took an unexpected form. And the new order was already spreading, creeping toward Vienna, toward the rest of the world. But the main thing was that something was happening; things were changing, the way they did in the theater.

"Well, thou hast seen thy God, Jokanaan," whispers Oscar Wilde's Salomé to the head of John the Baptist. "But me thou didst never. If thou hadst seen me, thou hadst loved me."

Seven riddles of the universe—Creation, force and matter, life, soul, consciousness, freedom of the will—and in addition the whole social question—had been put to the Occidental Oedipus, the cultured man of the nineteenth century. He turned the riddles over in his mind a little while and then stated that they had been solved, and that the social question was answered by the Communist Manifesto. God and the desert of the universe no longer held any mysteries for him; perhaps he would have become a totalitarian desperado right then and there, if he had not had one unsolved riddle left: the riddle of woman.

Salvation no longer existed, but thank God there was still sin. There was no longer an Eternal, but there was still the eternal feminine. The world spirit who brooded over the chaos had been secularized, but the daughter of the "earth spirit" was not yet nationalized. Her full-bosomed torso still existed to confound the puritanical iconoclasts of female suffrage. Woman still reigned behind the scenes of the world theater. She could still convert her favors into political power like the Theban state courtesan, Phryne, or withhold her favors in the interests of pacifism, like Aristophanes' Lysistrata.

Woman was *Le Sphinx* (a drawing-room tragedy by Octave Feuillet). She was *La Pauvre Lionne* (by Émile Augier, the moralist of the *honnêtes gens*). She was a pretty, expensive pet in whalebone corset, ermine wrap and *coiffure pleureuse*.

The true wild beast in lovely savagery——
If that you want to see, my ladies, come to me . . .

declaimed the actor-playwright Frank Wedekind in the prologue to his horror play, *Erdgeist*. Dressed in a red lion tamer's costume, he ushered forth his Lulu, that little prodigy for whom every eternal adolescent and Nietzschean was prepared to kill himself and all the rest of humanity on the spot.

"Go on, gentlemen, laugh. This is all so tragic, you know."

But his juggling with destinies succeeded only when he himself acted in his plays, and when he directed them, showing his universally adored wife Tilly balancing on the sphere while he cracked the whip. Each of his dramas was a variety show of wild and breakneck paradoxes. His art was a perilous *salto mortale,* a death-defying leap which ended with him.

Wedekind's vogue never extended beyond Germany, and even there he never attained complete respectability. He was considered a petty showman, not to be compared with the worldly Englishman who had learned, for all he said he hadn't, from Ibsen—the British Puck (or Caliban, if you will), George Bernard Shaw. Wedekind received full recognition in Germany late in his career, after the First World War, when the German expressionists appropriated his types: the prostitute, the athlete, the "masked gentleman" and his other poster allegories.

Perhaps it can be said that he created nothing lasting, except for the lasting memory one retains of the wonderful female equestrienne one saw as a child at one's first traveling circus; her pink sash can neither be forgotten, nor eclipsed by the costume of any other heroine on earth.

Wedekind was of American stock. He began his career as a publicist for a Swiss meat-extract firm and for a traveling circus. His passion, which he shared with the entire cosmopolitan world of his day, was the circus and vaudeville: untrammeled theater. For the circus was the place for the stylized acrobatics of modernism, the aerial feats of the intellect bottomside up on the flying trapeze. There the nose dive into illusion, which the stage hero merely talked about and which the stage director faked by a trick of lighting, was actually performed by artists who were in real danger of falling. There the heads of the audience were literally turned as they craned their necks to watch. The "split personality" of a Gioconda, even when projected by an Eleanora Duse, could not compare with the smiling lady in the box who was sawed physically in half. D'Annunzio's capricious *terza rima* could not compete with the suppleness of the Egyptian snake dancer in her sequined skin of scales. Gorki's "ragged barons" and poet-rogues might be more tragic, but they were certainly less amusing than the eccentrics with their sorrow painted on their faces and the poker-faced clowns in plus-fours perched high on their velocipedes.

Dulled to the social "repent ye" sermons of naturalism and bored by the vivisections of the feminine psyche—the surgery lasting through five acts in the same Chippendale décor—we flocked to the Wedekind type of music-hall art. Those were our earliest literary escapades. There was too much security in our lives; we wanted the uncertainty of the tightrope walker who balanced on the wire between the circus sky and the fatal fall. Escaping from the regular lessons of grammar and the rule of three, we longed for mystification of one kind or another, for mirror illusions or verbal prestidigitation.

We longed for a peep show, something scary, spectral, lascivious: Maeterlinck's Gothic-symbolist marionettes in dream temples (*Monna Vanna,* or virtue in dishabille); Edmond Rostand's fable in alexandrines about the pasha of the hen yard, Chantecler, and his alluringly stockinged hens; Oscar Métenier's Grand Guignol with Octave Mirbeau's dramatized penny dreadful about Chinese tortures, *Le Jardin des Supplices;* or, at the Abbey Theatre in Dublin, John Millington Synge's horrific burlesque, *The Playboy of the Western World,* a painfully funny picture of a hapless village fool and parricide.

But the best of them all was August Strindberg, the "wild Swede," the Swedenborgian, who threw his audiences into a nervous fever with his fakir's tricks. Props vanished, blocking out spaces in which breathless changes of scene led nowhere. The daughters of Indra, the atmospheric Brahma, came down into the poisonous vapors of the Third Circle, the earth, and went about starving for air. They went to the Growing Castle, which their earthly foster father, the master glazier, could not see. There lived the self-interned officer who every evening waited at the stage entrance after the performance for the great singer. But she never came out and at last, grown gray and childish, he had to go backward through all the torments of examinations down to the lowest preschool class of immaturity. But the poet wedded his sweetheart, Indra's daughter, and took her home to the airtight, tapestry-walled marital chamber without an exit. Before the barred door the theologian, the philosopher, the doctor and the lawyer quarreled over the truth, believed by the one, deduced by the other, investigated by the third and possibly provable by the fourth—the truth that was behind the door. And when the master glazier opened it they found out what was behind it: nonsense. Nothing. The solution.

But the worked-up audience, looking at reality through a Strindberg prism, asked themselves: What is Strindberg? Was he the Scandinavian genius? Or a paranoiac? A prestidigitator who wanted to put Brahmanism, Christianity, social consciousness and eroticism under a top hat and produce a seven-riddles-of-the-world omelette?

There was the Strindberg marriage, which was a strait jacket placed on the father by his old nurse and his wife. There were the Strindberg hells of daily life, the Strindberg mineralogy of nations, his nonsense chemistry (in his *Blue Book*). What an abstruse, glassy, grotesque cosmos it was! But where, from the Buddhist point of view, lay the optical illusion? Was it in the object, in the prism or in the observer?

It was nowhere; it consisted in the indivisible trinity. But this trinity was already in process of dissolution, for men analyzed such phenomena separately, isolating each single one as the whole of reality. In Strindberg the various fancies devoured one another like snakes in a pit. It was this quality about Strindberg which made "right-thinking people" dub his work the monstrous effusions of a sick mind.

"If you read Swedenborg," Strindberg wrote in his autobiographical *Gothic Rooms*, "you will find that his description of hells which are states of mind and not places coincide with these fancies. But there is a constant. Seek it and you will solve many a riddle."

But people wanted more precise directions than that. Where were they now? Was the destination some future paradise—or hell?

"Hell," replied George Bernard Shaw's Don Juan ("A Dream of Hell") "is the Home of the Unreal and of the seekers for Happiness. . . . The only refuge from Heaven, which is the home of the masters of reality—and the earth, which is the home of the slaves of reality. . . ."

There they stood, the Ibsens, Björnsons, Hauptmanns, the Strindbergs, Wedekinds, Maeterlincks and G.B.S.—though exactly where *he* stood you could never tell. There they were, making their pilgrimage to reality and back, across a hundred stages and a thousand changes of scene. There they were, bound and collected in my father's library. My father who died a freethinker and left them to me—the slave of reality.

Chapter V

The Growing Castle and the Abbeye de Thélème
—La Guillotine de la Liberté et la Bibliothèque
St. Geneviève—O saisons, o châteaux!

EVERYONE'S UTOPIA has a geographic locus, a Zion, a Vatican, a Regensburg Valhalla, a Kremlin, a castle that grows as long as you stand outside it, into which you enter only by an orthodox compromise and from which you emerge only by a cynical back door.

My father's castle was situated in Paris.

He had never been there, although Paris was the metropolis of his library. He dressed like a Frenchman, and even the style of his beard was French. He drank the *grands crus* of Burgundy, translated almost all the important French lyrics, but denied himself Paris—as, I suspect, a happily married man denies himself a secret sweetheart.

His sweetheart wore a Sphinx's hood; she was Colombine, *l'implacable enfant* of Verlaine; sometimes she was Baudelaire's mulatto woman; she trilled the *Chanson des Gueux* and *Chansons Rosses* of Jean Richepin and Aristide Bruant—the entire repertory of the *Lapin à Ghil* and the *Cafés Chantants*. His sweetheart was old Flemish songs of passion (adapted by Maeterlinck for the diseuse Yvette Guilbert, the siren-voiced vampire of Montmartre). His sweetheart was vice personified, attired in a Félicien Rops *négligé* or the habit of a nun of the Abbeye de Thélème,

93

above the main portal of which stood the antidogmatic dogma of Rabelais: *"Fais ce que vouldras!"*

This Paris of his was:

Les Litanies de Satan (Baudelaire).

La Carmagnole.

L'Après-Midi d'un Faune (Mallarmé).

It was Voltaire's *Écrasez l'Infâme* (the Church). And it was the *On y danse* of the mob at the annual celebration of the storming of the Bastille. And it was the relentless *J'accuse* of Zola the Dreyfusard. It was *le Caveau* of the first proletarian singers, Désaugiers and Béranger and *La Ballade de la Mauvaise Réputation* of *"pauvre Lélian—ce cochon de Verlaine."*

Above all it was the tabernacle of everything to which the adjective *free* could be applied—freethinking and "free love," the Free Theater (Antoine's *Théâtre Libre*), the free verse of Jules Laforgue and the free rhythms of the Belgian Verhaeren.

It was the puppet-play country of Alfred Jarry's *Ubu Roi—Ubu Enchainé:*

Act I. Scene II.

The Field of Mars

The three free men. The corporal.

We are free men and here is our corporal. Hurrah for liberty, liberty, liberty. We are free. Never forget that our duty is to be free. Walk a little slower or we'll arrive on time. Liberty is never arriving on time— never, never! Let us have our liberty drill. Let's disobey all together, one, two, three, you first, you second, you third. There's the difference. Every one of us marches in a different rhythm, even though it's more tiring. Let us disobey individually our freemen's corporal.

THE CORPORAL. Riot!

Collective disobedience under orders from the corporal of liberty in the "riot camp"—that would be total freedom for humanity, the freedom of all with respect to each. The next step after that kind of freedom was to press the muzzle of a revolver to one's temple—and that was the step Alfred Jarry took.

My father would go on so ardently about Paris that my mother actually urged him to take a trip there—with a jealous undertone equivalent to: "Why don't you introduce the woman to me?" Whereupon my father would promptly fall silent and would turn to his shelf of foreign poetry to pick out an "unbiased" poet—Sully Prudhomme or Swinburne or Walt Whitman—and set to work on one of his free translations, while my mother would go to her piano and take musical revenge by playing a bagatelle of César Franck.

In his heart my father knew that my mother's jealousy was justified. To be sure, he always insisted that in poetry he would not be deceived "either by the new natural philosophy or by the pious penitence that has become fashionable since Verlaine and Maeterlinck." He might repeat emphatically: "We who have smashed the bridges of dogma behind us must go forward with reasonless optimism toward the eternally longed-for goal." But he knew very well that his idolatry bordered on the mystical and irrational. The *divine Liberté* whom he worshiped had ordered her high priest, Robespierre, to guillotine her singers, Désorgues and Chénier—and then for a whim had had Robespierre himself beheaded by her deadly toy.

Yes, my father knew very well that *Liberté* was a fickle wench. He knew her past from that penetrating novel of the Revolution by the freethinker Anatole France: *The Gods Are Athirst*. He knew very well that all these goddesses of liberty had an unquenchable thirst for power. And this was even more true of the terrestrial, power-drunk demigods and the self-intoxicated demitalents such as Anatole France's hero, Evariste Gamelin, the student of David and the propaganda painter for liberty, who did not deviate by a brushstroke from the principles of the National Convention and who covered his defects as an artist with the crimson of death sentences. Even more horrible were the cold killers who were immune to any kind of intoxication, those state prosecutors for Liberty, the Fouquier-Tinville crew.

My father was also aware of how vulgar Liberty could be when she trafficked with politics, how chauvinistic or jingoistic. Political jargon could reduce her to a whore of Babylon. And yet he read with pounding heart the names of those who had dedicated themselves to her: Schiller and Heine, Pushkin and Victor Hugo.

"Liberty in art, liberty in society!" Hugo had declaimed. "That is the double banner which rallies all of youth, led by the élite of every generation. . . ."

Forward . . . toward the eternally longed-for goal.

"What I am afraid of is that this longing will eventually come to fulfillment," Heine had said. He had himself espoused the cause of political liberty, in order to forget the physical and spiritual torments of romantic *Welt-schmerz* and Byronic "ennui."

Heine died in suffering in Paris early in 1856—the year my father was born. Nine months before, Charles Baudelaire had published in the *Revue des Deux Mondes* his prologue to the *Fleurs du Mal:*

Au Lecteur

*Il ferait volontiers de la terre un débris
Et dans un baillement avalerait le monde;
C'est l'Ennui—L'oeuil chargé d'un pleur involontaire,
Il rêve d'échafauds en fumant son houka.
Tu le connais, lecteur, ce monstre délicat.*

After this description, could "ennui" deny that it was the father of Liberty? The paternity charge was as good as legally proved.

Charles Baudelaire begins his journal, *Mon Coeur Mis à Nu,* with the insight:

"*De la vaporisation et de la centralisation du Moi. Tout est là . . .*"

A reader heckles: "One moment please. Just what is there?"

"The thing-in-itself."

"Where?"

"You should have looked closer. If you had, you would perceive it now."

"I see nothing. What does it look like?"

"Like a soap bubble that has burst."

"How can I possibly see something when nothing is left of it?"

"Something is left. The content."

"A soap bubble has no contents. And after it has burst there is nothing left of it."

"There is. The impression of colorfulness and of beauty—or Baudelaire's euphony."

"Beauty and euphony are matters of interpretation."

". . . Like space and time."

"I beg your pardon! I can measure space with a yardstick and tell time by the clock."

"You can also determine both by Baudelaire's heart laid bare—the universe by the size of the heart and the time of life by the beat of the heart, by the relation of infinity and finiteness to the Self in itself, by metaphor."

"What is the essential of it, its form or its content?"

"Baudelaire's answer is: 'Love of beauty to the exclusion of all else is the necessary condition for the production of works of art.' "

"For instance, of soap bubbles. But what are soap bubbles good for?"

"Hm. The sea exists in order . . . well . . . in order to proclaim the immensity of creation and to promote shipping. Mountains and valleys teach us nobility, as well as humility and strategy. The fruits of the earth yield the blessing of work and planned economy. . . . Doesn't everything that exists exist for a purpose? The soap bubble for blowing . . . love so that man need not be alone in his ennui. Or, Baudelaire's albatross—soaring over the infinite seas of his onomatopoeia, it follows an infallibly euphonious instinct: AL-BA-TROS. But, captured by sailors, the target of their crude jokes, it waddles painfully around the quarterdeck:

The Lost Library

Exilé sur le sol au milieu des huées,
Ses ailes de géant l'empêchent de marcher.

And then it looks exactly the way poetry looked to that teleological helmsman, Sören Kierkegaard: 'An inadequate compromise with reality.' "

Baudelaire borrowed the phrase, *Mon coeur mis à nu,* from Edgar Allan Poe, whose most loyal interpreter Baudelaire was. Poe wrote:

> Suggested title: Heart Laid Bare. If any ambitious man have a fancy to revolutionize at one effort the universal world of human thought, human opinion and human sentiment, the opportunity is his own. All that he has to do is to write and publish a very little book: My Heart Laid Bare.

The albatross which Baudelaire had sighted on his crossing of the Atlantic was the Angel of the Odd, *l'ange du bizarre.*

Back from America, Baudelaire wrote in the preface to his translation of Edgar Allan Poe:

> Recently an unfortunate was brought into our courts whose brow was adorned with a strange and singular tattooing: No luck! Thus he wore above his eyes the label defining his life, like the title of a book, and the interrogation proved that this strange title was terribly true.

The message of the fallen angel Israfel ("whose heartstrings are a lute") whose cult Baudelaire introduced into Europe was:

99

I would define the poetry of words as the rhythmical creation of Beauty. Its sole arbiter is Taste. With the intellect or with the conscience it has only collateral relation. Unless incidentally, it has no concern whatever either with Duty or with Truth. . . . [E. A. Poe, *The Poetic Principle.*]

On the compass employed by the Occident in its explorations and voyages around the world, the markings show Truth in the east, Biblical Morality in the south, Reason in the west. But the magnetic needle Duty points inexorably toward the Pole Star of Purpose.

On the compass of the figurative adjacent sphere—intuition—the needle of Taste points infallibly toward the magnetic pole of Beauty.

The succession of fatal shipwrecks in which Occidental thought has repeatedly come to grief have all been caused by one illusion: that reason and knowledge are two fixed points on a transcendental continent, that they are the end of the world, so that no one can travel beyond them.

Again and again Occidental thought has steered by a compass whose card showed these twin arrows. Always Western thought has set sail toward a self-evident truth, and regularly it has been caught up and wrecked in the tornado of unforseeable passions. The wild winds which have buffeted it could only have been predicted musically.

> *De la musique avant toute chose* . . .
> *Et pour cela préfère l'impair.*
> (Music first of all . . .
> And therefore I prefer odd to even.)

For the musical system of co-ordinates was governed by the occult, by odd numbers, not by dualistic, evenly divisible numbers.

Plus vague et plus soluble dans l'air
Sans rien en lui qui pèse ou qui pose . . .

In the nine stanzas of his *Art Poétique* Paul Verlaine had provided the key to the West's white magic of numerals.

II.

Il faut aussi que tu n'ailles point
Choisir tes mots sans quelque méprise:
Rien de plus cher que la chanson grise
Ou l'Indécis au Précis se joint. . . .

IX.

Que ton vers soit la bonne aventure
Éparse au vent crispé du matin
Qui va fleurant la menthe et la thym . . .
Et tout le reste est littérature. . . .

Somewhat more didactically, the "symbolist" Stéphane Mallarmé, speaking as Monsieur le professeur de lycée, said: "Too much precision of meaning is ruinous to literature, which is necessarily vague." (*Le sens trop précis râture ta vague littérature.*)

A word to the wise . . .

Since my father was a translator, poetry was his professional reading matter. He studied the technique and nature of poetry in all languages and styles.

Of course, even the most felicitous translator is the second lover of the Lady Fancy whom the first has already deflowered. She accompanies the translator of the moment, who introduces her to us, like any belle walking with her current lover. Shakespeare's Dark Lady is not the same as the dark lady of his translator, the Catholic Romantic poet, Von Schlegel. One of François Villon's *filles de joye* behaves differently in the company of the Victorian Swinburne. One of Louise Labé's love sonnets has an altogether different sort of intensity in the original from what it has in Rainer Maria Rilke's version—it is as different as the Japanese print is from the copy sketched in charcoal by Degas.

My father never quite made up his mind whether poetry was translatable or untranslatable, whether the sound or the picture evoked through the language was what counted most.

What, for example, was the fundamental quality of the albatross: its phonetic or its physical structure?

What was the *tertium comparationis?* The similar fate of poet and albatross; the figure that Baudelaire had created, or the strange, odd sound and rhythm of the bird's name, which Baudelaire had borrowed from Coleridge's "Rime of the Ancient Mariner."

(When Coleridge wrote his poem of the distressed sailors to whom the albatross appeared as a consoling, miraculous symbol, it was the name itself which appealed to him. Then his fellow poet, Wordsworth, proposed to him the popular ballad idea that the starving sailors should kill the bird of good omen. From these two ideas sprang the theory of poetry embodied in their joint *Lyrical Ballads*.)

What is poetic? It is an insoluble, idle question—for every line of verse is the product of perfect idleness, *une oeuvre du désoeuvrement,* the iridescent soap bubble of gray ennui, of boredom and the lament over the shortness, the monotony, the very content of life—in short, over nothing. A soap bubble like reality, like our earth—for our planet too is one of many soap bubbles, one of the innumerable spherical variants in this universe which itself has no form, which includes all realities within itself and yet has no content. For the universe is idleness in itself, the ennui of creation.

Says Dostoevsky's Devil to Ivan Karamazov:

> Our present earth may have been repeated a billion times. Why, it's become extinct, been frozen, cracked, broken to bits, disintegrated into its elements; again "the water above the firmament," then again a comet, again a sun, again from the sun it becomes earth—and the same sequence may have been repeated endlessly and exactly the same to every detail. Most unseemly and insufferably tedious . . .

Fortunately for bored humanity and for literature, there are men of action who from time to time convert the soap bubbles into rubble heaps. For the fact is, or has been up to now at any rate, that all the colossal victories of the generals and the courage of their armies, all the fervor of the revolutionaries who free the people from their yoke—*et tout le reste*—would not last any longer than a soap bubble if these things were not condensed into literature and preserved in libraries. The men who make history owe their conquest of posterity solely to literature. For all their founding of cities, their extension of frontiers, their belts of fortresses, their thermae and sewage projects, are at best as static as their equestrian statues in bronze and marble. Only in the drama or in fiction do they come to life again.

No matter what terror the "greatest man of all times" aroused during his lifetime, his tyranny compares to later tyrannies as a shower of stones from a catapult compares to modern bombing. Acts kill themselves the moment they are committed. They become irrevocable; they cannot be rewritten like the plot of a drama or novel. No man of action, no Alexander the Great, Caligula or Jack the Ripper, can repeat his role—as even the poorest actor can do. No man of action can choose a better supporting cast which will do greater justice to the content of his life and give it new impetus. The next Caesar who steps on the stage inevitably steals the show from him. When Napoleon the Great, the Little Corporal, marched into Potsdam, he had the lid of Frederick the Great's coffin lifted so that he might look in. And Frederick could no more prevent him than could Napoleon stop another successful corporal from planting himself on his marble tomb in the Dôme des Invalides, arms folded in the Napoleonic manner. In fact, the real accomplishment of the first two was to die decently and be decently interred in a coffin. The Führer never made the grave.

In history their myths are no more substantial than those of Achilles or Goliath or even a Falstaff. As Byron says:

> What matters where we fall to fill the maws
> Of worms—on battle-plains or listed spot?
> Both are but theaters where the chief actors rot.

What history transmits to us are facts. "And there is nothing easier to arrange than facts," according to the historic statement of that Bishop Talleyrand who has gone down in history as a diplomat. History was never at the scene; an eyewitness does not make history. It is the historians who make it, and the tale is historically the more credible the more contradictions the historians dig up out of the reports of the eyewitnesses. But the writer is present at the scene of the action and he does not give a damn whether it happened mythologically, historically, in the present or in some distant utopia. He catches it red-handed, and in the moment that his work is produced, pantomimed or recited it has more reality for the spectator than all the archives of the historian who digs up evidence of this and that. It has more actuality than a historical event, photographed by the light of flashbulbs and telegraphed by interviewers, has for the millions of readers of the daily newspaper. Those readers see no more of the history-making figures or of historic incidents than Stendhal's Fabrice del Dongo saw of Napoleon and the Battle of Waterloo: a cloud of dust; or than the inmate of a concentration camp sees of the "class struggle": a barbed-wire fence.

In the realm of literature the facts do not count.

Whether the mob weeps for dead Caesar with Antony, or makes fun of the infatuated old fellow with Shaw's Cleopatra, is wholly up to the author—so long as the excitement he received from the bare historical facts can be transmitted to his audience.

The German philosopher of history, Theodor Lessing, has called history: "Conferring meaning upon meaninglessness."

The sole meaning of history is expressed in Homer's Plaint of Helen:

What a mournful lot Zeus sends us, that we henceforth shall
Become a song for the future generations of men.

Again and again the question recurs: what is the mission of literature? One answer might be that the Trojan war over Helen was fought in order to supply the material for the *Iliad*. And that the Attilas, the Genghis Khans, the Fredericks, the Peter the Greats and all their imitators ought to have fallen on their knees and thanked the libraries that a Shakespeare or a Racine would have mercy upon them, that an Ibsen or Strindberg would find them worth a part, that an Aristophanes or a Shaw would draw on them for comic relief. And they would do better to refrain from blaring out their opinions on the national or the social task of literature; and much better to refrain from burning books, liquidating writers and blowing their trumpets so loudly as to reduce all readers to utter imbecility—for in so doing they merely demonstrate that their place in the history of mankind is on the refuse heap.

If there is anything at all worth while in our existence, it is falling in love; and if there is any goal left, that goal is falling in love with beauty. If there is any purpose at all to our fever and fretting, it is to be fruitful, that is, creative—to increase and multiply, not the majorities or the population quotas of political slaughterhouses or industries, but ourselves alone. And if all our toil and travail is still rewarding, the reward is to go to bed with one's love, with one's dream, with one's indefinite yearning (*l'Indécis*), in order to mate it to the exact expression (*le Précis*); to touch and be touched, to enjoy and ejaculate, to perpetuate the orgasm, for art is the ∞, the sign of infinity in the mathematics of sensuality.

Why a marriage of two sounds—a rhyme, an assonance, a counterpoint—is artistically perfect, can no more be explained in general terms that the fact that one loves

God, the king, the fatherland or the people above all else. One wants to have for oneself what all crave: beauty, which is an image derived as much from one's own eternal wish-dream as from contemporary fashion.

It sometimes happens that a person lives with another for a long time, that an epoch lives with a work of art for a long time, without paying any particular attention to it, and is then suddenly overwhelmed by the experience. Whole generations had no ear for Johann Sebastian Bach's *St. Matthew Passion,* until the young baptized Jew Mendelssohn-Bartholdy heard what was in it. Generations made their pilgrimages past the Isenheim Altar of Matthias Grünewald and were blind to its colors until the converted ex-Zolaist, Joris Karl Huysmans, perceived there the splendor of decay glowing in all the colors of the rainbow.

My father read Rimbaud without appreciation and, like all his contemporaries, he left Ducasse (Lautréamont) unread. They were incomprehensible to him because they employed tonal values hitherto unheard. After Baudelaire, Verlaine, Mallarmé, there was a gap in the bookshelves, a gap the depth of a nuance. But it was easy for me, the inheritor of these books, to fill that gap, for since my father's day taste had changed. Less inhibited than my father, I went to Paris, which was still "worth a Mass," and recklessly drained Rimbaud to the dregs without regarding his warning:

VOICI le temps des assassins!

For I came to the Paris that my father had denied to himself. I came to his Growing Castle where the nineteenth century exhibited its lushest products, its salon celebrities, its Bal Musette vulgarities, its cosmetic beauty, the enormous belly of its markets. And I lusted after everything: after the lithe, lambent stonework of the Sainte Chapelle and the iron skeleton of the Eiffel Tower as well as the folds of every midinette's *jupon.*

Il faut être absolument moderne . . .

To that extent I listened to Rimbaud . . .

Des châteaux batis en os sort la musique inconnue.

For I heard that music like the rattling of bones from the châteaux. All that I saw and heard, of beauty and of ugliness, were the things I had read of before; and previous acquaintance made their beauty or ugliness all the more exciting, indescribably more exciting. It seemed inexhaustible. I already began to dream that I had rented a room in the Growing Castle for the rest of my life, that I was at the end of my wanderings.

À vendre les habitations et les migrations, sport, féeries, comforts parfaits, et le bruit, le mouvement et l'avenir qu'ils font.
(For sale: the dwellings and the migrations, the sport, the glamour, the modern conveniences and the noise, the bustle, and the future they all are making.)

To this sentence of Rimbaud's I did not listen.
Intoxicated by tradition, humbug, *clarté,* as though I had drunk a vin pommard, a Pastis and a Calvados—

The Lost Library

"d'une liqueur non taxée de la fabrique de Satan"—or to put it another way, delirious from the alchemy of words— like so many of my generation, I cried: "To the devil with literature! To the devil with the whole nineteenth century and all its heritage!"

I would do my own writing.

As it happened, a suitable subject crossed my path in the underground post office below the Paris stock market, where the harmless vermin of the foreign press had built their nests in six long-distance telephone booths. I made friends with an extraordinary specimen of the type, a kind of Grand Exalted Master of journalism. Formerly a neopathetic lyricist, he had been converted to Catholic belles-lettres by Léon Bloy, the baptizer of the literati. Then he became a Blavatsky anthroposophist and was now a foreign correspondent, a rather slippery customer. During the intervals between his telephone calls to Madrid, Cologne, Berlin and Rome—that is, from midnight to three o'clock in the morning—he went around impressing the foreigners who visited the cabarets on the Place Blanche. He was, I thought, a ready-made character for a novel.

I used conscientiously to accompany him on these nocturnal jaunts, taking mental notes while he talked about Mussolini, Marcel Proust, *Kama Sutra,* the Hindu handbook of love, and the qualities and qualifications of the various *poules de luxe.* But one night, as though he suspected that I had him in mind for a subject, he turned the conversation to an "idea for a book" which he had been considering for a long time:

109

The Lost Library

La vie intérieure de Demoiselle

ANTOINETTE BOURIGNON

écrite par elle-même

1683 / Amsterdam / Rue de la Bourse
chez Jean Riewerts & Pierre Arents

"There's a subject for you," he said, grinning. "You're welcome to it."

Antoinette was one of the illuminati, a much-maligned nun, a tremendously prolific writer—and in addition an irresistibly ugly nymphomaniac. She was excommunicated as a Jansenist, although she was as fierce as any Jesuit in her denunciation of the fatalistic, anti-Jesuitical doctrine of predestined grace expressed in Bishop Jansen's *Augustine.* She was the founder of the utopian colony on the "Island of Grace," Noordstrant, and the fraud involved in her sale of shares in the property caused, when it was discovered, a crash on the Amsterdam stock market. She was a self-canonized saint whose writings started street fights in Holland, France, Denmark, Germany, Italy and Switzerland. And now she was disturbing my Montmartre night life and forcing me to discard my plans for a novel on a modern subject. There were five volumes of her writings in the Bibliothèque St. Geneviève on the Place du Panthéon; they had been taken from the archives of the former convent of St. Germain.

And so once again I sat in a library every day, reading in order to write. And in annoyance I wrote:

The Lost Library

Libraries are the true cemeteries of ideas. These librarians, all gray in mimicry of the dust on their books, bringing folio volumes out into the dim light and then putting them back into their coffins, have the look and the gestures and the matter-of-factness of undertakers. And these bookworms, their lips quivering like madmen in dialogues with themselves, their eyes gazing vacantly into infinities, resemble the pallbearers at the grave of some dear one. Theirs is the same eagerness and the same anxiety to catch some glimpse of the terrors of the hereafter. For those who come here to poke among the relics of the past know that in some such place at some future day their own efforts, thoughts and musings will also be laid to eternal rest. Will that, then, be the end of it?

With growing irritation I read *La Vie Solitaire* by Antoinette Bourignon.

. . . A paradise of excess of Grace. Such as St. Theresa felt when a seraph pierced her and drew out her bowels with the red-hot tongs which he drove into her body. By virtue of divine love and ecstatic converse I spent days in insensate numbness. And those sweet tongues of flame, those delicate caresses from a hand supernally tender, so overwhelmed me that I implored God to withdraw from me. A fountain of sacred cantatas sprang out of my soul . . .

"One must be absolutely modern . . ."

Utterly exhausted, I went to the Café d'Harcourt to refresh myself with a few glasses of Vermouth di Cinzano. There I watched a masked procession of medical-school anatomy students and their sweethearts marching up the turbulent Boulevard St. Michel. Then, back in my flat, I opened Rimbaud.

Une Saison en Enfer

Ma santé fut menacée. La terreur venait. Je tombais dans des sommeils de plusieurs jours, et, levé, je continuais les rêves les plus tristes. J'étais mûr pour le trépas. . . .

J'avais été damné par l'arc-en-ciel. Le Bonheur était ma fatalité, mon remords, mon ver: ma vie serait toujours trop immense pour être dévouée à la force et à la beauté.

Le Bonheur. Sa dent, douce à la mort, m'avertissait au chant du coq—ad matutinam, au Christus venit,—*dans les plus sombres villes:*

> *O saisons, o châteaux,*
> *Quelle âme est sans défauts?*

(My health was threatened. Terror came. I fell into a sleep lasting many days, and, awake, I continued having the saddest dreams. I was ripe for death. . . .

I had been doomed by the rainbow. Felicity was my undoing, my remorse, my serpent: My life was to be always too vast to be devoted to force or beauty.

Felicity. Its fang, gentle unto death, awakened me at cockcrow—from *ad matutinam* to *Christus venit*—in the somberest cities.

> O seasons, O châteaux,
> What soul is whole?)

A man sans soul, sans youth, sans art, is sans *défauts*.

Chapter VI

The Universal Book—Blind Souls and Empty Space—Pre-Raphaelites and Futuristi—The Prosthetic Man with Replaceable Parts—The Last Man.

ARTHUR RIMBAUD's desertion from Montparnasse literature, his departure from the café, La Closerie des Lilas, to Ethiopia, from the life of genius to the ivory trade, was more significant for European civilization than the French Revolution and Napoleon and all socialist tracts had been. The things of the spirit rushed after him—and the great migration was on. His imitators aped only the violent gesture when, with intent to shock, they exposed their bare behinds to the public. And his successors in the sphere of action, without ever knowing anything about him, without having read him or any other original spirit, imitated his states of exaltation out of sheer funk at the immensity of life, and out of cravenness in the face of fortune. No fountain of sacred cantatas sprang from their souls; they coughed up undigested fragments of the *Malleus Maleficarum*, of Rousseau, Nietzsche, Marx and Sorel, and dumped their vomit into the funnels of loud-speakers.

À vendre: l'anarchie pour les masses; la satisfaction irrepressible pour les amateurs.
(For sale: anarchy to the masses; irrepressible self-complacency to the dilettantes.)

113

In his life as well as in his poetry, Rimbaud anticipated the fate of twentieth-century writers.

Precisely at the midpoint of his short life of thirty-seven years, when he was barely eighteen and at the height of his artistic achievement and of his joy in that achievement, he was overcome by dizziness, became sick to the stomach at the vision of anarchy being sold to the masses and at the sight of the irrepressible complacency of the dilettantes of violence.

"Damné par l'arc-en-ciel," he swung himself over the parapet of books, fled to the anonymity of the colonial soldiery—first having denied his gifts and cold-bloodedly turned his jealous friend Verlaine over to the Brussels police.

> *Fileur éternel des immobilités bleues*
> *Je regrette l'Europe aux anciens parapets.*

Too late!

The other Rimbaud, who survived the suicide of the poet, labored without memories and without nostalgia as the bookkeeper of a third-class export firm located at Lake Chad. Found feverish and delirious in the jungle, he was shipped back to Europe as unfit for work; he rotted away in a Marseilles hospital for tropical diseases. As weak as a child, he obeyed his pious sister and his harsh peasant mother and took the Sacraments before he died.

> *Pourquoi Christ ne m'aide-t-il pas, en donnant à mon*
> *âme noblesse et liberté. Hélas, l'Evangile a passé . . .*

Was this to be the end?

But biography describes only the periphery of life that

114

surrounds the timeless work, much as the Double Circle
—the circle of the whole cosmos and that of the ego—
encloses the triangle of the creative mind whose three sides
—according to the doctrine of the heretic Antoinette Bourignon—are labeled: *Formatio—Reformatio—Transfor-
matio*. Under that pattern all prophetical vision is sub-
sumed. . . . One may reject all books, but one never
escapes from one's dream library, as one never escapes
from anything that has once been an obsession. . . .
Everything that is has once been prefigured in dream.

Georg Christoph Lichtenberg, discoverer of the Lichtenberg electrical figures in physics, and classical German
aphorist, conceived of a "universal book composed of all
possible combinations of the alphabet, which would therefore have to contain everything that has ever been or will
ever be thought and written." The Book of the Apoca-
lypse makes no revelation which has not already been anticipated in the Scriptures. Dante is a pupil of Virgil.
Goethe took his Faust from Marlowe, Marlowe his *Doctor
Faustus* from a German puppet play. Thomas de Quincey
garnished his *Confessions of an English Opium-Eater*
with the histories of Titus Livius. Rimbaud confessed: "I
can no more explain myself than the beggar with his con-
tinual Pater Nosters and Ave Marias. I do not know how
to say more. . . ."

In none of the recesses of the intellect, not even in madness, does the mind escape from its forerunners. It can
invent no abstract design, no ornamental motif, which has
not been prefigured upon some butterfly's wing. Man's
reason is no more than a variant of the instincts, like the
sense of orientation of migratory birds or the sense for
symmetry of spiders and bees. Man's machine saurians,

his flying dragons, are plagiarisms of traditional fabulous monsters. Man will find nothing in the structure of the atom which was not already present within himself. If he "brings out the inner image"—as Dürer defined the artistic process—he produces only the likeness of a lover who has long been waiting for him.

Minski, in the Marquis de Sade's *Juliette,* travels between China and Kamchatka, makes of the naked bodies of girls his chairs and tables, dines upon the hams of boys. But he no more discovers a novel source of happiness than does the liberator of humanity who annihilates an enemy city in a flash.

The libraries provide incontrovertible proof that the highest sensations of pleasure and the deepest feelings of horror can be adequately described. Can be described even when multiplied by collective millions. "Numbers imitate space," Pascal said. And books imitate the universe of our thoughts, the heaven and hell of our minds.

The more salvation or happiness is generalized, that is, the more it is standardized, the more individuals there are who starve, die and vanish without leaving a trace on the statistics of successful achievement. Individual human lives would not be worth a scrap of paper if literature did not go on extracting some gold out of their quintessence. The stories of Tantalus and Job have expressed all torment. Boccaccio's *Decameron* and the forty-seven volumes of Maupassant's stories have traced every degree of the torment of love. Shakespeare's *Richard III* and Molière's *Tartuffe* have described all the rascality of which the human heart is capable.

Such is the canon that literature has established. Goethe

states it in the lines he puts into the mouth of his Torquato Tasso:

When the human self is silenced by his pain,
A god gave ME the gift to tell of mine.

That is what distinguishes the work of art from the chance product of the child who has not yet experienced his ego, the madman who has lost it, and the primitive who has not yet recognized it.

This gradual liberation of the ego in art has nothing in common with historical or political liberation, in which only the men on top are changed.

After the French Revolution the schoolteacher took over the office of shepherd of the soul, and the morality of the church was replaced by the morality of the ferrule— the latter, after the First World War, in turn by the morality of the "corporal" state.

Right up to late maturity the nineteenth century was haunted by the recurrent schoolboy's nightmare of the final examination. In all its dreams it endured the stern glance of the form master, prompt to punish every unchaste thought that bordered on the irrational or the transcendental. Every time it lifted the veils of naked truth just a little, it was terrified and awoke bathed in perspiration—but not failing, of course, as is the way with forbidden things, to repeat the dream at the next opportunity, and from time to time to peep a little higher and a little lower. Even so, however, the West had little time for dreaming. War followed close—as though it were the punishment feared.

The Lost Library

The short vacations between the compulsory education and the compulsory patriotism of Europe occurred at the time of my puberty, and I naturally exploited them fully to gather experience and to read. This is no place to talk of experiences, but as far as reading was concerned, I pursued byways in art, in spiritism, in sexual pathology. Somebody—I have forgotten whom—called Sigmund Freud a Columbus who discovered the new continent of the unconscious. But what attracted me were less the abstract topographical names—libido fixation, inferiority and Oedipus complexes, repression, et cetera—than the erotic character of this utopia where every tree was hung with Venus fruits and priapi sprouted out of the earth like asparagus.

Actually, it was no New World. Indian and Chinese philosophers had visited it long before, as their ideographs show—for example, the Rig Veda hymn to Purusha, the Self-World-Spirit incarnate, and Lao-tse's Tao, in which there exist neither punishable instincts nor a superego as judge; where good and evil graze peacefully together like the wolf beside the lamb, ruled solely by reason and harmony. And every artist of the West had also beached his boat on that continent and explored its interior. Some had even described its precise location—as, for example, Coleridge in his *Biographia Literaria* (1817): *"Citra et trans conscientiam communem*—that which lies on the other side of our natural consciousness . . ."* ("A Chapter of Request"). So that Freud should rather be compared to a Mercator who drew on the map of the "unconscious" the pleasure principle's parallels of longitude and latitude. Henceforth even the most unimaginative could guide themselves by the lines of the Freudian atlas. And as soon as his poetic account of a new water route to Far Eastern shores of love had become widely known, thousands of persons with artistic ambitions set sail upon the *mare tenebrum* of the dream components and hastened toward the land of densely thicketed virgin forests, of fetishes with titanic protuberances, and of coral-lipped blooms.

Not so far-reaching, but fraught with more mischief, was the effect of a similar system of speculation that also came from Vienna. This was *Sex and Character,* by Otto Weininger. Weininger advanced the thought that every person was irredeemably hermaphroditic, an epicene monster made up of male plus and female minus, or vice versa. His doctoral thesis completed, the author fell victim to a bout of the Jewish combination of self-love and self-hate, and killed himself. A number of infantile, overambitious suicide candidates seized eagerly on his doctrine.

Freud and Weininger expressed the inwardly directed irony of the Austrians, which is bad for Austrians and for anyone else who takes it seriously. For the Austrian's gay melancholy is only understandable after a few glasses of the local new wine, and his jocular morality makes sense only in the dialect speech of the local farces—the farces of Nestroy, the genius of the Viennese suburbs. On the basis of his natural frivolity, the Austrian sets up a world system—and it is not his fault, it is the other people's "misreading," if the thing collapses with disastrous results. The Austrian was only building castles in the air. Heaven forbid that anyone should place any portentous meaning on any of his constructions, whether they be the Freudian Id or one of Arthur Schnitzler's tragicomedies about lights-o'-love, or Hugo von Hofmannsthal's Hapsburg-Spanish ceremonials, or musicality in general.

The Lost Library

Freud and Weininger succeeded in inciting the two partners of the worst marriage made in heaven against one another, Weininger by playing off the potent male intelligence, the plus, against female feeling, the minus; Freud, the libido against the intellect.

This particular marital discord, the hysterical delusion that thought and feeling are an unnatural pairing of incompatible opposites, can be found in all religions and in almost all philosophies and social contracts. Often it is accompanied by shrill screeches of moralistic vituperation; often its outcome is the double suicide of the love-haters. Reconciliation between the two principles is possible only in art, which regards thinking and feeling as betrothed in *joie de vivre*, gives each its due and does not meddle with their relationship.

In the first voluptuous laziness of university life—at the time of life, that is, when a young man is out to show that he is no prude where either women or forbidden books are concerned—I hesitated, wondering where to satisfy my curiosity first. It had to be done as quickly as possible, for there was the daily threat of imminent conscription. While I was hesitating, a knowledgeable jack-of-all-trades recommended to me the writings of a seer named Madame Blavatsky. Her book was entitled *Isis Unveiled*.

A crucial decade older than myself, my friend played the part of Mephistopheles for me. He had the answer to every desire, whether it was the right Gretchen or the right magical books. As always when he lent me one of his secret books—maliciously, he had also lent me Freud and Weininger—I had to swear by all that was holy that I would return it to him "within a few days." In this case I put off returning the book week after week for many months. In the meantime he, as an "enemy alien," had moved away to an unknown address, and I had been sent to a military barracks. His loan finally became a part of my inherited library, and now in Vienna, when I was unpacking that library, the legitimate owner of *Isis Unveiled* could again not be located. He had disappeared in a concentration camp.

Ill-gotten gains bring no blessing. . . . The book was frightfully ponderous, really: an indigestible witches' broth concocted out of the Vedas, the Cabala, the Gnostics, astrology, astrophysics, mythological paleontology; a compilation of Zoroaster, Heraclites, Theophrastus, Eliphas Lévy; a slashing assault upon "modern science." But there were some pretty good prognoses in it:

> Between the years 1886 and 1897 there will be a large rent made in the veil of nature, and materialistic science will receive a death blow . . . crowned with the enunciation of the electrical nature of matter and the facts of radiant energy . . .

Punctually in 1895 Roentgen discovered X rays.

Helena Hahn—Madame Blavatsky after her brief marriage with a Czarist general whom she had "bewitched"— was a Russian, a contemporary of Dostoevsky (the dates of her birth and death were, respectively, ten years after his). She was for a time friendly with and later became a mortal foe of Annie Besant. A "spiritistic swindler," a "counterfeiter of the Veda ritual," a "thief and receiver of stolen goods who battened on the treasures of all secret doctrines"—so she has been described by some. And by others: "The priestess who has laid the foundation for the future religion of mankind." But no matter what was said about her, she was a personality of such forcefulness that no one who had ever met her ever forgot her. Even reading her left an enduring impression.

And I remembered her now, not only because her prophecies of "an approaching cataclysm at the end of a five-thousand-year cycle" seemed on the point of proving balefully true, but also because her terminology was inspired more by artistic analogies than by scientific logic. For the scientists, alas, have prepared quantitative and qualitative labels for all the "vital forces" on which the writers, painters and composers of all ages have squandered their lives, forever fearing that the slightest syllable, brushstroke or grace note might prove too crude, too direct. In psychoanalysis, that repair shop of the instincts, specialists label every sexual symbol. The scientists gabble about "mnemic engrams" and "engravings upon the brain structure"— while Madame Blavatsky at least preserved the aristocratic elegance of esotericism when she wrote:

> Dreams, forebodings, presentiments, prognostications are impressions left by our astral spirit on our brain, which receives them with greater or less distinctness.

Was her theory any the weaker because she claimed that she had received her ideas in spiritistic séances in Tibet? Was that any more incredible than Rimbaud's invention of the Brahman who explained the *Proverbs* to him? And was her passport to Tibet which had been granted by a mysterious Tartar shaman any less valid for the strange signature? Was it not just as "occult" as the visa stamp of some consul of a fictitious "British Empire"? Who were the "enlighteners" and who the "blind of soul"—to use Madame Blavatsky's language: the exact scientists who declared apodictically, "The ether is a hypothetical medium filling all of space," or the Blavatsky theosophists who asserted that they saw in the ether the "astral light," the *"anima mundi,"* the "workshop of nature"?

Madame Blavatsky had apparently learned from Egyptian and Chaldean papyri more about long-distance transmission of magic formulae (which become less effective as they become more public) than our wireless telegraphers and radio technicians:

> The divine intellect is veiled in man; his animal brain alone philosophizes. Formerly, magic was a universal science, entirely in the hands of the sacerdotal savant. Though the focus was jealously guarded in the sanctuaries, its ray illumined the whole of mankind. . . .

At that time I understood approximately as much about physics as I do today: virtually nothing. Yet, with blind reverence, I murmur the magic words "Compton effect," "Corpuscular theory versus wave theory," "oscillations in empty space," and so on. The Blavatsky view seems more comprehensible to me: "Space is not empty, but filled with models of all things that ever were, are or will be." For that space and those oscillations become visible in art. Now all works of art may be mere soap bubbles in empty space, without a demonstrable justification for being. And from the scientific point of view, Madame Blavatsky's doctrines may be untenable fallacies. But I was convinced of the truthfulness of her transcendental polemics, such as:

In their unbounded glorification of matter, they sing
the amorous commingling of the wandering atoms and
the loving interchange of protoplasms, and lament the
coquettish fickleness of "forces" which play so provok-
ingly at hide-and-seek with our grave professors in the
great drama of life, called by them "force correlation."
Proclaiming matter sole and autocratic sovereign of the
Boundless Universe, they would forcibly divorce her
from her consort, and place the widowed queen on the
great throne of nature made vacant by the exiled spirit.
Do they forget or are they utterly unaware of the fact
that in the absence of its legitimate sovereign, this
throne is but a whited sepulchre, inside which all is rottenness and corruption? That matter without the spirit
which vivifies it, and of which it is but the "gross purga-
tion," to use a hermetic expression, is nothing but a
skull-less corpse, whose limbs, in order to be moved in
predetermined directions, require an intelligent operator
at the great galvanic battery called LIFE.

In those days, however, it was more respectable to refer
to reliable philosophers like Henri Bergson than to Madame Blavatsky and her *Isis Unveiled.* If the subject came
up in good society, it was more dignified to say "élan vital"
than "an intelligent operator at the great galvanic battery
called LIFE."

"When, for example, my dear lady, I raise my hand
from A to B—like this—there are two wholly different
aspects to this movement. From inside, from my point of
view, it appears as a simple, continuous action. But from
your point of view it is a distinctive curve, isn't it? Oh,
by all means, imagine as many positions along this curve
as you please. But believe me, they are all generated absolutely automatically by the single, unitary action of mov-

ing my hand from A to B—— I beg your pardon! I assure
you I have nothing up my sleeve, nothing concealed anywhere else on my person—no need to search me. I've done
that on my own impulse, simply and solely out of my own
élan vital. Do you think I am joking, my dear lady? Pro-
priety prevents my going too far, as the phrase is. . . ."

Man's permanent plaint is directed against the injustice
of his morality. In the course of his life he employs all
available lawyer's tricks and alibis to combat death. Sometimes he invokes the law of the conservation of matter, like
Lavoisier; or he claims his astral hereditary right to two
additional existences, like the anthroposophist-theosophist
Dr. Rudolf Steiner; or he speaks, like H. G. Wells, of his
"physical inheritance." But theosophers or materialists,
reactionaries, revolutionaries or evolutionaries, all have
the same tendency to assure themselves of their continued
existence—whether in their nation, in the next generation,
in the here and the hereafter, in progress, in a greater
fatherland, in a better future or a better heaven.

To be sure, the hitch to this idea, for its inventor, is the
thought that when the happy future finally dawns, he will
no longer be around; and with a sidelong look to make sure
that death is not already peering over his shoulder, he
hastily makes a correction or two, adds a few brief eterni-
ties, a couple of hundred years of posthumous fame, a
couple of thousand-year Reichs. Or he takes a deep breath
and postpones the death sentence until the Last Judgment.

All his life man has been litigating against the historical, biological or divine limitation on the span of his life.
He protests against it, both as an individual and in solidarity with the rest of mankind. In the memory of man—if

not since the beginning of the world—this litigation has been going on; all that has changed is the wording of the pleas.

My father, for example, born in the second half of the nineteenth century, was politically and intellectually an heir of the revolutions of 1848; aesthetically and mystically he was an adherent of the Oxford artists' community, the Pre-Raphaelite Brotherhood—also an 1848 movement.

I recall their delicious-looking marzipan paintings, of knightly gallantry and of working girls led astray, hanging in the plush salons of silver-haired ladies—souvenirs of a tempestuous past smiling above the plump sofa cushions. Their evangelist, Dante Gabriel Rossetti, the Anglo-Italian painter-poet, had been inspired to found his Brotherhood by a posthumously published letter of John Keats. Keats, a genius excited into precocity by the fevers and euphoria of consumption, had suddenly fallen in love with the cubic forms of the Early Renaissance which he saw in reproductions of Milan church frescoes. "Magnificence of drapery beyond anything I ever saw, not excepting Raphael's—but grotesque to a curious pitch," he wrote.

Every gifted young artist dreams in his restless nights of that ultimate pleasure of "the curious pitch"—or as Baudelaire formulated it: "To conceive a whole canvas devoted to one lyrical or fantastic jest."

They had been a strange and boyishly brash bunch, these Pre-Raphaelites, affecting medieval garb and the picturesqueness of the artisan. They provided tuberoses and Arabian incense candles for their Madonna of the London suburbs, Elizabeth Siddall, who modeled for all of them,

126

the painters and the poets as well. Rossetti married her, buried his manuscripts in her grave, and then seven years later disinterred, disinfected and published them.

John Ruskin, whom they called their Wyclif, inveighed against the hypocritical perfectionist vanity of Victorian art-mercantilism. Their guild master, William Morris (ballad writer, weaver, cabinetmaker, designer of stained glass, printer of books) called for a revival of handicrafts. Charles Algernon Swinburne, their virtuoso in all lyrical techniques, wrote pagan paeans, Christian antiphons, Villonesque ballads and current political satire. And with the nostalgia of the child he cried out to the maternal waves:

> I will go back to the great sweet mother,
> Mother and lover of men, the sea . . .

And he made fun of the God-Father of Darwinian pantheism:

Once the mastodon was, pterodactyls were common as
  cocks.
Then the mammoth was God; now He is a prize-ox.
God, whom we see not, is; and God, who is not, we see.
Fiddle, we know, is diddle; and diddle, we take it, is dee.

Seated in the organ loft of his art, wishing to be sublime and yet widely heard, the Pre-Raphaelite counterpointed the disharmony of the nineteenth century in his requiem. Soon, "half in love with easeful death," he would lie down in the garden of Proserpine, upon her flower bed, to die. But meanwhile he drew all the stops of his poetic organ, from the *vox caelestis* down to the deepest cry of the *vox humana*. All his religious and revolutionary fervor spilled over into classical meters and died away in an oddly contemporary "curious pitch."

"We are all under sentence of Death. . . . Our one chance lies in expending that interval, in setting as many pulsations as possible into the given time. . . ." wrote Walter Pater, the critic-philosopher whom the Pre-Raphaelites had canonized.

"De profundis . . ."

"I am dying beyond my means," jested his former student at Oxford, Oscar Wilde, when sick unto death he was given a glass of champagne—in a cheap hotel in Paris where he had gone after his term in Reading Gaol.

This last bon mot of the dying nineteenth century was bequeathed to the heirs of "art for art's sake." In music the legacy was accepted by the poet-composer Claude Debussy; in painting by the color-lyricist, Odilon Redon, by the color-form symphonist, Kandinsky, and by the fugal cubists; in poetry by Jules Laforgue with his atonally rhymed elegies, and then by Guillaume Apollinaire in his *Calligrammes.*

When my father was young, the *avant-garde* consisted of the dandies, the Impressionists and the Pre-Raphaelites. In my youth, the *avant-garde* was a much more excitable group of dynamicists, futurists, expressionists.

My father had no qualms about placing in his library the science-fiction "anticipations" of H. G. Wells (and Huxley). He accepted the refashioning of man, "mankind in the making," as he accepted into his world order moving pictures and the phonograph. These were instruments of Progress. But he was decisively opposed to the dynamic experiments of "futurism"—which was the collective word used at the time to make fun of all post-impressionist art starting with Van Gogh's "color incendiarism."

That alone would have driven me into the arms of the new art. For whoever has denied himself a pleasure because it was decried as vice, whoever has never done anything foolish, who has refused to read a book because it was "banned by the censor"—has never been young. And so, solely from revolt against my father's authority, I was elated when on my way to school I was handed a leaflet put out by the Italian *futuristi*—the occasion being the opening of the first German Salon d'Automne in Berlin in 1913.

DESTROY THE MUSEUMS! BURN DOWN THE LIBRARIES! the leaflet was headed.

I stole into the two back rooms in a middle-class lodging house with pounding heart, as though I were entering a brothel. Exhibited there were Gino Severini's "simultaneous" mural-kaleidoscope, *Pan Pan Dance at Del Monico's;* Boccioni's kinetic, explosive portrait, *Laughter;* Delaunay's crumbling *Eiffel Tower;* square nudes and still lifes by Gleizes, Metzinger and Le Fauconnier; Kandinsky's "non-objective white forms." The rival "ultramodern abstractionists" and "Cézanne secessionists" confronted one another, and the formal debate degenerated into a brawl, so that the police had to be called in.

The chieftain and sponsor of the futuristi, F. T. Marinetti, was both a millionaire's son and a born orator. The handful of impecunious coffeehouse Bohemians who were his followers were easily persuaded that he was addressing the seething masses of the people before the final conflict.

At an improvised protest demonstration in Paris, he cried:

The artistic victory of the liberated word neatly cuts in half the history of human poetry from Homer to the latest lyrical sigh on earth . . .

He announced his futuristic projects in the superlatives of an industrial advertiser and with the crudity of extremist election propaganda:

Destroy syntax! Sabotage the adjective! Away with it, away with everything except the verb!

And he did not realize that he was only genuflecting to the symbolism of the evangelists Johannis and Mallarmé.

He adored slogans and bellowed like a circus barker his prophecy of "the creation of mechanical man with replaceable parts"—that is, the future prosthetic cripples of the World War.

But that too was only a borrowing from the late historian of literature, Hippolyte Taine: *"Il n'y a ici, comme partout, qu'un problème mécanique!"*

With his passion for novelties, Marinetti developed "typographic ideograms," advertising verse printed zigzag to catch the eye; he invented also the political trademark *Fascismo*. (Later, when he insisted on his author's rights to Fascismo, he incurred the disfavor of two competitors —the professional hero, Gabriele d'Annunzio, and the nationalistic gang leader, Benito Mussolini.) But almost a decade earlier, when he first appeared in public in the squares of Milan, the "most mechanized city in the world," he had anticipated what were to be the standard tricks of totalitarian parades: the Roman-dictator gestures, the laurel wreath crowning his shaved skull, the megaphone voice and the doctrine of "annihilation of the individual." "The Ego must be extirpated from literature."

He had provided also the prescription for sterilized mass murder: *"Guerra sola igiene del mondo."* What a non-plus-ultra modern, what a truly futuristic dictum! And yet what an ancient text!

For had not, at the beginning of the previous century, the orthodox, Catholic, blackly reactionary writer Joseph de Maistre raved in the same fashion? *"La guerre divine . . . l'effusion du sang: une vertu expiatoire . . ."?* And had not, at the end of the nineteenth century, Arthur Rimbaud cried out deliriously in *Les Illuminations: "Je songe à une guerre, de droit ou de force, de logique bien imprévue. . . . C'est aussi simple qu'une phrase musicale . . ."?*

Oh, yes, war is as simple as the musical phrases of the bucolic poets who perish amid the screaming of human abattoirs. . . .

Until his unnoted death in 1938, just before the overture to the murderous, polyphonic second symphony of swift annihilation, F. T. Marinetti went on repeating parrotlike the futurist's blabber at international writers' congresses. He was servile as a worn-out court jester who had been lent by his Duce to foreign fairs:

Aggression, courage and heroism are characteristically futurist and characteristically fascist.

In *My Heart Laid Bare* Baudelaire had noted:

A supplement to military metaphors:
The poets of combat.
The vanguard writers.

This use of military metaphors does not indicate militant souls, but submissive ones made for conformity, the souls of lackeys, of bastards who can think only with the herd.

And yet Baudelaire himself had been a "poète de combat" of the Revolution of 1848, an *avant-gardist* with Delacroix, Manet and Daumier. He too had given himself up to exaggerated illusions about the future, like every imaginative young man. "Eighteen forty-eight," he confesses ruefully, "was amusing only because everyone fashioned utopias like castles in Spain. Eighteen forty-eight was charming only in being so excessively ridiculous."

Baudelaire's green peruque, with which he scandalized the guests of the Café Ruche, the lily that Rossetti. flaunted in Piccadilly, the glass hat that Marinetti wore in the Roman cafés—these eccentricities were the cockades of a secret resistance movement against the prevailing self-righteous philistinism in taste. Only by having the courage to be ridiculous did the "dandy"—the Baudelairian knight-errant—combat the cliché-spewing dragon of the Great Majority, a monster swollen with vulgarity and fear of life.

"Can you imagine a dandy talking to the people for any reason but to flout them?" Baudelaire mocked.

The genuine "dandy" is apparently becoming extinct and is imitated only by a few persevering dilettantes. One of the last of the true dandies in France was Guillaume Apollinaire. According to his own statement, he was the illegitimate son of a Roman woman and a Polish nobleman, born in a sleeping car between Italy and Monaco. He was the herald of the "antitradition futurists" and the "cubist painters"—both his phrases. Proud of his

"Frenchness," he promptly challenged anyone who questioned it to a duel, only to decamp, scared to death by his own gesture. But he went on throwing literary challenges into the face of Europe and all Europe's modern technology.

À Travers L'Europe

Rotsoge
Ton visage écarlate ton biplan transformable en hydroplan
Ta maison ronde où il nage un hareng saur
Il me faut la clef des paupières . . .
J'ai cherché longtemps sur les routes
Tant d'yeux sont clos au bord des routes . . .
Ouvre ouvre ouvre ouvre ouvre
Regarde, mais regarde donc
Le vieux se lave les pieds dans la cuvette . . .
Et toi tu me montres un violet epouvantable . . .
Mais tes cheveux sont le trolley
À travers l'Europe vétue de petits feux multicolores . . .

All his life Apollinaire writhed under the charge that he was un-French (*un métèque*). With the outbreak of the First World War he wanted to prove his loyalty. And so he died the common heroic death of the period—died on the eve of the Armistice, November 9, 1918—"*d'une logique bien imprévue.*"

Around this same time the Russian futurist Gumilyov, former big-game hunter in Africa, ex-soldier of the Czarist army and *avant-garde* poet of the proletarian world revolution, was indulging in fantasies about:

Lands where giants still dwell in sunlit groves,
Where dwarfs bicker with the birds for nests.
If only they won't start counting all the stars now!
If only the world is not explored to its end!

But since the world was already explored to its end, the Bolsheviks shot him in 1921 because he remained a man of little faith. His divorced wife, the poet Achmanova, was exiled to the end of the world, Siberia.

Exactly one year before the nineteenth century was finally laid to rest—in 1913, that is—a verbally and rhythmically monstrous contribution was sent in to the German *avant-garde* expressionist magazine *Sturm*. The title of the piece was *Der Letzte* (The Last Man).

> . . . Laughter. I laugh. Three days plummet. Shout. Three days eternities. And you've not yet fallen, you're not yet smashed. Damned sky! Blue husk. Puff cigarettes and scatter ashes. All together. The trench. The trenches . . .
> Mother womb. Father womb. Mother, can't see you. Mother, you kiss. Roughly. Hold me. I am falling, see! I am falling. . . .

This terrifyingly prophetic monologue was read by only a small group and was not published in *Sturm* until 1915 when it was reported that "Captain August Stramm has fallen on the Russian front, the last man of his company."

In civil life he had been a clerk in the post office and had once written a paper on *The History of Postage Stamps in the District of Magdeburg.* He was happily married to a writer of conventional short stories, lived an altogether innocuous existence until there suddenly appeared in the crazy, maligned Bohemian magazine a series of his "verse cycles": a torrent of:
nouns

verbs

nouns

phonetic orgasms,

monosyllabic, spasmodic dramas: *Happening, Rudimentary, Worlds' End.* Out of them, after his death, the intrinsic expressionistic art of the linguistic fugue was born: a doctrine of harmonics consisting of pure sound—associations—an outbreak of glossolalia.

The editor of *Sturm* also put out separate publications, thin pamphlets with yellow covers. They were no longer books. It was as though the new writing had already been hit by two war shortages: the scarcity of paper and the impoverishment of language. The poetry of mutilated syllables was an early parallel to the spare skeletons of expressionism in the graphic arts (especially to the expressionistic woodcuts and linoleum blocks). Here were the same explosions of black and white, the same mosaics of ruins. Much later, when the sight of chaotic conditions had become commonplace, the expressionistic mode came into fashion. But at the beginning, since these expressionistic pieces were previsions which had not yet been confirmed by apocalyptic destruction throughout Europe, they met with furious opposition. At exhibitions the public, which loved its peace, lashed out with canes against those samples of "destructive art." The respectable literary critics were almost speechless with indignation at the "fuss kicked up by these no-account coffeehouse rowdies" who were again attacking stable tradition.

Yet, without the shelter the coffeehouses afforded, tradition would never have survived the war. In them, and with the aid of the yellow pamphlets published by *Sturm,* I found my way back to it.

Chapter VII

IN THE European cafés more books, and often greater ones, have been planned than are housed in all the libraries of the world put together—and more deeds than have been committed in world history.

Wrote Thomas Babington Macaulay in his *History of England:*

> The coffee house must not be dismissed with a cursory mention. It might indeed at that have been not improperly called a most important political institution. . . . Nobody was excluded from these places . . . every shade of religious and political opinion had its own headquarters. There were houses near St. James Park where fops congregated. . . . The conversation was in that dialect which, long after it had ceased to be spoken in fashionable circles, continued, in the mouth of Lord Foppington, to excite the mirth of theaters. . . . There the talk was about poetical justice and the unities of place and time. There was a faction for Perrault and the moderns, a faction for Boileau and the ancients. One group debated whether *Paradise Lost* ought not to have been in rhyme. . . .

For in the cafés it often happened that a single bon mot, a nobody's flash of wit, could incinerate the whole bombas-

136

tic verbal edifice of a celebrity. There, around one-legged marble tables, the councils met to decide whether paradise, since it was lost anyway, was better off with or without rhymes. There, in conclave, the ecclesiastics of an aesthetic vatican conferred all night long over who should be the next pope of literature, until, with the sun rose puffs of white tobacco smoke.

In these bazaars of Occidental Bohemia, in these mosques of quarrelsome nomad sects, there was agreement only in the common worship of naked femininity. It did not need to be a specific woman.

Had Chloe ever guarded sheep, or only watched over the dreams of lascivious pastoral poets? Was Carmen really a Polish Jewess, as Théophile Gautier irreverently asserted? Enraptured by the story his colleague Prosper Mérimée told at a café table, Gautier had gone to Seville to look up the girl, and in bed she had told him the same fantastic tale of jealousy that she had told Mérimée. And the poet of the Paris Café Select who was called "The Serbian Rimbaud"—I have long since forgotten his name—whom did he mean when he recited his ode, *La Chevelure Incendiaire,* in return for an apéritif? Was he talking about Lily B.—or about Karl Marx? And had the bard of the U.S.S.R., Mayakovsky, killed himself out of disappointment with the Revolution or out of jealousy over red-haired Lily B.? In times of political upheaval all passions are questionable. But who in the cafés would venture to ask a passion for its passport? Who inquired what mistress had been inspiration for the poem that a Parnassien, sitting over his morning coffee—and glancing frequently up at his image reflected in the two wall mirrors—would hastily scribble down?

The Lost Library

I am speaking here of an imaginary library of stillborn, neglected or apparently dead books which were germinating or about to be published at the time I began going to the coffeehouses. I am speaking of the literature of a cultural empire that has fallen. Probably the decline of Bohemia should be dated from August 1, 1914—for every historical date is the date of a catastrophe. Murger's *La Vie de Bohème,* which had its origins in the Café Momus, had become the nickname for the only United States of Europe. But Europe never understood the significance of this republic because it could think of states only in terms of a bureaucracy and fixed frontier posts.

At the end of his life, which he called a tragedy in fifty-five acts, fifty-five-year-old Oscar Wilde, an exile in Paris, complained that now he was doing his writing in a café where they had run out of ink.

But where in the Europe of today are there any real cafés? The café has become a peddler's booth for the black market; every apéritif means a financial hangover, and every female has become a political amazon of one party or the other. The free superstate of Bohemia has been annihilated now that all Europe has been turned into a gypsy camp. The ivory tower, that defiant metaphor for the solitary, strong personality, has been bombed—that ivory tower which Sainte-Beuve erected for the militant romantic and former professional soldier, Alfred de Vigny:

. . . *Et Vigny, plus secret*
Comme en sa tour d'ivoire avant midi rentrait . . . [from *Consolations*]

138

The Lost Library

When I stepped into the Berlin Café Megalomania
(*Café Groessenwahn,* the nickname of the Café des Westens) for the first time, I left Prussianism behind forever
and entered the terrority of Bohemia, where the inhabitants spoke and wrote in foreign languages: Symbolism,
neopathos, in the idioms of the English "Georgians" and
the Stefan George circle, in the argot of theatrical dress-
ing rooms and music halls, and in a silent speech and
unwritten writing which only the initiate understood.

At the beginning I saw a Dostoevsky in every man that
wore a Russian smock; a Barbey d'Aurevilly in every
threadbare, sarcastic, elderly fop; Gauguin's Noa Noa in
every dark-complexioned, full-lipped model. But eventually I became more familiar with Bohemia's *Almanach de
Gotha.*

Acceptance into any one of the literary circles was
equivalent to swearing an oath of allegiance to the prevailing artistic views of that circle. It was a vow not to pub-
lish a line anywhere but in the circle's publication, to obey
the rules of order governing the circle's aesthetics and the
circle's women; and to fight the circle's polemics to the last
drop of ink. "And it was easier," wrote Aurelian Scholl,
the pamphleteer, "for a man to change his opinions than
to change his café." For three centuries the feuds of
Bohemia had been going on—table against table, café
against café. The feuds continued there because they had
begun there.

The oldest coffeehouses had been set up by Turks in the
age of Sultan Suliman II; their sign was the sultan's
beverage, coffee, and the croissant, baked in the shape of
the Turkish crescent moon. Coffee had become the "lit-

erary beverage," as Balzac called it. And the cafés had become, true to their origins in Asia Minor, the breeding places of great schismatic movements (or isms).

In eighteenth-century London there was James Harrington's liberalistic Rota Club in Mille's Coffee House. And at the Turk's Head there was a band of political brigands around Daniel Defoe and John Law (writer on economics and later financial dictator of France). In Paris around the same time the first cafés were opened by the Armenians, Pascal and Grégoire of Aleppo, and by the Levantine "Procope" (Foire de St. Germain).

C. de Merry, the author of *Café* (1837), an epic in two cantos, recounts in his preface:

> It was at the Café Procope that Voltaire, J. B. Rousseau [the writer of odes] and Piron met. They would discuss the failure or success of a new tragedy. The intrigues that started there disgusted the Men of Genius and helped not a little to discredit the Théâtre Français.

The names of the cafés stand for the battlefields on which for three hundred years this strange republic of Bohemia steadfastly held out against the massed armament of so-called "good taste" and so-called "common sense."

The *Encyclopédie—ce magasin de toutes les choses utiles*—was conceived by Voltaire, Diderot and D'Alembert in the Café de la Régence—where afterward the author of a *Dialogue sur l'Amour,* Buonaparte, first created a stir and played his first games of chess.

In the Café Guerbois (Faubourg des Batignolles) Emile Zola, Théodore Duret, Manet, Degas, Whistler and Renoir conducted the revolt of *plein-air* painting against the École des Beaux Arts and the five Academies of the Institut de France.

In the Closerie des Lilas the Montparnassiens, the alchemists of the vowel (Verlaine and Rimbaud) and the magicians of the verb (the Symbolists) were attacked by the social *chansonniers* of the "Free Republic of Montmartre" (Aristide Bruant—immortalized by Toulouse-Lautrec's posters—and Jean Richepin and Xanrof).

In the Café d'Harcourt (Place de la Sorbonne) the teacher of dictators, Georges Sorel, argued with his friend Charles Péguy and delivered lectures on his theodicy of "violence" and the social uselessness of literature. And in the Café de la Rotonde on Montparnasse, the headquarters for the *fauves* and the first expressionists, the Russian journalist in exile, Vladimir Ulianov (Lenin), nursed his disgust with the goings-on around him and brooded over censorship schemes which would protect his "innocent proletariat" from such excesses on the part of the *imaginisti*.

In Vienna in the Café Central was to be met Lenin's colleague, Comrade Leo Bronstein (Trotsky), playing chess with Austria's foreign minister. And back to back with him—though neither knew the other—sat the professor of nerve pathology, Sigmund Freud.

The Berlin literature of revolt, then, had its conspiratorial center at the Café des Westens, alias the Café Megalomania. Its waiter was Richard, red-haired, hunchbacked and a bringer of luck, a man who could keep a secret and who held his counsel as to the innumerable plans for books and political attacks that he overheard. (He took the plans with him to his grave, and they remained unrevealed and unfulfilled.) Richard was a storehouse of information that would have been invaluable to a literary historian. He knew all about the amorous intrigues, the aberrations, the lost and betrayed illusions and the unpaid checks of later world celebrities. On the debit side of his ledger was the vagabond Peter Hille, soiled with the dirt of all the highways of Europe, who carried in his knapsack a whole collection of choice ideas and drafts for poems which enriched the work of more illustrious poets down to Franz Werfel. There was also the flame-bearded, redheaded anarchist and balladmonger, Erich Muehsam, whose polemical humanitarian pamphlet *Kain* had been subsidized by Richard, and whose brow already seemed branded for murder by a dehumanized tyrant.

And there was a certain Paul Scheerbarth, bloated by beer like the frog in the fable. He was a shabby visionary who sat at the farthermost rear table of the Café Megalomania and dreamed up his "astral novelettes." One of these stories concerned the inhabitants of the planet Venus, whose sole means of communication was cloud painting in concave and convex colored forms. A henpecked husband, he wrote the tale of Liwuhna and Kaidoh, lovers who mated in the ether to become an inseparable couple and finally "a white-hot flaming wheel going out in the universal night." Always looking for a place to live—he was regularly evicted by his landlords—Scheerbarth conceived his "glass architecture," skyscrapers and spherical houses of crystal and steel. He was, besides, something of an inventor, and tinkered with models for a perpetual-motion machine with which he would be able to move mountains and transform any landscape architectonically. But in both the macrocosmic toy of science and in his microcosmic poetic models, if gears F and H turned, J and K did not—or vice versa. The ultimate result, he announced triumphantly, was that he had failed at everything; it was a great relief to him when he thought of the frightful misuse his machine could have been put to by mankind. The potentiality of mankind for evil was the true perpetual-motion machine, and that machine started rolling again on August 1, 1914. With the general mobilization of all patriots, Scheerbarth embarked on a course of passive resistance, and committed suicide by refusing to take any nourishment.

Diplomatically waiting on tables, Richard was the go-between among all these conceited, difficult guests who took their talents as seriously as army officers take their decorations. He smoothed their love affairs and tempered the antagonisms between the two extremes: the politically and aesthetically radical magazine *Aktion,* published by the social revolutionaries under the editorship of Franz Pfemert and his wife, a radical Russian noblewoman; and the orthodox organ of expressionism, *Sturm,* which was run by the frenetic psalmist Else Lasker-Schüler (who also called herself Tino of Bagdad and the Prince of Thebes). She was the jealous platonic friend of Franz Marc, the painter of "animal destinies," and her astral body was always in Palestine—"the mentally remotest land on earth"—where she ultimately died in exile.

Es pocht eine Sehnsucht an die Welt
An der wir sterben muessen.
(A nostalgia knocks outside the world which will be the death of us.)

In the Café Megalomania there sat enthroned at her side her second temporary prince consort, Herwarth Walden, the regent of Late Expressionism. This wood sprite with his eternally restless, shifting, bespectacled eyes and his mane of straw-colored hair possessed the powers of a troll to bewitch and to produce treasures. Whatever he accepted and published—alchemistic essays by the gold-seeker, Strindberg; the satanist novel, *The Hammock,* by the Dane Aage von Kohl; a farce on the carnival of death which was the Russo-Japanese War; the painter Kokoshka's one-act satyr play, *Murderers, the Hope of Women;* whatever he exhibited—Kandinsky's *White Form;* Chagall's *Moi et le Village;* Marc's *Tower of the Blue Horses;* whatever he touched seemed to acquire immortality from the contact with his spidery, heavily be-ringed fingers.

The prodigal son of banker parents, Walden had sold his *Sturm* on street corners in Berlin, Zürich and Paris. The group of painters and poets who gathered around him were completely under his spell. He had them convinced that they were living in the Year One of the new millennium of art. The wrath and the ridicule of public and critics meant nothing to them compared to the curses Walden hurled at anyone who deviated by an iota or a brushstroke from his own aesthetic gospel.

Thus, having become the absolute monarch of the "Sturm Art Salon," Walden threw opulent banquets to which he invited art-loving officials of the state, general staff officers and police censors, initiating them into the technique of the most advanced painting and into the linguistic secrets of August Stramm. The banquets paid off: during the war, when even the arts were put to military uses, his important connections certified to his indispensability on the home front. In tune with the times, he added a patriotic eleventh commandment to his abstract laws of art: "Let everyone be a Prussian after his fashion—after his fashion—but let him be one! For in earthly things the Prussians are artists."

Haughty to the last, he was expelled from his country by a dictatorship of dilettanti. By now gray and wretched, he sought refuge in Soviet Russia. There he continued to proclaim his expressionism as "the highest artistic ideal of the world proletariat."

But that was carrying folly too far. He was charged with "dissemination of counterrevolutionary, antipopular, formalistic false doctrines and incorrigible hermetism," and was liquidated.

It was a strange swarm that gathered in the Café Megalomania: larvae and pupae in every stage of metamorphosis. Displaced poets. If Else Lasker-Schüler was a disheveled reincarnation of Sulamith—"black, but comely as the tents of Kedar, as the curtains of Solomon"—Theodor Däubler of Trieste, writer of epics, was a Silenus in a tattered lounge suit—with pagan appetites in eating, drinking, smoking and poeticizing. Däubler was eternally traveling, was always everywhere at once. At one and the same time he turned up in the Paris Latin Quarter restaurant, Le Furet, the headquarters of the Greco-French poet, Moréas (*Les Stances*); in Rome with the medium Eusepia Palladino; in Bucharest with Carmen Sylva, the poetry-writing Queen Elizabeth of Rumania; in Danzig with the Polish macabre novelist Przybyszewski, Strindberg's colleague; and in Riga as the guest of the Freemason Count Alessandro Cagliostro (born in 1743), now residing on his estates under the name of

The Lost Library

Baron von Uexkuell—so Däubler said. Whenever Däubler came into the Café Megalomania he would be carrying all his possessions in a suitcase: a shirt, toothbrush and three thick packages containing his poem *Das Nordlicht*, in *terza rima*.

"On the shore of the Caspian Sea," he would begin one of his recitations, which lasted all night long, "at the foot of Mount Ararat, ravens announced to me the primal sound RA-Ra-Ra, the Egyptian name for God, the art-creating Destroyer. . . ."

At one of *Sturm's* exhibitions of Kandinsky, Däubler tangled with Dr. Rudolf Steiner, the Hungarian *arbiter elegantiarum* of theosophy. Steiner was speaking about his project for a "Goetheanum," a temple dedicated to theosophic-gnostic-Faustian art, which was to be established on the Bavarian side of Lake Constance amid a colony of villas for propertied lovers of esoterics.

"Dilettante!" Däubler snorted. "You ought to know that Germany possesses no astral planes. . . ."

Däubler was at home in the studios of Picasso, Matisse and Modigliani; he was just as much at home among the dead. He chatted fluently in ancient Greek with the skeletons of monks on Mount Athos, and in Sanskrit with Buddhist adepts. In my dead father's darkened library, during the war, he conjured up improvised ghost stories, while Rainer Maria Rilke, sitting like a specter himself, watched through his lorgnette.

He had fallen out with Gabriele d'Annunzio, whom he accused of having secularized the secret treasure of the Renaissance—the synthesis of Platonism and Christianity.

He incurred Herwarth Walden's wrath when he defended the pen drawings of Georg Grosz, who was, he

146

declared, the only contemporary demonographer. Walden attacked Grosz for having corrupted the pure, childlike lines of his favorite, Paul Klee.

It was through Däubler that I made friends with Grosz, who sat on the terrace of the Café Groessenwahn dressed in a loud-checked jacket, with face powdered white like a circus clown, posing as "the saddest man in Europe." And Grosz introduced me to Dadaism.

This movement had started in Zurich in the middle of the First World War among intellectual deserters from all the warring nations. The head and founder of the movement was Hugo Ball, a Catholic essayist and hagiographer, a pale, quiet, tall person. In a cheap Berlin music hall he had fallen in love with a Danish singer, Emmy Hennings, elevated her to the status of his wife and disciple, and founded the Cabaret Voltaire for her to perform in.

There, after recitations by Emmy Hennings from the French writers Max Jacob and Blaise Cendrars, Franz Werfel's satyr play, *The Word-Makers of the Age,* would be given, and some musical selections by, say, Debussy. Last of all, Hugo Ball, wearing a batlike cloak made of cardboard and a blue-and-white striped shaman's hat, recited his "sound poems" until his voice took on "the ancient cadences of priestly lamentations" and he was "carried off the platform as soaked in perspiration as a witch doctor."

One evening, so the legend goes, Ball was with the Rumanian Tristan Tzara and the German Richard Huelsenbeck, two writers of *poèmes simultanés* in the Apollinaire manner. In search of a stage name for a girl dancer, they reached for a French dictionary and opened it by chance to the word *dada*—hobbyhorse.

Ball is alleged to have said: "Here, gentlemen, you have the ism of all isms—Dada-ism!"

Whatever the true story, his abracadabra spread with magical swiftness and conquered one cosmopolitan café after the other in all the belligerent countries.

The cafés have diverted me—as they did then—from my father's library, whose natural growth was stopped by his death and by the First World War.

It may be terribly tactless of me to devote space to mere literary puerility when discussing so serious and significant a product of the human spirit as European literature. My only excuse is that what others call "puerility" I prefer to think of as an outburst of youthful impetuosity. And even the mature men who never forget the seriousness of the times must occasionally appeal to youthful instincts in order to encourage both young and old who are fit for war to dress up as soldiers and play with the murderous precision toys of their armaments industry.

But in the interest of historical accuracy I must emphasize that Dadaism was merely an eczema of youthful heroism. For those were solemn times and for the most part Poesy was appropriately solemn—as is always the case when the high priests whet their metaphors on the altars of patriotism.

Tens of thousands must be struck by the holy madness,
Tens of thousands must be swept by the holy sickness,
Tens of thousands by the holy war,

sang Stefan George when his beloved youths, his Siegfrieds, marched off to war. The German poets worked overtime turning out war verse. Weak though they might be in other respects, they were certainly strong on patriotism.

From the literary point of view, wars, civil and international, seem to have been sent by the gods solely in order to stir poets out of their brooding on the nonsense of existence and punish them for their sinful pride in their meager creative talent, as Apollo punished Marsyas.

In my father's library I grew up all too well sheltered. I was coddled in the illusion that human catastrophes could be averted—just as could venereal disease by timely medical treatment—by cosmopolitanism in literature, by scientific control of all experiments dangerous to the common welfare, by a general strike on the part of the international brotherhood of workers. I had seen only the pacifistic, humanitarian side of the library, and its essential skepticism toward all heavenly and earthly—particularly earthly—authority. And when the library was searched for defeatist literature, for writings dangerous to military security—every world-conquering movement starts to worry about sedition within its borders before anything else—my father was arrested, which no doubt hastened his death and helped to send him to a civilian grave.

But as soon as the mobilization order was plastered on the advertising columns, on top of all the announcements of the theater and other entertainments, the library changed its tone. Whenever disaster strikes and you want to read in order to forget it, you always find that everything you read applies to the disaster. And so it was that whatever book I opened suddenly proved to have a "heroic" side. Suddenly these books no longer spoke of the dear reader or the esteemed author; they were concerned only with volunteers who presented their cleanly washed bodies to the inspection of a state medical officer—he too "a man of culture" who had now exchanged the Hippocratic oath for the oath to the flag.

The classics were sent to the front as "comforters" for the soldiers, along with woolen socks and ersatz chocolate. All the newly published books had a clinging odor of hospitals and antiseptic and pus. And just as the general staffs published their casualty lists, all the publishing houses put out their "anthologies of our fallen authors."

Posthumous tribute was also paid to writers whose style had been rejected in peacetime as "decadent and morbid." War hallowed the warrior. The girls at home, who once would have laughed at the sight of the louse-ridden poor devils back from the front on furloughs, now swooned to embrace them. And, similarly, the home-front critics applauded the feeblest literary effusion if it had been "baptized in fire," and particularly if the author had died "for us."

It was thus, in France, that Charles Péguy won fame and emerged from the obscurity of his secondhand bookshop on the Rue de la Sorbonne. Péguy, Dreyfusard and worshiper of Joan of Arc, was a compatriot and confrere of the prophet of violence, Georges Sorel, who was destined to survive him and come out strongly for Lenin and Mussolini. On the thirtieth day of the First World War, whose coming he had feared ten years before, Officer Charles Péguy met "solemn death"—shot in the head.

Heureux ceux qui sont morts pour la terre charnelle,
Heureux ceux qui sont morts d'une mort solennelle,
Ils se sont recouchés dedans ce Hosannah
Qu'ils avaient désappris devant que d'être nés . . .
(Happy are those who died for the sensual earth,

Happy are those who died a solemn death,
They have returned to that Hosannah
Which they had unlearned before they were born.)

And on the Italian side Gabriele d'Annunzio made a propaganda flight well above the scene of the mass killing and took up Péguy's refrain:

> *Beati i misericordiosi perche avranno da tergere un sangue splendente* . . .
> *Beati i puri cuore, beati i ritornati con la vittorie perche vedranno il viso novelle di Roma, la fronte ric-coronata di Dante.*
>
> (Happy and blessed are they because they shall have glorious blood to spill.
>
> Happy and pure in heart—how happy are those who will return victoriously, for they shall see the new Rome and the newly adorned brow of Dante.)

Hugo Ball was every bit as dedicated and in earnest when he hurled Dadaist ridicule at the uniformed inferno and the collective martyrdom of the times. At heart he was no less militant than the war veteran Cervantes when the Spaniard took up his pen in order "to make everyone see what an abomination are the senseless books on chivalry, so that there will be no more of them."

For Hugo Ball, "buffoonery was only the opposite pole of the sublime." "The power of the artist," he wrote, "rests on fear and awe. Our age has converted these into terror and horror." His Dadaism belonged to the tradition of that frightening mummery with which Satan amused his sinister cohorts and impressed the mob. "I cannot turn back alone," Ball wrote reminiscently, years afterward. "All those ideas must go along with me."

Long after Dada had developed from the stage name of

a dancer to the title of a movement in the history of art, and long after Hugo Ball was through with it—when, in fact, he was close to death—he wrote: "Unhappily transcendence is often so misunderstood that climbing beyond the corporeal world becomes a matter of climbing over corpses."

Hugo Ball was forgotten by the time he died of cancer in Switzerland in 1925. Dadaism passed beyond him and became commonplace. For he believed: "We shall be resurrected as we were begotten (in paradise and in the spirit), not as we have been injured in the world."

It is a misconception of Dadaism to credit it with a specific artistic or philosophic program. Actually, the Dadaist differed from all other 'ists' in that he had no program at all. Everything that existed and expressed itself was for him "dada"—*eo ipso*. The Lucullan gorging of the war profiteers as well as the lotus-eating of the aesthetes, a proletarian street demonstration and a ministerial oration, the highest intellectual values of occidental culture (printed on Japanese paper) and the devalued paper money of the inflation, vice and patriotism, a lynching or an official execution, the whole Breughelesque "tournament between the carnival and the fast"—it was all so much "dada."

From the Dadaist point of view there were two types of people on the face of the earth: on the one side the Dadaist, who saw how funny the madhouse was; and on the other side the solid mass of paranoid idiots who thought themselves normal and resented being made fun of.

For the rest, the ear of the Dadaist transposed everything he heard, whether in verse, in official prose, in stock-exchange quotations, in addresses from pulpits and platforms, into: "Dada-dada-dada . . . blablablablah . . ."

The Chief Dada of the Berlin Section, an unsuccessful architect named Baader, delivered an impromptu address at the opening session of the German National Assembly at the Weimar Court Theater. He declared—amid universal protests from ultraright to ultraleft—that the establishment of the German Republic which had just taken place was a "Dadaist demonstration." In Paris a "Dadaist court" conducted a monster trial of the nationalist poet Maurice Barrès (*Du sang, de la volupté, et de la mort*), Member of the Academy. He was found guilty and sentenced to death.

Unfortunately no movement, no matter what its direction, can go on indefinitely without wearing out. One group of the Dadaists afterward veered toward a radicalism more concerned with *Realpolitik,* in a bid for popular support; another group refined Dadaism into Surrealism.

Then, like all new developments, this one too looked around for a suitable ancestor. I first heard the name of that father of Surrealism in the hangout of the Parisian Dadaists, the Bar Cintra in the Passage de l'Opéra, where it was whispered from ear to ear with that harsh, importunate urgency with which a certain type of hawker tries to pass off his "guaranteed unique, unbelievably daring erotica."

"Rimbaud is a girl's school writer compared to him—a pale imitation of him. Rimbaud's work came out eight years after he first published—first edition 1868, Imprimerie Balitout; the little book has been lost. Republished by Blaise Cendrars, following the text of the second edition of 1890—but still virtually unknown. And the man's atheism: a super De Sade." And Remy de Gourmont said of him, *"Il ne voit dans le monde que lui et Dieu—et Dieu le gène."*

Always looking for the newest novelties, for unexperienced sensations, I promptly rushed to read the first complete edition of his works, which had just been compiled by our fellow Dadaist Philippe Soupault. And opening the pages of this most modern author of the past, I read:

> . . . *Depuis les temps reculés, placés au-delà de l'histoire, où, dans de subtiles métamorphoses, je ravageais, à diverses époques, les contrées du globe par les conquêtes et le carnage, et répandais la guerre civile au milieu des citoyens, n'ai-je pas déjà écrasé sous mes talons, membre par membre ou collectivement, des générations entières, dont il ne serait pas difficile de concevoir le chiffre innombrable? Le passé radieux a fait de brillantes promesses à l'avenir: il les tiendra! Pour le ratissage de mes phrases, j'emploierai forcément la méthode naturelle, en rétrogradant jusque chez les sauvages, afin qu'ils me donnent des leçons. . . .*

(From time immemorial, times beyond history, I have appeared in subtle metamorphoses at various eras; I have devastated the countries of the globe with conquest and carnage and have spread civil war among the citizens. Have I not crushed under my heels, member by member or collectively, whole generations, so that the hosts of them cannot be numbered? The glorious past has made wonderful promises to the future—it will keep them! To polish my sentences I shall necessarily employ the method of nature, retrogressing to the savages in order to learn from them.)

[From *Les Chants de Maldoror*, Chant sixième, par Isidore Ducasse. (Born in Montevideo, 1846; died in Paris, 1870. Called Le Comte de Lautréamont after a character in Eugène Sue's novel, *The Mysteries of Paris*.)]

Chapter VIII

Retrogressing — The Tower of Babel — The Faubourg St. Germain—L'édifice immense de souvenir—There Is No "Earlier" or "Later" in the Temporal Universe.

RETROGRESSING . . . *En rétrogradant* . . . The vicious circle turns once more upon itself.

Rimbaud's drunken ship *Montparnasse Vingtième Siècle* sped with billowing sails toward the bogeyman jungles of the primitive Henri Rousseau (*Le Douanier*). Jean Jacques Rousseau had earlier recommended the nature cure for a sick social morality, and now taste turned back to the primitives to learn from them and be healed. The artists were once more in advance of their time; they were returning to crudity, to the awkward, archaic work of the African Negro's kraal, a good while before Europe, galloping along gaily on the nag Progress, had reached the brink of cave life.

Man in his free, natural state, uncorrupted by the intellect, man as noble savage, imbecile or child, is a born artist—so the argument ran. The mass man is akin to the noble savage, for he is simple and virtuous, healthy in his feelings and normal in his judgments. He may sometimes go a bit overboard in revolutionary exuberance; but in his economically conditioned drive for social perfection he always acts purposefully and sanely—in contrast to those crazy individualists who tear everything down.

155

"Happy is the common man!" sighed the "better sort." "Poverty is a great radiance from within," said their poet, Rainer Maria Rilke.

And "society," those who really set the pace, who were philanthropic, liberal and socially minded, became enthusiastic about the proletariat, Negro art and ragtime. Their sons, the *jeunesse dorée,* went crazy over stage divas dressed in the cottons of factory workers, as the nobility had once tumbled in the hay with shepherdesses. The money aristocracy made up to the plebes to secure timely indulgence for the sins of capitalism, and to obtain protection against the advancing Asiatic hordes. Shuddering with admiration, the wealthy ladies watched street demonstrations of the unemployed under the windows of their villas. From their boxes they looked on at the Red revues and barricade dramas which they had financed. Their eyes were glued to the stage, where the speaking choruses of the united proletarians of all countries trampled on the corpse of bourgeois civilization in the glare of the kleig lights.

A vanishing upper crust was hypnotized by the sight of the herd, by the cries of "Forward!" and "Down with!" and by the hordes dancing around the individual burning at the stake. Singing laudatory songs, composing penitential verse, the prominent literary figures gave up their "at homes" and their artists' balls in favor of the mass meetings of the race-and-class scourgers. And the icy historical materialists were seized with a burning desire for an immortal collective soul. The stubbornest dialecticians went sleepwalking on their roofs, baying at the moon of instinctual logic.

Wrote the sociologist Gustave Le Bon:

The way men think in the mass is totally different from their psychology as individuals. Reason exercises only the slightest influence on the collective psyche. The collective psyche is governed by a special logic of its own, collective logic. [*Enseignements Psychologiques de la Guerre Européenne*].

This type of logic bears a close resemblance to "prelogical thinking," which was investigated by the ethnologist Lévy-Bruhl. He concluded that the peculiarity of precivilized society was expressed in "the law of participation." In the perils of nature, in the struggle against predatory beasts and in the demonism of fetishes, the savage feels personally involved; he feels that he participates in a fierce communal will, in the communal act—just as the collective man participates in war, in revolution, in the glory and terrorism of his leader fetishes.

El sueño de la razón produce monstruos ("The dream of reason engenders monsters") was the title that Goya gave to one of his "Caprichos." By this he meant that reason without imagination gives birth to impossible, useless ideas. United with reason, imagination is the mother of all arts.

But the opposite is also true: imagination without reason brings forth monstrosities also, and by such amphibia, spawned in cold blood, we are surrounded today. By amphibia who squat in the marshes, enveloped in miasmic fogs, who croak about a "decline of the West" and who breed in the morass of the Unconscious. Wherever the wild currents of history flood over civilizations, they are there, paddling around in the mud.

In the brackish backwaters of a Montparnasse café a Dadaist friend played a practical joke on me by introducing me to one such batrachian. And this slimy, characterless, colorless creature who adapted himself to every fashion, every type of decadence and barbarism, who acted as a spy for all sides and betrayed all sides—in short, this objective critic—immediately made a note of my name. Soon afterward we ran into each other at an intimate reception given by the royal poetess Anna, Comtesse de Noailles—the Wallachian princess and the muse of Red meetings. This time he invited me to his home.

His address alone betrayed the sort he was. The place was on the Rue le Regrattier on the aristocratic Isle of St. Louis, where a person lived either for reasons of economy or because he was a *ci-devant,* an archconservative. The few guests at this miser's very frugal dinner were wholly appropriate; they were drawn from the ranks of the artistic, political or sexual epicenes.

The quiet conversation among the guests, some of whom were handing around copies of their most recent books, had been going on for some time before a pair of portieres opened and the host slipped into the room. Pursing his lips as though he were remarking on some indiscretion in high society, he said: "Our dear Marcel Proust's soul has departed from his body."

Immediately the conversation took on the muted tones of mourners at an open grave. Each of the writers present seemed to be concerned with only two questions: how to formulate the obituary notice, and what magazine to offer it to.

The qualities of their dead "confrere" had suddenly become apparent for the first time.

"A genius of retrospection."

"I shall never forget my own words the last time I saw

him: 'Marcel, your residence is in the blind alley of Latin genius.' "

"Vain as his whole work may be, the fact that he introduced psychoanalysis into literature will remain to his credit."

"A male Mlle. de Scudéry of depraved capitalism."

Each succeeding comment was wittier and more malapropos than the one before.

When we start to read Marcel Proust, our first impression may be of embarrassment. Why are we being bothered with all this family? Who are these Combray grandparents in an advanced state of petrifaction, these moldy aunts and uncles? Why is he trying to impress us with phantoms out of the fashionable world and the *Almanach de Gotha* (which, by the way, he learned by heart)? It is embarrassing and annoying to such an extent that we hesitate whether to lay the book aside at once, or to go on reading precisely from the fascination which embarrassing material always exercises.

Proust talks about himself with the excessive excitement of a hypochondriac, neurotic boy. His adolescent love affairs are magnified out of all proportions. He is affected about a social clique who, with their biting puns, their trivial aesthetic sophistries and their gossip, get on the outsider's nerves. The temptation is to give up—if it were not that you are already caught up by his diction as by a virtuoso's scintillating prelude of arabesque passages —Debussy? Ravel? You grow restless; you don't know what is going on; all you know is that somewhere close by someone is improvising incessantly, brilliantly, and that everything is vibrating with the music. And in this musical confusion of the senses you see it through, more and more stimulated, fastening on an *aperçu* here by which a duchess exposes a weakness, or there on an ambassador's *bon mot* which will destroy a career, a marriage and a life; fascinated by the impudent frivolity of the well-brought-up, by the wittily turned propositions of a homosexual in the manner of Monsieur de Charlus.

And at last you are amused; you laugh understandingly at this society. And later, when you are really familiar with Proust, you laugh uproariously.

It is only afterward, when the last Proustian chord has faded, that you feel the shock. You realize that you have been in Tartarus, among highly spiritualized chauvinists, among witty, subtle Jew-baiters involved in the scandalous Dreyfus affair; that you have drifted to the landscaped brink of an abyss whose dangers you were unable to estimate because it was bottomless and only dimly illuminated now and then by a Proustian digression.

"Each profession understands the other, and each vice understands the other vices also. . . ."

It is only after it is all over that you realize you should have seen through these conceited, gossipy, bickering phantoms; that you should have taken the warnings of Anatole France or Proust's Bergotte to heart and looked into their family background in Balzac.

Balzac's *Comédie Humaine* had been dedicated in all seriousness to the zoologist, Saint Hilaire. It classified every ruling instinct of the genus homo sapiens—the avarice, the parasitism, the habits of copulation. As a reader of Balzac you ought to have been prepared for the worst. Like Balzac, Proust started his story off in the *juste milieu,* and as in Balzac the surprised reader of Proust unexpectedly finds himself among the perpetrators of vicious star-chamber politics, among the corsairs of high finance, at the other end of the world from the demimonde.

There was nothing new about the basic material in *Cities of the Plain* (*Sodome et Gomorrhe*). Yet since the days of the Marquis de Sade and Balzac this passion that Proust described had become so anemically sublimated, so refined, that we were once more intrigued by its elaborate ceremonials. After finishing the book, you become suspicious and you ask yourself: is it possible that an ancestor of Proust's friend, the Marquis de Saint Loup en Braye, was ever mixed up with Balzac's murderer-priest, Herrera-Vautrin? Could a mistress of the Baron de Nucingen have been the great-grandmother of Odette de Crécy (Madame Swann)?

Combray, the little provincial town in Normandy, was —in Proust's childhood, at any rate—one of those *"cabinets des antiques"* described by Balzac, filled with moth-eaten nobles, and the seat of two rival clans: the circle around the anti-Dreyfusard Duc de Guermantes, and the circle around the "progressive" Verdurins who went in for Wagner's music and radical socialism. And on the other side of the street—*du côté de chez* Swann (as Proust called him, but in reality Mr. Charles Hirsch)— was the cultivated scion of the race of usurers (in Balzac: Gobseck and Rigou).

Proust had not exaggerated when he showed how ripe for collapse France was, how little fight there was among her so-called best elements. His prognosis was confirmed when the next onslaught came, after his death. His caustic satire and his mania for skillfully vivisecting every motion, every sensation, proved to be entirely justified.

Hereditary decadence and asthma, which affected him from early youth, had predestined Proust to be what he became. He was so constantly in a state of sexual over-excitement, so frayed by the fevers he ran every morning, so exhausted, that a madeleine dipped into a cup of tea— offered to him by his secretly desired mother—was sufficient to produce in him a violent hemorrhage of painfully sweet memories. But at his cradle he had also received the gift of genius from the good fairy. He could descend with the somnambulistic sureness of an Orpheus down into the bowels of his mundane past. He followed his beloved memory, and all the Cerberuses of the drawing rooms, clacking their false teeth and growling in their throats, could not harm or stop him. The insatiable maw of time with its Never Again closed around him as gently, as tenderly as his own palate tasted the crumbs of memory.

No sooner had the warm liquid, and the crumbs with it, touched my palate than a shudder ran through my whole body, and I stopped, intent upon the extraordinary changes that were taking place. An exquisite pleasure had invaded my senses, but individual, detached, with no suggestion of its origin. And at once the vicissitudes of life had become indifferent to me, its disasters innocuous, its brevity illusory—this new sensation having had on me the effect which love has of filling me with a precious essence; or rather this essence was not in me, it was myself. . . .

I retrace my thoughts (*Je rétrograde par la pensée*) to the moment at which I drank the first spoonful of tea. . . . And suddenly the memory returns.

Suddenly, thinking back upon Proust, all the modern writers seemed to me old, terribly old—and our host was like a ghost appearing out of the miasmic atmosphere of a sickroom when he repeated:

"My dear Marcel Proust's soul has departed from his body . . . or shall I say, his half-soul," he added.

This cheap mot was all that occurred to this miser—and was simply a pretext for getting in the "my dear Proust," thus putting forward his claim to the literary inheritance. But not even this witticism was entirely his own; it had simply been given to him by the circumstances in order to characterize him as a Proustian creation—which was what he was, he and his whole circle. They were as much an invention as the anecdote they told:

"When our late confrere, our unforgettable friend Marcel Proust who has, alas, died so young, lay on his deathbed, he asked to have his manuscripts back in order to correct a death scene he had described in the light of what he was experiencing."

Proust was no sooner buried than posterity began honoring the tomb of his reminiscences with more editions and critical commentaries than he would ever have longed for in his moments of wildest ambition. Even one of his harshest critics (and one who now has almost caught up with him in the race for fame), André Gide, paid his last debt to Proust and made his apology: if he had ever chanced to offend the departed novelist by, say, rejecting manuscripts of his, it had been only because a certain stylistic unevenness had irritated him—in particular Proust's somewhat arbitrary use of the tenses and his excessive abuse of subjunctives.

But Proust had good reasons for such aberrations; he followed the grammar and syntax of predictions and prophetic dreams rather than the grammar and syntax of an actual course of events. Thus, in the *passé défini* account of a tradition he was already anticipating the present decay; in the indicative mood of his love for the still-immature, imperfect Gilberte he already sensed the pain she could give him; he was aware of the subjunctive of doubt, the possibility of a general betrayal of all emotions, the corruption of all ties.

For he was always retrogressing, *en rétrogradant.*

Retracing his thoughts to the symbols of his childhood, and even farther back, to the archetypes of the primitives.

But who are the authentic primitives, the really unspoiled ones?

Are they Darwinian pre-stages of man? Or Rousseauian savages living in sexual and classless innocence? Are they the people who dwelt in Paradise before humanity erected its Tower of Babel, building floor upon floor, first for the family, then for the clan, then for the priesthood, for the absolute monarch, for the state composed of individuals—higher and higher to the very summit: the almost divine collective?

Early in the nineteenth century the German philosopher of "subjective idealism," Schelling, hearing Alexander von Humboldt's account of his travels among the natives of the South Sea islands, wondered whether these peoples were really "savages." Might they not be, he suggested, degenerate descendants of mighty cultures that had been swept from the face of the earth? Herman Melville too, when a prisoner of the Typee cannibals in the Marquesas Islands, thought he could detect in the wooden masks of their idols the lingering traces of once divinely beautiful works of art.

The Lost Library

Why not? Perhaps ultimately their cannibalistic legends, their inarticulate litanies, their complex dance rituals often lasting for a year on end, are indeed survivals of noble literatures gone to seed under the misguided despotism of priests and witch doctors. And how far back in time would those literatures reach, since in all of them dragons occur—faithful descriptions of the giant saurians: the Singhalese dragon of the eclipse, Shavo, who swallows the sun and moon; the dragon of the Athanasian heresy who was beheaded by St. George; the hydra of the counterrevolution which emerges afresh, raising its seven cliché heads, from every political struggle. Are these not fragmentary figures from antediluvian poetries?

At any rate, wherever I find these beasts mentioned, even in newspaper editorials, I marvel anew at how ancient they are. I have felt this way ever since I began rummaging through medieval bestiaries, studying the characteristics of lintwurms and griffons in order to write my *Das Neubestellte Abenteuerliche Tierhaus* (published 1923), a zoology of fabulous beasts and their role in mysticism and superstition. (I began this back in Vienna in 1921 when I had lodgings near the basilisk house in the Schoenlaternengasse.)

At the time I asked myself where in man's memory the recollection of such monsters survived? For our paleontologists place the beginnings of man long after the age of the saurians. But possibly all culture is only part of a process of dissolution; perhaps we who are still alive are only a kind of fungus flourishing on the decayed fauna of a planet that is dying. And therefore all our splendid achievements, technical as well as intellectual, are nothing but necessary, and of course unconscious, disintegrating

165

agents useful for cleansing the earth's crust of the last cadavers.

"Oh, but then," I went on, once having got into this vein, "the monsters still have one place left where they can disport themselves: the sea. There is a gigantic laboratory of monstrosities where a nature gone mad goes on experimenting—putting mammals into the bodies of fish, planting animals like flowers in the soil, shaping spiny cucumbers and filigree fans. . . . The things that are being feverishly created down there, the symbols that are being spawned there, can't be imagined. Divers at best get only a glimpse of the outer edges; but occasionally the salt seas disgorge their products on the beach, or wash them into the ports where sailors spin their yarns, and where a sailor might have a bit of the arm of the kraken dangling from his pants pocket. . . ."

(I carried these ideas around with me for a long while, until I reached America, where a literary pickpocket snatched them from me.)

Monsters die out—the symbols survive—*et tout le reste est littérature.*

The symbols with which reality overwhelms us are really innate with us—just as susceptibility to certain diseases is innate in our organs. Nowhere is that proved so drastically, so indubitably, as in the life of a creative personality, especially of a writer—the positiveness of the proof corresponding to the degree of his originality. First of all, everyone who plays any part in his destiny, who hoodwinks, seduces or persecutes him, will be drawn from the reservoir of the characters he himself has invented. And the countries, environments, events through which he must pass are those which were created beforehand for him, created for him prenatally. And he will die a death that rhymes with his last sigh.

Perhaps—for perhaps is the word with which to precede any stab at the truth—perhaps this is the source of the great consolation, the reassurance which a work of art brings us: that it prelives the divine and infernal tensions which are unbearable to us as human beings. Literature is the sole credible source of news on that incident in Nothingness which we call existence; the only report in which the event and expression are intermingled and of like nature. Not the writer but his fate chooses his subjects for him.

Joseph Conrad, author of the parable of the captain who had to choose between the raging typhoon and the wicked wife, wrote of himself:

Though I have often been classed as a writer of the sea, I have always felt that I had no specialty in that or in any other specified subject. It is true: sea life has been my life. It has been my own self-satisfying possession. When the change came over the spirit of my dreams (Calderon says that Life is Dream), my past had by the very force of things to enter for a considerable part into the body of my work, become one of the sources of what I may call for want of a better word, my inspiration—of the inner forces which set the pen in motion.

Joseph Conrad (Teodor Jósef Konrad Korzeniowski) was born in the Ukraine, the son of an intellectual leader of the illegal Polish nationalist party. His father was one night taken away by the soldiers of Czar Alexander II, and his mother died soon afterward. The orphaned Joseph

Conrad was raised by a rich uncle. But that was not his past. His fate dictated for him not the life of a Polish Irredentist, but the life of a first-rate English novelist of the sea and the tropics. When the change came over the spirit of his dreams—at the age of seventeen—he ran away to sea, at Marseilles. He became a patriot of the oceans and a master in the British merchant marine; he steered for those "mysterious coasts where a spiteful Nemesis lay in wait." A passenger who knew something about writing, John Galsworthy, recognized his talent, and Conrad quitted the merchant marine. Writing became for him a sailor's hobby. He settled down in the coastal garden of the English language because all his life he had felt attracted by its foreignness; he cultivated its soil and planted exotic flowers of style. This was resented—just as the English miss he married was always resentful and shocked when he brought his down-at-heels friends from shipboard and the colonies home, even as his characters did in his books. His wife never got used to the lordly way he would introduce a half-dead, delirious Negro, two dissolute bookkeepers who had been bearing the white man's burden in Africa, or the blinded wreck of a tropical captain—the scum of the jungles and the East Indies, white and colored, racked by swamp fever and cholera. By such doings he shocked not only the literary critics and his wife, but even his best friend, Ford Madox Ford, who allegedly gave him lessons in English. His wife claimed in her memoirs that he never completely acclimated himself to the English language; he would talk French when he was in high spirits and swear in Polish during a spell of malaria.

The Lost Library

Conrad the sailor had reversed Rimbaud's course, had emerged from the intoxicating romanticism of the sea and the jungles into the adventure of literature. A pirate captain in command of mutinous souls, he was gaped at by his landlubber readers as though he were a jinx, a phantom from the Flying Dutchman. And he brought his curse with him into literature—even down on my father's library, which went under in the flood of barbarism.

I must anticipate and digress somewhat to tell about a minor episode which took place in Marseilles, the city where Rimbaud died and where Conrad shipped out to sea. In the general panic after the barbarian invasion, almost the entire intelligentsia of Europe had fled to Marseilles. One pitch-black night when the mistral was raging I was caught by the blackout on the Cannebière. Since it was necessary to keep out of the way of the Sûreté Nationale, the Vichy-French servants of the Huns, I slipped into the familiar refuge of Snappy's Bar. I found the place full of sailors whose ships flew forbidden flags. I went around asking the routine questions about the next sailing of one of those ghost ships—for often, in exchange for filthy lucre and a few humble words, the sailors would smuggle aboard a phantom passenger. One sailor, who looked like a regular Robert Louis Stevenson pirate, sent me over to a corner table almost hidden by the swirling tobacco smoke. There sat a master of the camouflaged English merchant marine. He was tall, haughty, grim, with pointed beard, and bore an amazing resemblance to Joseph Conrad. When I made my request, he looked me up and down sharply, but at the same time with so much kindliness and understanding that I was beginning to be hopeful. Then I heard a voice I shall never forget, a sea-seasoned voice whispering to the man with the beard:

"Beware of enlisting any lad with lean brow and hollow eyes; given to unseasonable meditativeness; and who offers to ship with the Phaedon . . . Beware of such a one . . . !"

Without understanding what he meant, I realized that the answer would be no. I turned about and slipped out of Snappy's Bar—and went on begging at all the overseas consulate doors for a visa. When I finally did get across and beached at the New York Public Library in Manhattan, I discovered that the warning to Joseph Conrad's double in Snappy's Bar had been a passage from the Jonah Sermon in Herman Melville's *Moby Dick*.

I do not know whether Conrad had read Melville. But artistic influences are often transmitted telepathically. And Conrad cruised in the same fateful waters, amid the same typhoons that had driven Melville toward the wilds of the Self. Conrad too penetrated into the interior, into Melville's "world of the mind; wherein the wanderer may gaze round, with more of wonder than Balboa's band roving through the golden Aztecs' glades."

Like Jonah, Melville was also a prophet who had abandoned his post and fled from his mission. But flight did not avail Melville either. He too was swallowed up by the sea monster, by the black maw of the white sperm whale, his Moby Dick, who spewed him out again at the place where he was destined to remain: in nineteenth-century literature. For no creature born from the womb can escape the allegory of its existence. Jonah's whale, Melville's Moby Dick, Baudelaire's albatross, Goethe's Me-

phisto, Dostoevsky's Idiot, Flaubert's Madame Bovary—
all these are only figures that represent something else.
But what?

The whale—let's keep this to ourselves—is not a real
whale at all. It is the womb of the Creator. Moby Dick
is the sperm that impregnates the great mother, the sea.
Faust's Gretchen becomes in Nietzsche the Blond Beast,
in Ibsen the sweetheart who saves Pastor Brand from
the Kierkegaardian falcon. And the falcon in turn is Ivan
Karamazov's devil. The Idiot is Dostoevsky's Slavic
Jesus Christ. And the Saviour is found again in Richard
Wagner's Parsifal, who redeems the sins of music as
Flaubert redeemed the adulteress, Madame Bovary. And
who was Madame Bovary? *"Madame Bovary, c'est moi,"*
Flaubert always said. But Rimbaud said: *"JE est un
autre."*

What is the I? What is the We? Is man the last
gasp of a crucified Deity? Or is he the plaything of someone who pretends to be God and is really Satan? Is he the
main character in the memoirs of a verbose old man?

Is he the hero of a literary odyssey of the twentieth
century, like James Joyce's Ulysses?

Copies to be sent . . . to all the great libraries of the
world, including Alexandria . . . Someone was to read
them there after a few thousand years, a mahamanvan-
tara. Pico della Mirandola like. Ay, very like a whale.
When one reads these strange pages of one long gone
one feels that one is at once with one who once . . .

And so when Europe was about to be destroyed like
the library at Alexandria, I spent an entire day and a
thousand and one nights emptying boxes full of books,

coursing through the bewitched woods where Perrault's fairies and Grimm's witches and robber captains lurk, making my way through Kipling's jungles, Alice's Wonderland and Strindberg's *Dream Play,* climbing up to Nietzsche's Superman and down into Huysmans' Là-Bas, traveling into the materialist utopia of H. G. Wells's *Mankind in the Making* and Back to Methusaleh with the progressive skeptic, George Bernard Shaw, searching through Dostoevsky's *House of the Dead* and stowing away on Joseph Conrad's *Narcissus.* And here I am, poorer than Sindbad the sailor, pillaged down to my last book, wearing the borrowed clothes of translation, begging for a hearing on my own account. So, my dear reader, let me pause for breath under the portico of your Public Library—the temple of American democracy—before I proceed.

For I have come to realize that my present and my future carry the hereditary taint of my books, the taint of two thousand years of intellectual inbreeding—the European tradition. My father's library, like my last home in Vienna, like the capuchin tomb of the Hapsburgs, like the Christian medieval state of the last Eternal Austria, like the Turkish mocha in the last coffeehouses, like the *"Heurige Wein"* in the Grinzing taverns, like each of the things I loved with my whole being, like France's Liberté to which I swore eternal fealty, like the Third Reich which smashed them all—all these things still exist only in the pluperfect tense, or in a *passé défini,* and the vain search for a lost age could be successful only in an optative mood, in the "might have been." The "remembrance of things past" is a vain enterprise.

PART II

The Lost Library

Chapter IX

Encounter with the Spirit of the Library after the Great Revolution of the Books.

THE WHITE, sixteen-volume set of Proust's *A la Recherche du Temps Perdu* in the *Nouvelle Revue Française* edition was the last addition I made to my father's collection of books before I left them. They did not come back into my possession again until I was in exile in Vienna. Before my exile, living here and there in Europe, I had not let myself be weighed down with possessions. What volumes of modern literature came my way, as gifts or, often, as loans—in fact everything I had read between the First and the Second World Wars—had either been returned to the owners or left in hotel closets, rooming-house fireplaces or the baggage racks of railroad cars.

Now, settled in my Viennese cloister, it took me about a week to restore the original mosaic of the library. Often, to determine where a book went, I had to resort to my visual memory, for sometimes my knowledge of the book was limited to the binding alone—to the gilt leather or the red velvet binding of a Pre-Raphaelite poet, or to a coarse-grained cloth covering an unbound manuscript (like a sturdy peasant girl's blouse). For I had been given sometimes to imagining the entire contents of a book from the format, the typography and the title.

Not so my father. He had always laughed at the stereotype question of simple-minded visitors: "Oh, Herr

Redakteur, have you really read all these books?" But he
could in fact boast of having assimilated them all, and of
knowing all about everything—from Goethe's theory of
colors to Vaihinger's philosophy of "As If" and Du Bois-
Reymond's *Ignorabimus*.

Finally the job was done and the three walls of my
furnished room in Vienna were covered. Returning late
at night and switching on the floor lamp, I felt that the
books formed a magical pentagram and other necromantic
patterns, producing an atmosphere that was both home-
like and eerie, and bringing the dead to life. It seemed
as though now, for the first time, I was really entering
upon my inheritance; as though I were once more in the
room where my father had died, from which he had just
been carried out, while his soul still lingered among all
the objects—like the open pages of books which continue
to flutter closed, like a drop of ink clinging to the tip of a
pen. It was as though only a moment before I had looked
at the heavy boards of the book which had dropped from
his dying hand—the first edition of Kant's *Critique of
Pure Reason,* the thing-in-itself in its uncompromising, as
yet unattenuated original form. It was as if I had just
picked the book up from the rug and placed it back on
its shelf—being, even at his death, as pedantic as he had
reared me to be.

For when that had happened, when he had suddenly
turned purple in the middle of a sentence from Kant, when
his lifeless weight had fallen into my arms—in that second
which was a fraction of eternity, I was like the sorcerer's
apprentice to whom the magician has left his apparatus.
The real magic he had taken with him into the hereafter.
The magic formula which I knew by heart, knew in my

sleep, was: Knowledge. It was the Open-Sesame! which let you into the treasure cave where was stored the philosopher's stone or the "glowing matter," the cosmic-ray diadem of the Trinity, the pure surplus-value gold of socialism. Once you owned these you had power over all the forces of nature and over the psychophysical nature of human beings. The Aladdin's lamp of the nineteenth century was science. No matter what happened to me I had only to remember the spell, and the genie of a book would appear to aid and counsel me.

But on the day of my father's death all the spirits had just been called up for military service. The university lecture halls had been taken over for military training and emergency hospital wards. The professors had been promoted to noncommissioned officers who now processed us, the academic cannon fodder, and delivered us into the hands of the generals.

After graduating from my compulsory military service —the most thoroughgoing kind of re-education from thinking and skepticism—I had placed all my hopes on the defeat of tradition. I no longer went back to the library. I only glanced at it as a visitor now and then, as I glanced at the rest of my father's belongings which stood unchanged in their old places in my mother's Berlin apartment. My further literary education, my *éducation sentimentale,* went on in the public places that flourished in the swamp of general demoralization. These were the sailors' cafés and the dives frequented by the men back from the mud and the trenches, places where poetry was a suggestive hit song and beauty the legs of some night-club singer. I studied the linguistics of the soldier's argot and learned the killer jargon of the patriotic "Free Corps" members, who spat out such vigorous phrases when they were drunk that a Shakespeare would have stooped to pick them up. I rounded out my education at the cellar meetings of the underground Reds, where the pack, hot for blood, howled furious imitations of the call of the cell leader.

It was as though the famous "public" had multiplied a millionfold, had sprung up out of the earth after a titanic bomb burst. Its numbers were being swelled incessantly from the parades of demonstrators who marched through the streets. It rolled on, a black flood reaching to the shores of the Volga and the foothills of the Urals, spilling out of the skyscraper reefs of the United States. The hordes stood elbow to elbow: Ernst Toller's "Mass Man," Alexander Blok's "slant-eyed, greedy-eyed Scythian tribes," Isaak Babel's mounted armies of Budyenny, Mayakovsky's "strangling battalions of angels with hammer and sickle," whose pounding syncopations roared like waves of applause. . . . All this was music to the ears of struggling young writers enthralled by sight of success.

A blast of Siberian weather swept down over Europe from the Bolshevist movie, *Storm over Asia,* and from the blizzard epic of comradeship, Alexander Blok's *The Twelve*—he himself was the thirteenth and was lost in the snow. The general temperature had.dropped so sharply that the postwar writers of all countries thronged into the warm mass meetings. And to get the chill out of their bones they talked faster and faster and went in for ever more strenuous linguistic gymnastics. Moreover, their breath, in everything they wrote, smelled strongly of vodka.

Against this assault, the wall that my father had built up for me volume by volume did not stand for long. Cracks appeared, and nothing that was being manufactured by belles-lettres was of sufficient format to fill the breaches. The "vitalistic" or "politico-biological" stereotype philosophy of the day seemed only to make matters worse.

But from the second half of the winter of 1932-1933 on, when Germany too succumbed to the totalitarian ice age and chilled the air throughout Europe so that it was difficult to sleep or breathe, and when those who had escaped with a whole skin and taken refuge abroad would start up at night with chattering teeth every time the floor boards creaked—then I began to long again for those books. If only I had them with me so that I might warm my soul on them!

My nostalgia for the books increased after I received one of those silly, coded letters in which the terrified sender who had remained in Germany tried to give a warning in the language of flippancy. What had happened was nothing special, nothing but the typical brutality of the new order.

> Yesterday we had visitors late at night who were very annoyed at not finding you here. Everyone had a high old time, so that this morning we had a lot of work picking up the pieces of dishware and furniture and what remains of your father's library . . .

But then my colleague Camill Hoffmann, press attaché of the Czech Embassy in Berlin, informed me that most of the library was on the way to me as diplomatic baggage. He was helping it to escape, as he had helped, under far greater risk, a number of living pariahs. As soon as I heard from him that the books were on their way, I began haunting each arrival of the Orient Express (Berlin-Vienna-Bucharest-Constantinople) at the West Station in Vienna as diligently as though I too, like the majority of the people on the platform, were waiting for some relative who had luckily escaped from "over there."

My sense of spiritual isolation on the crumbling island of Austria eased somewhat when I had the books again and they were able to speak to me. At first I rained questions on them—especially on the omniscient nineteenth-century authors. But the more often I did that, the more I became aware that it was rather I who ought to be submitting to examination. How had it come about, how had things gone so far, that such vast intellectual assets could possibly have been devalued so that they were no longer worth a copper; that humanism could have been allowed to get so ragged and tattered; that every inspired thought could have been reduced to nonsense and ugliness; that in spite of constant ideological social hygiene, in spite of all the investigations of literary criticism, in spite of all curative ideals, a paralysis of the brain had hit with such sudden force?

There had been many early diagnoses of the condition, but they had been pooh-poohed and disregarded because they had been offered by artistic, hence pathologically inclined individuals. That was so, for example, of the classical prognosis by Heinrich Heine early in the nineteenth century:

> Kantians will appear who will not hear of piety in the phenomenal world, who will tear up the soil of our European life with swords and axes in order to cut out the

very last roots of the past. Armed Fichteans will appear on the scene whose fanatical insistence on getting their way will not be curbed by either fear or selfishness; for these people live in the spirit and defy matter. . . . But even more frightful will be the natural philosophers who will take part actively in a new German revolution and identify themselves with the work of destruction.

Later in the century, Fyodor Dostoevsky cried out from Russia:

Tyranny will become first a habit and then a disease. . . . Blood intoxicates, and minds will be opened to the worst abnormalities. Such degeneracy can take place that abnormalities will seem like pure joys. . . . The opportunity for going on such a rampage often infects a whole people. Society despises the hired executioner, but not one who is provided with unlimited power. . . .

The most precise medical prognosis was formulated in the 1800's by a Swiss university professor of cultural history (who would listen to him?), Jakob Burckhardt:

Conditions in Europe may one day shift overnight to a state of rapid decay, and what now appear to be the positive forces will suddenly reveal their fatal weakness.

On the other hand, there were a number of my father's "famous contemporaries" who were still alive and therefore still writing. They, although they had "seen it coming"—"it" being the European madness—now presented a sad spectacle of conformism. But the fact that prophecies had proved true did not hold much comfort. Out of the collection of books, out of the peculiar pattern they formed, I kept hearing my father's voice, chiding, remonstrating, becoming more and more urgent, so that, instead of seeking for further arguments among the books, I turned and addressed him.

—Let me speak now. Let me try to report what has been going on since you departed—what your books, and we along with them, have come to.

Do you remember your last visitor, that impetuous student, a volunteer on his way to the front, who sat before this wall of books when you called me in and said: "I want you to meet Herr Ernst Toller, who impresses me as someone very unusual."

Just what you felt to be unusual—the enthusiasm with which he spoke to you (I was listening from the other side of the door) or the few poems which I found on your desk after . . . after . . . you were no longer here—you never had a chance to tell me. Did you suspect that his unusual destiny lay in the discrepancy between his revolutionist's nature and his poetic drive? Certainly you little thought that the oddness of his life—and that was the most tragic part of it—was to become the usual fate of writers in our day.

The rift of the times cut straight through his heart, to use your favorite phrase of Heinrich Heine's.

But that is quickly quoted, and like every metaphor it only cools the feverish imagination, is only poetry's local anesthetic. It does not tell how deep the rift goes. If the thing can be described briefly in any figure of speech, it is this: In your times fates turned into books; in ours, books made our evil fates.

You may say: "That was your fault. I bequeathed

my books to you as I handed on my experience. You were supposed to learn from them, to deduce the good and to distinguish it from the bad. In other words, to sharpen and temper your judgment. From my books and the experiences in them you, your generation, might have profited—at least as much as our generation did, whose legacy was no larger. Where then must the blame be laid? On the books—or on you?"

On us? Well! Or perhaps on there being all too many books? On the reckless, spendthrift proliferation in all the fields of knowledge, which one of your early contemporaries, an American named Edgar Allan Poe, even then called a plague of your times? Didn't you try to convince us that everything was fixed, everything was established, that there was no use trying to shake any of it? And that, as Professor Haeckel, your professional solver of the riddles of the universe, put it: "There will be nothing at all left for our grandchildren to worry about"?

What was there left for our scientists, writers and political men to do but to insist that our guilt was inherited? And they insisted until it drove us mad. Whereupon they tried to persuade us that there was a method in this very madness, that *you* are to blame for it, if only because you did not stick consistently to the road of progress. The one school roars: Sweep all the trash away! The other analyzes the madness back to our parents' bed—they call it our Oedipus complex which drives us to kill our fathers in dreams in order to possess our mothers. They find the root of all evil in our parents' household, that is, in the period of our childhood. Youthful experiences count for everything with them. . . . But experiences can make you more stupid, more wicked or more cowardly whether they come to you through your parents or through the printed pages.

You, our parents, pounded into us the lessons you learned from experience, and we have learned either to pound them into others or to swallow the beatings in silence. And when I say beatings, I mean just that: nationalized, systematized brutality going as far as the torture that levels everything, equalizes all feeling; I mean, too, the humiliation of every individual to produce a collective consciencelessness.

"Crueler than Nero," I read recently as I was leafing through one of your Victorian satirists. I don't know who was being apostrophized. Perhaps Amor—or was it the Emperor Franz Joseph, or Kaiser Wilhelm II, or Nicholas, Czar of all the Russias?

Nero . . . ?

We lack sufficiently primitive expressions for calling for help, and we lack names with which to identify our murderers. The nameless horror so mocks all attempts at description that someday people will simply read swiftly by it, just as you read by such a sentence in Tacitus as the following. (I happen to remember it only because I had to write it ten times as punishment for getting a Latin case wrong.)

"After the execution of so many noble men there awoke in Nero the desire to exterminate virtue altogether."

Virtus (*virtutem* in the accusative!)—Nero exterminated a word!

Well, then, Ernst Toller later wrote plays which you would indeed have called unusual. They testified to times

184

of distress that would have been inconceivable to you. Those were times when language was rationed like every crust of bread, when people had to make do with old, discarded verbal trash. But Ernst Toller managed nevertheless to preserve a certain dignified bearing, and that you would have respected. You would have respected him and his co-fighters, all literati, who wanted to set up on the ruins of your bankrupt pacifism a free syndicalist republic in Bavaria. They did, for a brief while, under the presidency of a Kantian, Dr. Kurt Eisner, who was shot in the back by a patriotic young nobleman, Count Arco. The Minister of Education was Gustav Landauer, one of our finest Shakespearian scholars. He was trampled to death by the troops of the Weimar Republic, the first German republic. Ernst Toller, Eisner's secretary, and the anarchist ballad singer of the Café Groessenwahn—do you remember him, Ernst Muehsam?—got away with only seven years' imprisonment. In prison Toller wrote his most successful plays: *The Machine Wreckers* (Gerhart Hauptmann's *Weavers* brought up to date), *Hinkemann,* a tragedy in the manner of Wedekind dealing with a crippled veteran who lost his masculinity—his *membrum virile*— on the field of honor and became a circus strong man, a castrated Hercules.

No, I have no copies of Toller. I did not know where to put them in your library. Compared with the classics of the naturalist school his works were planless, constructed too haphazardly. Their tremendous effect on us is hard to evaluate objectively; you have to consider the fact that we were all in a state of nervous agitation. And to understand the abrupt entrances and the disjointed dialogues of his characters you have to remember—that is, remember a time that came after yours—the kind of audience the author was addressing. His audience sat behind the muzzles of machine guns.

Here is one passage that has remained in my memory. I first heard it at a Toller première in Berlin at which a number of patriotic vigilantes, the notorious *Feme* killers, threw stink bombs.

UNKNOWN: The Cause above all.
I love the men of the future.
WOMAN: Man above all!
For the sake of the Cause
You will sacrifice
The men of the present.
UNKNOWN: For the sake of the Cause I must sacrifice them.

In a similar vein Dostoevsky's Grand Inquisitor defended the cruelties of his doctrine of salvation against the Saviour himself. But nowadays the inquisitor and the saviour appear on the stage as one and the same person, opposing humaneness as the worst of heresies. Against their united abuse of power, Toller defended individual men and the present time.

Toller had the gifts to become the Danton of a German Revolution and a Schiller of the theater; but since these two gifts were incompatible, since they were separated by the rift through his heart, nothing reached perfection. Again and again, to his despair, his "unknowns" exploited his dramatic passions for the shabbiest political, party-line ends.

I never knew him when he was not head over heels in love—in love with freedom, with the plan for a drama,

186

with the most elegant society women. And how successful
he was with the ladies—for they were taken with his sensual, defiant rebel's face. He had the head of an improved
Danton—and once, as a chief of the Bavarian Syndicalist
Republic (for it was syndicalist, not soviet), three thousand marks' reward were placed on that head. In afterdays it decorated the book supplements of newspapers,
bearing the caption: "Latest portrait of the celebrated
militant dramatist."

In love, intoxicated with ideas, sleepless, he sped from
mass meetings to world congresses of intellectuals and
P.E.N. club dinners, making speeches that always brought
about a dramatic turn of the tide. The premières of his
plays in all the capitals of Europe—they were given in
national theaters and in the clubrooms of students' and
workers' cultural groups—always produced furious disputes. He would appear at a writers' banquet in the
U.S.S.R., at a street demonstration of the French Popular
Front, in an airplane flying over the battlefields of the
Spanish Civil War. He returned from these adventures
with his ideals as impaired as his Hinkemann's manhood,
and set sail for America. To what end? I did not know it
then, but it was to find a hero's death, the only one still
open to a writer in our times: suicide in a New York hotel.
He killed himself out of unrequited love—for a woman
. . . or rather for the Revolution . . . or even more, for
the stage. For no playwright ever gets over the nights he
has spent on the boards.

After the tragic catharsis of the vainly heroic struggle
for freedom in Spain, which had inspired him as it had all
the best contemporary writers, he found his dual role of
agitator and poet more difficult than ever. He played it

wearily, with less and less conviction, exhausted like all the rest of us by exile.

Exile! Yet what better item could a writer desire for his biography than that he was sharing exile with Ovid and Dante and Tasso, Heine, Büchner, Hugo and Zola. And certainly in the beginning the experience of exile stimulated him and renewed his spirit of defiance. It warmed his heart to witness the hospitality of foreign lands for the uncompromising, innocent victims of persecution. But like every group in misfortune, the exiles used up their stock of fellow feeling, bored one another with complaints about the quality of Eternal Justice, and wore themselves out petitioning for an identity card or for an extension of their permits to stay.

Even banishment loses dignity when its cause is so mean —the coming to power of a mangy cur, abused and disregarded until it went mad—a street mongrel raised on the garbage of jingoism and trained by universal education until it became rabid whenever it came across anything that smelled of intelligence. . . . But I am anticipating.

Without a résumé of literary activity after the First World War, the outbreak of which you lived to experience, it would not be possible to understand what came out of the books in your library, what came of their ideals and their utopias.

By a miracle, it seemed, and with the military assistance of America, the civilization of France and England won out in the end in that war. The literati of those countries were pleased to engage in disputations between red and black converts who awaited, respectively, all earthly happiness from the Moscow Communist synod, or heavenly salvation from the Roman Vatican; between scholars like the immoralist André Gide and the mystic Paul Claudel; and between such dueling masters of paradox as George Bernard Shaw, the Fabian, and G. K. Chesterton, the orthodox Catholic. These contestants, at any rate, were still each other's peers; their personal lives were dignified and their literary form impeccable. The battles were fought within the limits of the art of composition. There was not yet any of the personal mud throwing and character assassination which became normal when literature entered the arena of collectivistic politics.

In Germany things were different. There had been the wretched collapse of the German blood-and-iron colossus, and the ridiculous exit of the Kaiser, a ham actor who had tried to play the part of a Byzantine Emperor. Germany witnessed the pandemonium of civil war and the sybaritic excesses of the inflation. The art which followed from all this—in the history of literature it has been given the name of Expressionism—can best be compared to an amusement park, with chambers of horror and waxworks poetry, with Indians-in-war-paint novels and plenty of raw humor to bring the house down. It was a political carnival, with no lack of literary pickpockets and bravos hanging around the fringes of the crowd. For refined society there were the dithyrambic, iambic, nobly revolutionary exhibitions of the "Young Germany" group, under the direction of Max Reinhardt. He produced the linguistic firecrackers of Georg Kaiser (*Gas, Nebeneinander, Von Morgens bis Mitternachts*) and Karl Sternheim's "antiheroic middle-class travesties," scenes of demonstrating workers and mutinying soldiers, dramas of smuggling, social wretchedness and sexual yearning, of *Feme* killings and parricides. (The parricides: Reinhold Sorge's *Bett-*

ler; Walter Hasenclever's *Sohn;* Franz Werfel's *Spiegelmensch.*)
Behind the scenes a lost generation loafed around. . . .

At this point I stopped speaking, in order not to frighten away the Spirit of the Nineteenth Century.

After a long, meditative pause, I heard him say: "So that was what all your revolting petered out into, after the overthrow of a despotism against which our best minds, our writers, scientists and men of the people had fought. So it ended in parricide and—a lost generation."

Yes, I replied, but that expression is not mine. It did not come out of the Germany that had lost the war and all sense of proportion; it did not come out of our Old World at all. It was a slogan of American literature, and its spokesman was not one of our harried literati, but a brawny, full-blooded American named Ernest Hemingway (who borrowed the phrase from good old Gertrude Stein, grandma of modernism).

In other words, the spokesman was a descendant of one-time emigrants from Europe, of nonconformist Pilgrims who took nothing from the Old World into the wilderness but Bibles. He was a child of that colonial nation which was now offering the highest bid at the auction sale of Western culture. Learned his trade as a reporter for a local dairy farmers' newspaper, educated himself by contact with Frenchmen and Englishmen, swelled with pride when his teachers called on America for military help, and came over to Europe not as a dollar tourist, but as an ambulance driver. And then he discovered in Europe not the Uffizi galleries and the Louvre, but trenches, shellholes, field hospitals and military brothels; a grand massacre in-

stead of a hallowed tradition; a "lost generation" instead
of the legitimate heirs of all the ages. But in the end he
became a lover of Latin culture anyway.

"Un nouveau mal de siècle," Marcel Arland called our
suffering. *"La délectation morose, le masochisme, l'in-
quiétude . . ."*

"There is one thing that concerns me more than all of
literature—myself!" Arland cried.

And his compatriot, Henry de Montherlant, who at the
beginning of the war urged youth to learn the "taste for
tragedy and practice teamplay on the battlefield as on a
football field," now wailed defeatedly: "One by one I have
seen my reasons for action disappear—religion, the desire
for glory and the liking *(goût)* for myself."

The new disease of the twentieth century was the old
Romantic unrest, "the profound reality of the self," as the
neopositivist, antirationalist philosopher, Henri Bergson,
expressed it—putting the best construction on the matter.

The disease hit Italy as *Fascismo,* introduced by the
futurist Marinetti and the Renaissance-imitator Gabriele
d'Annunzio, and it spread epidemically through the activi-
ties of a socialist newspaperman, Benito Mussolini. But
the nations which had remained neutral observers during
the war also caught it. In a lecture the Spanish neo-
Kantian, Ortega y Gasset, warned his students:

There are in fact generations which are untrue to
themselves. Instead of resolutely attacking the tasks
which have been set them, they turn a deaf ear to the
insistent calls of their mission. They prefer to lean com-
fortably on the ideas, institutions and pleasures of their
forefathers. It is clear that historical obligations cannot be shirked with impunity. I have the impression

that the present generation in all of Europe, but especially in Spain, belongs to this type of shirker.

"To put it more explicitly," said the Spirit of the Nineteenth Century, "the present generation has betrayed us to the enemies of the spirit. They have disregarded the watchword of Victor Hugo: *'Certe, il viendra le rude et fatal châtiment.'*

"Have we not left you a monument in the graves of our revolutionaries who fell in 1848, and in the court-martialed members of the Commune of 1871, who were shot against the wall of the Cimétière Père-Lachaise? *Monumentum aere perennius.* Our books were written against the Napoleonic dictatorship, against the Kaiser's Caesarean delusions, against the Czarist Cossack terror. Did none of your intellectual leaders learn from those books what his historic duty was: after the abolition of slavery in the ancient city state, after the abolition of serfdom in medieval feudalism, to proceed to the abolition of wage slavery under capitalism and so to attain to a classless, cosmopolitan society where good living, technology and culture would be enjoyed by all?"

Oh, yes, I replied, that was far from forgotten. One of your books has become the Bible, the Old and New Testament together, of our era. It is believed in a thousand times more passionately than the Bible in Luther's translation. That book, a nominalistic, numerological drawing-up of accounts with the exploiters of man's heritage, was written by one of your German forty-eighters, a dialectician trained in the school of Hegel. None of your fervent advocates of the Rights of Man could have foreseen, any more than did the Nazarene's apostles, in how much blood and sweat and tears we would be swamped as a result of that book. You all underestimated it—Marx's *Das Kapital*.

You never realized that as the four Gospels overthrew the Roman Empire, as the *Encyclopédie* and the *Social Contract* and Beaumarchais' *Figaro* overturned Bourbon absolutism, so *Das Kapital* would help to destroy Russian Czarism. It took no more than "ten days that shook the world"—in the phrase used by an ecstatic American reporter (John Reed) to telegraph the news to the world. (For his services as a chronicler he was honored by burial in the Kremlin, near the Red Savior.)

Yes, with the aid of this German redemptionary doctrine, reactionary, serf-ridden, illiterate Russia smashed the apparently impregnable fortress. Astounded, everyone turned his head toward Moscow, as the best minds had turned toward Paris at the end of the eighteenth century, after the storming of the Bastille. What Goethe said then, when the armies of the French Revolution defeated the Prussian mercenaries at Valmy, was repeated when the Slav Bolshevist armies triumphed over the interventionists of Allied Europe:

"This place and this day mark the beginning of a new era for humanity, and you can say that you were there. . . ."

We were there.

In the van were the old *avant-garde* of the nineteenth century, who still survived. In Russia as in the French Convention the leaders of the new state were intellectuals, sprung from the educated classes. A keen polemicist and amateur generalissimo in charge of the red *levée en masse* (Trotsky) announced in his manifesto, *Literature and*

193

Revolution: "The human average will be raised to the level of an Aristotle, a Goethe, a Marx."

That was not utopianism; that was just another item on the agenda.

Terror in the streets, executions of monarchists, the burning of churches and monasteries—how could these things possibly frighten us? For had they not all been versified and dramatized by your eighteenth and nineteenth-century classic and romantic writers? We had been educated to discount the atrocity stories which the exiled and dispossessed abroad would always invent. All their cries, all their invective against the despoilers of their homeland, could not compete with the fanfares of the new *"Marseillaise"*—the good old *Internationale* written by De Geyter to the text of Pottier, a mediocre party scribe of the Paris Commune of 1871. Mediocrity never hurts an anthem.

How could we writers have withheld our approbation from so generous and freedom-loving a regime, which allowed complete liberty to science and to every modern trend in art—somewhat as a victorious general gives his troops leave to have a good time in the conquered city. Thus, in Moscow, there were the "Serapion Brothers," a group of "café literature" anchorites who took their name from one of E. T. A. Hoffmann's stories; the "Acmeisti," who consistently practiced Mallarméan symbolism and Lafcadio Hearn's linguistic ritual, the "raging and racking and rioting of words"; the Russian futurists headed by Vladimir Mayakovsky, whom Lunacharsky made an official of the Commissariat for People's Education.

Mayakovsky coined the latest incendiary slogans: "It is

time to plug the museums and the libraries full of bullet holes."

"Machine-gun batteries—very well! But when are you going to get around to the onslaught against Pushkin and the other generals of classicism?"

Libraries were pulped by the "class guard on the literary front." What did we care? The foundations for larger cultural structures were already being laid. Gifted men were collapsing? Well, their place was instantly taken by a more robust type, a type closer to the people. And celebrated foreigners sent their declarations of sympathy to Russia—Anatole France somewhat smirkingly, Romain Rolland and Henri Barbusse enthusiastically, H. G. Wells formally. But the old Bolshevik, Maxim Gorki, nursed a grudge from a safe distance—in his luxurious villa on the Isle of Capri.

Naturally, measures were taken to make sure that no workers' poet would be able to accumulate capital as a result of his talents. Those who rose to fame too swiftly had to submit to examination by a jury of comrades who would not countenance any artistic privileges. The social-use value of a play was decided by a free vote of the majority of the audience. Those who could not demonstrate that they loved the comrades more than literature were sent to be re-educated by digging ditches. The scarcity of intellectual products was overcome once and for all. Propaganda verses, proletarian epics, photoplays and stage plays featuring knights of the class struggle, were turned out on the assembly line. Standing on rotating platforms or in rushing elevators, drama recruits under Theatrical Sergeant Meyerhold pounded out their *agitprop* slogans. Stanislavski's old guard of carefully trained performers, and Wachtangoff's and Tairoff's living marionettes, performing in unheated but jammed halls, served to lift the morale of a populace worn out by hunger and civil war, or of weary soldiers of the people grimly enduring the cannonades of White armies who had been supplied with arms from abroad.

The movement forward, or at any rate the sense of motion, was so hectic that everybody involved lost the ability to think and feel. He could hear nothing inside his empty head but the watchword of the Comrade Chief Engineer: "Revolutions are the locomotives of world history."

And the ukase in *Literature and Revolution* of the Comrade General in command of the redoubtable armored train: "Your art is not identical with the proletarian Revolution. You are nothing but artists who won't go all the way with us . . . Fellow travelers!"

Woe to the fellow traveler whose car was attached to the Russian armored train! Inability to stop and rest anywhere was hard on the constitution. And the tempo was terrific; woe to him who could not keep up with it!

Sergey Essenin, son of a peasant, poet, vagabond and imagist, gave up first—at the age of thirty. "Why the devil did I shout in my poems, I love the people! You don't need my poetry any more, and you don't give a damn for me." After this he hanged himself in a hotel in Leningrad (formerly St. Petersburg). It was said of him, as it was later of Ernst Toller, that his suicide was due to personal troubles, to disappointment in love.

Just a weakling! Just a fellow traveler! One less of the lost generation. One after the other they went like that—and at such a pace that there was no time to fit their books into the proper literary categories.

The Lost Library

In the beginning they had all been burning with excitement, with eagerness to join the struggle, to participate in the Revolution. They had even run with utter recklessness to see who would win the Progress obstacle race. The favorites had been Lafcadio Wluiki, of André Gide's stable, who committed murder because he was "curious about himself"; and the Italian futurist, Giovanni Papini, who extolled "universal suicide" and the "motorized cavalry of the Bolshevist poets' phalanx. . . ."

To tell the truth, the literati did not put up much of a struggle. As soon as the armored cars started off, they fell under the wheels. They were not equal to the imposing tasks of materialist history, and the locomotives ran over them. It was their own fault for thrusting themselves forward, for abandoning the schedule and overstepping the prescribed party line. What they should have done was to stand in rank and file like their organized colleagues and sing praises to the revolutionary prescience of the engineer. That was the only way that they could avoid being crushed.

Of course the workers' movement of Europe had been rather put to shame. To think that with its resources of French vitality, British tenacity and German efficiency it had been outstripped by the Slavic backwoodsmen. But Europe's humanistic culture, theorizing and weakness for books were a handicap. These feelings had robbed the European literati of the ruthlessness essential to a revolution.

Some time before, in the nineteenth century, Europe had been under the spell of Russian literature as it was now under the spell of the Russian Revolution. Europe had been attracted by the self-destructive fanaticism, the grim gallows humor, the contagious insanity and the pan-Slavic mysticism of that literature.

> Yes, we are Scythians, we are Asiatics.
> Once more we ask you, Old World,
> To join with us as brothers for the Feast.
> They ask but once, the barbarians of the East.

There was a sinister undertone to this ultimatum from the new classicist of the Revolution, Alexander Blok. And even more sinister was his silence afterward. He vanished without a trace from the sight of his Western admirers, to whom he had been praised as the most eminent poet of Soviet literature. Not another syllable was heard from him, nothing but, one day, a few terse obituaries written by embarrassed comrades who wore smiles of pity.

Next!

"The dead man takes hold of the living man who becomes his successor, the continuer of his interrupted life," wrote Proust in the second volume, *Within a Budding Grove,* of his *Remembrance of Things Past.*

Proust was my last addition to my father's library. For how else could it have become the rendezvous of the nineteenth century with the lost generation of the twentieth?

Chapter X

Monologue with the Spirit of the Nineteenth Century, Continued—Of the Beautiful Lady and Literary Vanity—And of the genus irritabile vatum.

BUT WHY in Vienna? the Spirit asked.

That too was not accidental, for a meeting with the past always takes place in a danger zone, always exposes us to the perils of being buried by an avalanche. The threat of the avalanche hung over Vienna and all the rest of Austria; both were snowed in within the narrow valley of their tradition.

"This dualism of feeling: that we belong to Austria and belong culturally to the German totality . . ." This, in the words of Austria's last classicist, Hugo von Hofmannsthal, was the dichotomy in which the Austrian lived from day to day, drifted with the current, and at night clambered in through the window of his old peasant-aristocratic, Slavic-Jewish mistress—running the risk of being caught in bed with her by the German totality.

Of course I knew that Austria was in a precarious situation. But I had been driven into linguistic exile and I suffered from spiritual malnutrition. That is why I went to Vienna, where my colleagues at least were still at home —although they too were no longer quite safe, so that by day they ventured no farther than the nearest coffeehouse, and did not dare to enter a tavern before dark.

The Lost Library

The bars were the meeting places of those long-standing adversaries of the days of the monarchy, the veterans of fading red socialism and the black-and-yellow legitimists. The latter conducted their arguments in the five vowels of the Hapsburg doctrine, which were all that they had left: A-E-I-O-U: Austria Erit in Orbe Ultima!

And today, Christmas night, walking through snow-covered baroque lanes after one of those discussions of literature that had already become meaningless—they were conducted like lovers' talk in whispers, for fear of the eavesdropping vigilantes of the Greater German Totality—walking back to my books, I repeated A-E-I-O-U. My association with them was Rimbaud's magic formula:

A noir, E blanc, I rouge, O bleu, voyelles
Je dirai quelque jour vos naissances latentes.

In front of St. Stephen's Cathedral, where funeral bells and Bach's toccata and fugue on the organ called "dying Vienna" to the last midnight mass, some young ruffians shouted out anticapitalist, anticlerical and anti-Semitic obscenities—extracts from those trashy books and pamphlets which you, Father, had kept in the "poison cupboard" as cultural curiosities, and which I had read in secret.

"Tomorrow," I heard one young fellow say, "we'll string them all up: the blacks and the reds and the Yids; we'll take care of the ones with a lot of books first."

And I did not breathe easy until I had shut the door behind me, and saw my father's library before me again.

"Well, then, what has brought you back?" the Spirit asked me. "The realization that you don't know where to go on from here—or that you don't know anything at all? The prodigal son of the lost generation returning to the religion of his fathers, of the nineteenth century? To Comte's positivism: the acknowledgment of the Higher Being, Reason, which you must not only make your model, but continually strive to improve? . . . Yes, you've attended to Friedrich Nietzsche's 'transvaluation of all values'; you've applied yourselves to that. But have you also taken note of Nietzsche's reminder of indebtedness: 'The parents have paid the expenses for what a man is'? Or is there something else that is worrying you, all you prodigal sons of the lost generation?"

Yes, there is. At this ghostly midnight hour, the two of us alone with a library full of systems for enchantment, full of learned spells, seraphic diabolisms, mesmeric mass suggestions, the sole means of communication that remains to me is the ABC—the literary cipher we use for setting down what is worrying us.

The Soviet Russian poet, Alexander Blok—I must again cite one of our dead against your ghosts; for where else should I get the authority to speak in the names of all of us?—even that soldier of progress as I later learned was worried about something. There was a blot on his revolutionary poetic past: the lines he wrote in his youth "To a Beautiful Lady." Two of those lines, even in dull prose translation, are a sharp, unequivocal self-accusation:

"It was my destiny to love her in heaven only in order to betray her on earth."

There it was, the frank confession that he was a betrayer. After this it could surprise no one when he became an apostate and betrayed his second mistress, the earthly daughter of the people—the Party—in favor of his earlier, heavenly sweetheart. He went back to the beautiful lady of his youthful poetry whom he had loved before he jilted her for a buxom public illusion.

He could be forgiven for his first infidelity, since it was directed against a beautiful lady, that is, against the bourgeoisie. But there was no pardon after he broke his vows to the Central Committee of the entire working class.

On the lips of a woman the accusation, "You have betrayed me," is dangerous enough, but the matter can be righted with a caress. Issuing from the mouthpiece of the stern wooden idols of freedom it becomes a brutal denunciation: You have committed treason against the Cause! No sanctuaries are open to the political outcast. Naked force, which holds nothing sacred but itself, has torn down all the altars, including the altar of Pure Art which even the church respected. The outcast can no longer sleep. Inevitably on some night fists will pound on the door of his dream refuge, will drag him out to some filthy puddle by a damp wall, and strip him one by one of his ideals, his honor, his life.

As Flaubert said: "There are honors which dishonor. . . ."

Ambition and the will to live are inseparable from each other. The oxygen of honor nourishes the flame of life and the spark of ego at the heart of it, so long as the ego does not flare up into the conflagration of love, or smother itself in the smoke of hatred, or go out entirely in the stale air of a prison or a concentration camp—or die in the course of interrogations. No criminal has ever been so hardened that he would not defend with tooth and claw his own conception of honor.

Stubborn to the last, he will boast like Stendhal's zealot priest, Julien Sorel, when he is locked in the death cell for having attempted murder from ordinary jealousy: "I am isolated in this dungeon, but I have not lived in isolation on earth, for I had the powerful idea of duty. The duty which I imposed upon myself, whether right or wrong . . ."

For no ordinary mortal is free from ambition; and he would rather let himself be beheaded for it than deviate by a hairbreadth from his sense of honor, his duty—whether right or wrong.

Only the ninefold wise men, the stylite saints who have stripped themselves of all possessions except *cogito, ergo sum,* who have weeded out every incipient desire in themselves, who with crippled egos sit on their heights and meditate on good and evil—only they have thoroughly killed off vanity, or think they have.

But what all of us, great and small, the geniuses and the petty talents, are "worried about," is our vanity. Without it, how would any work of art have come into being, have been composed in notes, chiseled out of stone, painted on canvas, cut in wood or written down on paper? If *vanitas, vanitatum vanitas* were not more powerful than *thanatos,* Orpheus would never have returned from Hades, Dante would never have left Inferno, Dostoevsky would never have escaped the House of the Dead, Marcel Proust would have faded away in his sickroom without ever becoming a writer. He kept himself going only by injecting himself every day with a dose of ambition, by repeating stubbornly: *"Tu auras le prix Goncourt! Tu auras le prix Goncourt!"*

And he got the Goncourt prize; it was his extreme unction.

Were an author's vanity not a stronger motive force than even the erotic impulse, Shakespeare, "desiring this man's art and that man's scope," would never have immortalized for us his Dark Lady, nor François Villon his Fat Margot, nor Alexander Blok his Beautiful Lady; we would never have confessed in verse our secret loves.

Even so ascetic a thinker as Pascal could not get along without applause from "at least three or four persons." Nor can there be any objection to a writer's selling his soul to his vanity, so long as he remains within the magic circle of his profession and preserves his artistic arrogance; so long as he does not sell his vanity into the service of the power libertines, the army officers' clubs or the political brothels. For, once vanity's desire for recognition has been awakened, he will find her an expensive mistress. Then she will beautify herself for every national gigolo and *caudillo,* and change her fashions according to the taste of every mob and every regiment.

It's always silly and hopeless to dig down into an author's biography or examine his texts microscopically in order to find out what his Beautiful Lady was actually like. For no matter how he has described her—as an Aphrodite Callipygia or a Dantean Beatrice with face turned heavenward, or like Byron as

so soft, so calm, so eloquent,

or like Baudelaire,

Comme un animal fort qui surveille sa proie—

she invariably proves to be only the wish-image of his vanity.

He is the victim of that particular illusion which Goethe's Mephisto predicted for Faust, that since he had

drunk of the witch's brew, every woman would look like
Helen to him:
Du siehst mit diesem Trank im Leibe
Bald Helenen in jedem Weibe.

Don't deny that all your nineteenth-century books, too,
were consecrated to vanity. Every one of them shows it.
If you tried to hide the fact, it was only out of false artistic
prudery. The writers who made no bones about the func-
tion of vanity were the ones you scorned as "decadents."
I open the first history of literature that comes to hand:

Decadents: Adherents of a school originating in
France. Chief representatives: Baudelaire, Verlaine,
Rimbaud, Mallarmé; also called Symbolists; introduced
into England by Oscar Wilde . . .

Vanity—what a strange goddess! When she brings
forth her greatest achievements in art, she is called decadence, but no one finds it at all reprehensible when a nation's vanity is coextensive with its ruins.

"I should like to know what actually inspires those deeds
which are publicly said to be done for the Fatherland."
This question was raised by the Great German writer
of aphorisms, Georg Christoph Lichtenberg. He was a
hunchback—therefore not fit for military service.
Vanity! There is the answer. And those are the vainest
who woo the lowest taste of their time while referring to
the "verdict of posterity" and "historical justice." But as
Tolstoy said: "The man who plays a part in a drama of
history never understands its significance. And if he ven-
tures to look into it, he is stricken with impotence."

The Lost Library

That is true. But no one acting in it has the faintest idea what the *tragedia humana* has in mind to do with him, and in what way he is intended, before he steps off the stage into the grave, to influence posterity. Nobody knows whether he embodies an individual's destiny or a cosmic one. When the roof collapses on a man's head, he will never learn before he breathes his last whether saturation bombing has destroyed the city, whether the planet is being annihilated in a collision with another heavenly body—or whether nothing more has taken place than an explosion of the gas stove in the room above.

In the same way it is impossible for contemporary literature, which is to say the written expression *in extremis* of our fellow sufferers, to offer an objective estimate of its importance in relation to a catastrophe as vast as the one in which we have been immersed for half a generation. It is a human, all-too-human weakness, and we are tempted into it by vanity, to confuse the monstrousness of events and the timeless importance of the art concerned with them, to mistake the colossal theme of a war or a revolution for the caliber of the artist. Nothing turns out quite so wretched as what was produced in the course of a jubilant mood.

The nervous haste with which all these "proletarian shock troops of poetry," these "Red intellectual workers" and "lyrical associations for racial rebirth," produced "literature" was only a symptom of the dilatation of the concept of honor as a result of hypertension between the collective vanity and the "profound reality of the self."

But what literary man dared to admit that he had a weak heart? He preferred to neglect his secret love and even his style rather than miss a dance at the newest political masquerade ball; he broke off with the beautiful lady who was his true love, his real vanity, to the last, until he could no longer go on and had to collapse like Vladimir Mayakovsky, the Don Juan of the masses, the powerful fellow who could hold up two men in his outstretched arms, the linguistic athlete who pressed the "Thousand Streets" to his breast:

I am yours, Oh planetarian proletariat!

He had been the show horse in the dictatorial circus; now he was utterly used up, kicked at by the liveried trainers and the stable hands of the press, humiliated and reduced to a comic stopgap performer. Finally, before he killed himself, he paid tribute to truth and scribbled the lines:

Lili, love me!
Comrade Government! My family is Lili.
As the phrase is, the case is closed,
The skiff of love was shattered by the waves of life. . . .
I am quits with existence.
Down below, where the world vanishes into tundras and the storm whips up the Arctic Ocean . . . into my chains I will still scratch the name LILI with my fingernails, and even in the darkness of the prison will kiss those chains. . . .

The letters of suicides are in one respect like poems: only in the rarest cases do they reveal their ultimate motives. So often the writer deceives himself just as much as he does others. And so there is no way of knowing whether the prison referred to in these lines was meant only figuratively, or whether it was a real threat.

"But what are you telling me now?" the Spirit demanded, with every indication that he was losing patience. "What is all this about a lost generation and a literature of suicides, when in the same breath you mention—as if it were the worst kind of nemesis—a revolution! It sounds to me as though this revolution of yours went far beyond the great French Revolution and completed the work for which our Liberals, Chartists, Socialists and forty-eighters—you mentioned only Marx—labored in order to lay the foundation for a future society that would no longer be ruled by vile Mammon. It is a terrible thought that all of your writers were on the wrong side of the barricades of liberty. I can't imagine that all of you turned away from the revolution just because it brought with it, as it must necessarily have done, certain evils, certain unfortunate concomitants. You sound embittered, prejudiced, like a politicaster; your talk is unworthy of a free writer."

No writer, I replied, whether he is a love poet or dramatist or novelist has the right any longer to be "unpolitical." That is the first commandment of this dictatorship of liberty. The writer's imagination and his aesthetics become *ipso facto* a confession of political faith.

For what sort of creature is this Beauty whom the majority worships?

At best she is the "photogenic Venus" of Hollywood, the American metropolis of the motion-picture industry; otherwise she is the kulak's daughter Eva in the Russian Communist paradise who has been taken to a clinic and had her soul surgically removed, the state paying the cost of the operation.

Ever since the whole world has become enlightened, it

208

has been getting gloomier and gloomier. Since technology has replaced religion, we admire the miracles of the machine. And since the nonexistence of God has become a proved fact, each of the iconoclasts has set up his One and Only surrogate god to fill the philosophical vacuum: "class consciousness" and the "voice of the blood," or (among the magi of science) "the quantum of the dual nature of light" and "the nuclear image of the curved universe," or finally, at the nadir of anthropomorphism, the collective god in human form, "Our Leader," and "Father of the proletariat, son of all the peoples." Moreover, society swarms with augurs who prophesy by the twitching of the psychic intestines, with "the anointed" who proclaim doctrines of redemption in the wildest language and who give body to their starved, skeletal theories with corpses.

One warning against this coming age of idolatry is to be found in the jeremiad of a poet who was just beginning to be appreciated when your century came to an end:

Respondez! Respondez! . . .
Let death be inaugurated!
Let nothing but copies at second hand be permitted to exist upon the earth!
Let the earth desert God, nor let there ever henceforth be mentioned the name of God!
Let there be money, business, imports, exports, custom, authority, precedents, pallor, dyspepsia, smut, ignorance, unbelief! . . .
Let the shadows be furnished with genitals! Let the substance be deprived of genitals!

This to be found in a book by Walt Whitman, the American, which was published in 1856—the year you, Father, were born. Didn't you pay any attention to it? He made himself clear—copies at second hand, shadows with genitals and the substance castrated. He was speaking of nothing less than the demiurge of the gnostics.

This almighty freak was named quite expressly by one of our modern Walt Whitman disciples, the apostle of *poésie pure,* Paul Valéry. In a Socratic dialogue, *Eupalinos ou l'Architecte,* he wrote:

> The demiurge pursues his aims without taking thought of their effect upon his creatures. He is not troubled by the problems that arise from the disparity between his aims and yours. He has given you the means of life and even some things in which to take pleasure, but not exactly what you wanted. But I come right after him. He may cheat me several times, and we shall see some ruins. But one can always, and with profit, look at a defective work as a step which brings us closer to Beauty.

Yes, what came after your demiurge of the nineteenth century was Eupalinos the architect who suffered no compunctions over a few ruins—namely the reduction to ruins of all European civilization; and who employed the heaps of bones and rubble merely as steps for him to climb up to the temple of his illusion of beauty.

That Eupalinos drafted construction plans suitable to the particular climate of the materialistic religions. He was the "mining engineer of the soul," the "constructive demolisher of formalism" and the "future master builder of chaos"—I am quoting literally the titles conferred on him by our totalitarian real-estate speculators, all of whom ordered him to build a façade of terror in order to conceal their frightful mistress behind it: their own Fear. For that mistress reigns over our modern Pericles more power-fully than any intellectual Aspasia, more murderously than any worldly Poppaea Sabina over her Nero.

Our great anatomist of the pleasure principle, Sigmund Freud—you knew him as a young doctor specializing in psychic disorders—has attributed this attitude of mind to our *Civilization and its Discontents*. This book of his is a valuable, objective eyewitness report on contemporary culture.

He writes:

The crucial problem for humanity seems to me to be whether and to what extent human cultural development will succeed in overcoming the disturbance of social life which results from the instinct for aggression and self-destruction. In this connection the present time is perhaps particularly interesting. Men have now come so far in the control of natural forces that it would be easy for them to exterminate each other to the last man. They know that, and from that knowledge comes a good part of their present unrest, unhappiness and anxiety. And we may expect that the other one of the two "heavenly powers," the eternal Eros, will make an effort to win out in the struggle with the also immortal antagonist. . . .

We see how vast the anxiety has become when even this dauntless moral revolutionary cautiously encases "heavenly powers" in quotation marks. In his old age, he began to wonder whether the libido was not, after all, dominated by the fear of death. He himself barely escaped the death camp by fleeing from Vienna, and he did not live to see the victory of the other heavenly power, Eternal Eros, any more than I shall live to see it. Of that, more later . . .

You wanted to know on which side of the barricades I, or rather most writers, stand today—on the right side or the left. The barricade you mean presumably divides humanity into poor and rich. That is the social question, which we call the Marxist question. However, there is another barrier that splits mankind: pleasure and unpleasure. That barrier is named the Freudian one, in honor of the antiprophet.

Well, in the murderous philosophical or religious war which has been waged since the First World War, and in which all the horrors of the instincts of aggression and self-destruction have been brought into play, literature stands either behind Marx or at the side of Freud. And it should be noted that the two of them, although authors themselves, commanded writers to keep out of their fields.

("They [writers] are," Freud said, "limited by the necessity for producing intellectual and aesthetic pleasure as well as certain emotional effects, and therefore they cannot forbear to change the stuff of reality.")

Both schools suspected art. In the great Marxian church of the proletariat it was despised as a capitalist privilege; in the Freudian temple of Eros it was treated as a mental disease. Consequently, what prevailed in place of *joie de vivre* was intense anxiety.

Our worst calamity is the loss of humor. That accounts for the epidemic of suicides among writers. Only those withstood it who still had a sense of humor, either individually or in sects. Louis Aragon, onetime French Dadaist, described such a sect in his picaresque novel *Le Paysan de Paris:*

The Lost Library

I announce to the world this event of the utmost importance: a new vice is about to be born; one madness the more has been given to man: SURREALISM, child of frenzy and of the shadow . . .

I happen to know the birthplace—the "Café of the Last European." And so, before the hour of ghosts is past and the thronging phantoms must go back into their cloth and leather coffins, I should like to take this opportunity to tell the beginning of the story. I haven't quite room enough, within the framework of this kind of literary history, to tell the whole story.

It took place on board the drunken ship *Montparnasse,* around the time that the cry rang out:

"The great Proust is dead!"

(And a number of the passengers insisted that what they had heard was: "The great Pan is dead!")

In any case, when the anniversary of that unhappy day approached, I was on the point of leaving my hotel for my evening walk past the darkly wooded Jardin du Luxembourg and up the slope of Montparnasse. I went to the hotel desk before leaving and found some printed matter in my mail.

It turned out to be a new publication entitled, *De Proust à Dada.* There was a dedication on the flyleaf, *"Hommage de l'Auteur"*—and the author proved to be that very literary amphibian whom I mentioned a while back, that friend of Proust who had served his guests at his home on the Île St. Louis with the piping-hot news of Proust's demise.

As soon as I glanced into the uncut brochure, I stumbled on the name of the very Dadaist who had once introduced me to the author. The passage in question read:

Not only are his ideas dangerous, but his personality as well. Gide, who knew him, turned pale when his name was pronounced; Gide knew the terrible results which might follow if his irresponsibility were translated into acts.

As always during the first thaws of spring, the café terraces of Montparnasse had overflowed onto the sidewalk. Climbing the Rue Vavin I saw above me the night owls fluttering around the corner of the Tabac du Dôme —and I was astonished that I had already come so far, for I had been brooding about the venomous attack upon my Dadaist colleague, and I was rather expecting to meet him at his usual café table.

I thrust my way through the noisy crowd to the underground room of the Café Select and saw him at once. He waved a friendly distracted greeting at me; he was in the midst of a discussion and was lunging at his opponent with swollen comb, like a Gallic fighting cock. The object under discussion, I soon discovered, was our fellow writer André Gide, whose "immoralism" my friend was plucking to bits; nothing was left of Gide, according to him, but "the abashed hypocrisy of a penitential Jansenist."

"Gide's *acte gratuit de liberté*," he crowed, "is just another sign of his miserliness. Things have to be free. He even wants freedom for nothing. His pederasty is merely the rear guard of his paternal conscience and the reverse side of the uprooted Norman mama's boy."

"Born in Paris of a father from Uzès and a mother from Normandy, where can I possibly strike roots?" André Gide had once written, defending himself against a chauvinist critic, Léon Daudet. The "dangerous Dadaist" had pounced on this statement. Gide had continued: "I have therefore chosen traveling. I have done more than that; I have written a book highly premeditated in its madness. . . ."

"*Fils à papa, toi-même!*" the Spanish Gidean, X. del Y. . . . murmured, in a voice loud enough for all at the table to hear. He was parrying the Dadaist's allusion, for everybody knew that the Dadaist was the "*fils d'un préfet de police*"—a police commissioner's son.

"Gide," the Dadaist went on, "Gide moralizes. That means that he violates the Marquis de Sade's maxim: 'The author must never moralize, only the character, and even he only when he is forced to do so by circumstances.' "

"Apropos of immoralism," a blond, monocled young man intervened—let us call him Karl Schmidt—"are you acquainted, gentlemen, with the *Extraordinary Adventures of Julio Jurenito?*" He took a book out of his brief case. "It's magnificent. A direct hit, I tell you. Just listen to this." And he began reading from the novel in declamatory tones:

Julio Jurenito taught hatred of the present; and in order for this hatred to be strong and mighty, to our astonished gaze he opened slightly the door that leads to the great, inevitable morrow. . . .

"Well, isn't that the purest flower of our Nietzsche?"

"Absolutely. Even the *furor teutonicus* is there," the Spaniard remarked. "I was in Berlin recently. All your hysterical playwrights shout themselves hoarse in this same stylistic jargon. *From Morn to Midnight* (by Georg Kaiser) was the name of one play I saw. You might hear something like that on the drill ground of a Prussian madhouse. 'Strong and mighty' all right. And you get the same line from every peroxide Gretchen who dances naked in your night clubs. Blood and soil—or cocaine and swastika!"

"You're all wrong," Herr Karl Schmidt spluttered, waving the book around. "Thus spake Zarathustra—excuse me, I meant: thus spake a Russian. . . . You will never understand our energetic and sentimentally enthusiatic, our intense and measureless soul, which has been able to impose upon us a form of inwardness, to use the phrase of one of our Stefan George disciples. . . . You have to have been born a German who suffered in the war, or else be a Julio Jurenito, in order to grasp the profound jests in which our hatred expresses itself. Just listen to this, all of you:

> Jurenito, the Master, would stand before all the courts of the world, before the revolutionary tribunals of the U.S.S.R. and before the wisest marabous of Central Africa as a traitor, a liar and the ideological author of countless crimes . . .

Ha ha ha! Magnificent! And why? Because this marvelous writer possesses a German sense of humor. He has wonderfully funny ideas. Just listen to this, for example:

> In the near future there will take place before a reverent public the solemn extermination of the Jewish people in Budapest, Kiev, Jaffa and Algiers. . . .

Prima, primissima! Your Dadaism could well use a slice of that loaf, just the way it's come out of the oven. That's a good sample of the 'New German objectivity,' our latest literary achievement. Of course only the Faustian Ger-

216

man soul is capable of such an experience—or the Kara-mazovian Russian soul."

"You've been taken in again," a slender, black-haired Bohemian jeered. "The author you so wildly admire is a Jew, and he intended that as bitter irony."

"Jew or Teuton, no matter!" Karl Schmidt replied, polishing his monocle. "Where art is concerned we make no distinctions of race, as long as the Cause is served. *Je prends mon bien où je le trouve*, I believe Molière said."

"*Arrêtez-vous, Monsieur!*" the Dadaist ordered him. "Before you go on with your annexations of foreign ideas, I should like you to request authorization from the copyright owner of *Jurenito*. Here he comes right now."

The sense of expectation you get before the personal appearance of a celebrated writer whom you know only from his books is similar to the shivers that run through you when the ghost of some famous personage in history is supposed to manifest himself at a séance by tipping tables. In fact, the more critical you are of the writer, the more nervous you feel.

I had, I thought, a very precise idea of the personality of the author and of his Julio Jurenito, since I assumed that both were the same, and since I also had picked up a good deal of information about his private life in the cafés of Montparnasse. For many habitués remembered him from the days when he had been a follower of the white-bearded Symbolist *maître* Francis Jammes, the "converted faun," as Gide called him; when he had flirted with Catholicism and even wanted to enter a monastery. Then, at the outbreak of the First World War he had returned home to Russia and enlisted under the banners of patriotic Czarist poetry. It was also said that during the October days that shook the world he had been captured by the Bolsheviki, but released and pardoned by his colleague, who had risen to be the Red generalissimo. In any case he joined the revolutionary league of writers, the Serapion Brothers. And when that group was suspected of "Menshevik counterrevolutionary tendencies," he had turned up on Montparnasse again in semivoluntary exile.

In a corner of the Café Tabac du Dôme he hatched out *The Extraordinary Adventures of Julio Jurenito,* which was translated into many languages and was a success almost everywhere except in his native Russia. In the book he mocked all modern reform systems, and in the final chapter went to the limits of cynicism about the radical abolition of humanitarianism in his own country.

At the moment he was supposed to be a favorite of the Russophile immoralist, André Gide.

The discussion at the table halted while he slowly descended the cellar steps of the Café Select, accompanied by two ladies. He took mincing steps like a doddering old man, and in spite of the warmth of the evening he wore a heavy woolen scarf wound around his neck and tight up against his unshaven chin. He paused, ran his five fingers through his graying mane, transfixed each of us in turn with the impudent stare of a sly adolescent, and said something in Russian which made the ladies laugh.

"Pardon me: Karl Schmidt!" the blond young man said, springing to his feet and clicking his heels loudly. "Chairman of the German Jurenito Club . . ."

"*Très bien!*" the author replied, as though complimenting a schoolboy who had learned his lesson well. "*Vous pouvez disposer,* Schmidt! *Et bon soir, chers amis!* We have just come from the Faubourg St. Germain meeting of the Friends of New Russia. There were lectures on the aims and tasks of Soviet proletarian art by a German Junker philosopher, a Chilean professor of mathematics and the poetess Madame la Comtesse de Noailles. . . ."

"Yes, wasn't it terribly funny!" said his wife, who was still giggling, to the other lady. But the other lady put on the stern expression of a nun and said something in Russian, apparently a reprimand to the effect that such a joke was improper before strangers.

"What is incredible and funny today can be deadly earnest tomorrow," the author of *Jurenito* said. "What do you think, *mon cher Dadaiste?* Humor is after all within your province as a policeman."

"Humor is sacred," the Spanish Gidean protested. "The only one who was ever blessed by it was the martyr Don Quixote when he accomplished the miracle of having Cervantes write his biography—and that was, according to our philosopher Miguel de Unamuno, as magnificent a step as the foundation of the Jesuits by St. Ignatius de Loyola."

"The pogroms conducted by Jurenito and his disciples," Herr Karl Schmidt cried enthusiastically, "are as sublime in their humor as our Hoelderlin is in his *weltschmerz!*"

The complimented author grinned.

"Schmidt," the Dadaist demanded angrily, "are you acquainted with the functional parts of humor? What is humor? The long hair of genius. Humor? The sex appeal that stewing chickens, symphony orchestras and *Weltanschauung* don't have. . . . Humor? A pair of eyes forgotten in a mirror . . . Humor? Its erotic zones: the top hats and chest decorations . . . Its *"mal au coeur"*: André Gide! *L'acte pur* in Dostoevsky sauce . . . Its perversities: *La plus grande France! La patrie! La na-*

tion!—ah—that old whore! *Deutschlandüberalles!*—And Mayakovsky's masses infected with Bolshevism . . ."

At the mention of the most famous of Soviet writers the author of *Jurenito* turned pale and the young Russian girl blushed, because it is written in books that people turn pale with envy and red when they are secretly in love.

"Humor, sir," the Dadaist continued, hammering away at Karl Schmidt, who was smirking and shamelessly flirting with the Russian girl, "humor is love of the absolute; it is the courage, for the sake of a joke and with breaking heart, to kill every rival and oneself as well. Humor—humor is Surrealism; it is . . ." And he went on and on like a lover consumed by jealousy who refuses to omit any arguments; for it was obvious that he had fallen for the young Russian girl and was already seeing everything with her eyes alone.

And those eyes of hers glowed like a pair of signal lights, flashing at each of us in turn, and each of us thought they were signaling to him. . . .

But to what have I digressed?

Originally I set out to present a piece of literary history, utilizing the technical devices of modernism and setting down all its categories, such as:

1) Futurism (Marinetti, Mayakovsky) and introspectivism (Proust).

2) Automatic writing—the trancelike setting down of emotional associations (August Stramm and, among the French Surrealists, Breton, Soupault, Éluard).

3) The interior monologue of Dujardin; the Delphic oracles of the average mind in its no-man's odyssey (taken

down stenographically by James Joyce in his voluminous
Ulysses).

4) The German epic drama of social dynamism (the
Erwin Piscator workshop theaters).

5) American montage novels, presenting simultaneous
big-city lives in slow motion (John Dos Passos: *Manhattan Transfer, The 42nd Parallel*).

I don't seem quite to have got to all of it. But that is
what happens to you when you talk to the spirit of books
—especially to the spirit of books of the nineteenth century—and when you catch something of their sentimental
airs. The same thing occurs in a drunken conversation,
if you have ever listened to one. You get the impression
that the parties to it are not so much answering one another as obstinately replying to some imaginary interlocutor. It is what happens to you especially when the talker is
a sensitive writer who persuades himself that the daemon
of his ego or the archetype·of his collective is speaking
through him.

That was the way it was at our café table. None of us
had any idea of the significance of our alcoholic or erotic
excitement. The Dadaist did not guess to what frightful
things his "irresponsibility," his Surrealism, would lead
him; nor the Spaniard his religion of Don Quixotism; nor
Herr Karl Schmidt his German romantic-classical delusions; nor I my peculiar character. Not even the author
of *Jurenito* suspected the depths of self-betrayal to which
his satiric gifts would bring him, although it was he who
had plotted the whole tragicomedy when he introduced to
us the young Russian girl with the irritating way of
widening her eyes.

The Lost Library

In fact even today he and all his Jurenito disciples would reject as a dirty (bourgeois-capitalist) lie that they had ever acted for any other reason than strict historically conditioned necessity. Certainly never out of jealousy over a pair of too bold eyes!

And they would certainly brand the following tale as a silly legend: that after our café table group had long since broken up and all of us were scattered to the four winds, a forgotten pair of eyes in the mirror of the underground café room continued to stare at the gloomy cellar steps where the author of *Jurenito,* his embroidered scarf wrapped around his bristly chin, had turned around once more and with a sarcastic curl to his St. Bernard dog's lips had growled, quoting himself:

"You gypsies, never again will you be permitted to form so picturesque a sect, so miniature a caste. It is your destiny as it is mine to vanish, to be resurrected again in the remote days when mankind has been stripped of purpose, liberated from purpose. . . ."

And although the first part of the prophecy has come true, the author would repudiate those words—as he would if only he still could repudiate his Jurenito, who was so dreadfully right about him.

It soon developed that the dominant personality in our café group was not he—though he was published everywhere except in Russia—but the gentle Russian girl whom he had patronized because she seemed so forsaken and "didn't know a soul." She achieved her position without doing very much talking, simply by her way of looking at each person so that he felt that she alone understood him. So that, in fact, he was convinced that now for the first time he understood himself. She was considered "very intelligent," though whenever she opened her lips to say something it was always something unimportant or a scrap of a thought she had picked up from others. She purred frequently in Russian, which was Greek to most of the others, but to the author of *Jurenito* it was his mother tongue and it made him homesick, so that his humor gradually trickled away and was gone.

She particularly disturbed us when her gaze suddenly darkened, as though she were the medium of a sinister power which was determined to seize the soul of one of us —but which one?

A number of events following one another in quick succession broke up our circle.

Mayakovsky's suicide created a gap in literature which a number of exiled Russian authors tried to fill, including the author of *Jurenito*. He rushed off precipitately to Moscow, taking along his smiling wife as an earnest of his good faith, and penitently assured a People's Commissar of the Cheka, "You are the greatest liberators of men, because the splendid yoke that you impose on them is welded, not of gold, but of solid iron." (The words he used in dead seriousness were the very ones he had mockingly put into the mouth of his Jurenito.) Taken back into the fold, he recanted all his Parisian "Western heresies" and hurled his anathema against his Latin seducers, and especially against the "malicious old man, the apostate with a filthy mind, the perjured shedder of crocodile tears —that fellow traveler, André Gide."

The proclamation of the German racial dictatorship was the occasion for Herr Karl Schmidt—the prototype of Jurenito's disciple of the same name—to proceed to "the solemn extermination of the Jewish people."

"I hope, madame," he said, bowing courteously to the Russian girl, "to see you here again when we march into Paris."

The Spanish Gidean misogynist stuck it out to the last in the cellar of the Café Select, until the French Republic withdrew his visitor's visa at the time the Spanish Civil War broke out. From Barcelona he rode to battle against the windmill giants of fascism, which were grinding his people to flour dust. But like Don Quixote when he wanted to liberate the galley slaves, he was first stoned by his comrades and then shot for deviating from the line of the Union Internationale des Ecrivains Russes. He left behind a volume of unpublished sonnets, anarchistic in form: "Ay, *ojos!* Ay, Dulcinea!"

Then came the schism within Surrealism when the fellow founder, Louis Aragon, quit. He had just returned from a tour of the Soviet Union and had promptly telegraphed his spontaneous conversion to the U.I.E.R. (Union Internationale des Ecrivains Russes).

The former Dadaist brought home the bride, as the fairy tales have it; the gentle Russian girl married him, and in her arms he became a humorless policeman of literature on the left, an exemplary patriot and a troubadour singing of her eyes. With him she consoled herself for her loss of Mayakovsky, who had rejected her and, for the sake of her sister Lili B., had deserted from the party and from life.

Chapter XI

The Devil's Automaton—Circe and Lady Chatterley—Apage, Satanas!

Now THE STORY is over, though not the night of the accursed Growing Dungeon which I have tried somehow to slide past. Now the fever of inspiration has dropped, and dry, stale criticism puts forth its claims again. And now the Spirit of the profoundly silent library tells me that the tale won't hold water, that it is written in no particular style, neither naturalistic, nor Symbolic, nor Surrealistic, nor psychological, nor fantastical.

It began as a Vie de Bohème. It began in the springtime of Paris, the best European climate for artistic creation. But our attention strayed to a bunch of cynical *arrivistes,* and we talked about their opportunism instead of their ideals.

"Where is the inner conflict? Where is the eternal meaning? Where is the spiritual atmosphere?"

Hm, I shall have to make up for that as well as I can, although the times are out of joint and everything is in a state of philosophical anarchy.

"Aha!"

None of those Aha's, if you please—none of those interjections of self-righteousness and malice. They don't apply to us. Our nihilism is operating with a smoothness never before achieved, a lack of friction that extends down to the most intimate sense reflexes. Our passions have been reduced to a minimal expenditure of emotion, like the expenditure of energy of an industrial worker working under the Taylor system. Our excesses are as disciplined as the calisthenics of a regiment.

Our intellectual atmosphere, the landscape of the modern Westerner, so to speak, is dynamic. That is, things are moving day and night; therefore even our leisure-time conduct and the flights of imagination are subject to strict traffic regulations. It is extremely important that no accidents should hold up general transportation and the expeditions into the stratosphere. Where once many roads led to Rome, all highways now lead to the factory, the laboratory or the concentration camp. The land of the Golden Fleece, the ocean strand and the mountain passes to the Absolute are fenced off with high-tension wires. Heretics are hunted down, deviationists are shot. Nobody knows what the laws governing existence are; nobody knows what actually matters.

"It seems obvious that life is concerned with life and not with the result of it," Goethe once said. He was still able to say that. Today people want to see results, records. It is also no longer quite the thing to refer to Goethe. For although his name appears still in the syllabi of Germanic literature and even in crossword puzzles, his Mephistophelian intuition is altogether alien to us. We are striving to atomize the cosmos and cannot possibly hold with his view that "no matter what you do with it, excellence is unfathomable."

And certainly our program of happiness for the collective mass completely contradicts his view that: "The highest good for human creatures still is personality."

In fact, personality, individuality, is now the capital

crime. There are restrictions on everything: ecstasy, bliss and sensual pleasure. The personality's peculiar powers have been stripped from it; the demonstration of joy has become obligatory; the mysterious regions have been illuminated with floodlights; amplifying microphones eavesdrop on the soul's whispered conversations; love is filmed for the newsreels so that Comrade Everyman may have a look at these things after his day's work is done.

I am no longer I myself; we have become public creatures.

The inadequacy of bygone communities linked by common beliefs was just that—that the personality always slipped through the mesh of the net; that in exchange for some renunciations it was given conditional freedom until death, and during this period of probation it could make fun of the solemn authorities after the manner of a Rabelais or Swift.

That sort of laxness is over and done with.

Heaven and hell have become one country, ruled by one Central Committee.

A grim welfare commission with a weakness for invoking divine punishment has placed all pleasure under the police supervision of German romantic transcendental philosophy.

Paragraph one of the Criminal Code reads: "Mind determines existence!" (*Das Bewusstsein bestimmt das Sein.*)

"Well, what is there objectionable about that?" the Spirit of the Nineteenth Century asked. "Isn't that perfectly proper? *'L'esprit seul peut tout changer!'* as Beaumarchais' Figaro calls out to the aristocrats in their stalls."

The Lost Library

Yes, the spirit can change everything by setting up the guillotines of *égalité* in the Place de la "Concorde," and seeing to it that the heads roll—the heads of all those who think differently. So much for that. Now, for the survivors who do not think at all, the regulation is turned upside down.

Paragraph two: "Existence determines mind."

And in their forced-labor camps we have learned how slavishly the mind obeys to the letter the most miserable conditions of existence. How willingly men surrender their human dignity bit by bit for an extra ration of bread —and how swiftly they cease to be human.

When he was still young and a Marxist, the novelist André Malraux philosophized in *Man's Fate:*

It is very rare for man to be able to endure—how shall I say?—his human condition. . . . Everything that men accept, beyond their own self-interest, in order to make themselves kill, tends more or less confusedly to justify this condition by recasting it into a principle of dignity—Christianity for the slave, nationalism for the citizen, communism for the worker. . . . It is always necessary for men to intoxicate themselves.

"Our goal is the total recasting of man," Leon Trotsky, the engineer of the soul, announced in his *Literature and Revolution*—and he perished as a result of the process.

It is obvious that so marvelously complicated a life factory as the modern state has become must naturally seize completely not only the means of production, but the means for intoxication as well. And these artistic intoxicants rate high, for by inducing laughter they increase produc-

228

tivity and by inducing fears they narcotize anxiety, while by their aphrodisiac effects they stimulate propagation and increase the supply of human factory-fodder.

The employee of the state, whether he serves the monster switchboard of the bureaucracy or the machine itself, is subject to a painfully close inspection of body and soul to insure that he is not harboring any unauthorized personality traits. For by the slightest incautious thought, by a single emotion that slips by the guard, the individual can be pulled into the gears and crushed by them. And this, of course, would injure the oversensitive administrative apparatus. For a degenerate art, especially a degenerate literature, is far more likely than scientific speculation, or even than religion, the "opium of the people," to promote individualism and other antiauthoritarian "venereal diseases."

But I am afraid I have gone off on trains of thought which the Spirit of the Nineteenth Century cannot possibly follow. My attempt to write a simple but contemporary history of ideas and amours has failed. It will be better if I here give the floor to the influential literary critic who has discussed a successful, state-approved novel of collective love which contains all the elements: inner conflict, eternal meaning and the intellectual atmosphere, strictly in accord with the prescription. The name of the critic as well as of the author under discussion may be concealed, since both have dedicated themselves to anonymous service as workers on the literary front. It is enough for us to know that the hero of the novel under discussion is the Soviet Russian people, and that the villain is a certain Volodya.

The Lost Library

How many dismal, melancholy Volodyas, infatuated with poetry, philosophy and their own *Weltschmerz,* have we not had in Russian novels? And not only in Russian novels. In all European countries during the nineteenth century this psychic plague appeared. The French called it "ennui"; the English, after their most prominent representative of it, "Byronism." The great German dramatist Georg Büchner wrote: "There are people who are unhappy only because they exist." The young Russian Volodya, too, grows morbid in the year 1930 over the meaninglessness of existence. . . . Confronting a world that really has a meaning, a goal, a faith, he fails. Volodya's melancholic loneliness is terribly intensified because, as he himself feels, he is no longer facing narrow-minded complacency, but a genuine community of belief whose members labor in the co-ops and foundries as—to quote the novelist—"in the old days a man embraced a girl or prayed to God."

The great project of recasting an omnipotent group of men, a project whose success all the statistics testify to, is something that the author makes visible through a hundred mental processes—whose result will one day be called: the new Russian man. Foolish and malicious Central and West Europeans who read the basic Bolshevist slogans seem to think that there is no room in our society for the kiss of a lover, the fragrance of flowers, a pleasing poem, the smile of a girl in love and the tears of one who has been jilted; that we have time only for a frantic pursuit of iron, iron, iron. In this novel they can discover that even without great individuals . . . there can be highly personal weeping, laughing, loving, hating, ambition and laziness. The unforgivable fault of these Volodyas is their inability to understand that ultimately every private smile flows into new will to work for the community, that all weeping is subdued by the certainty of being sheltered within a common aim. . . .

The Lost Library

Bodies are broken in factory accidents [the reviewer continues enthusiastically], minds go under from the slightest impact of a harsh era. A new climate has suddenly come into being, and in it men are shooting up with luxuriant fresh growth, and other men are being destroyed. . . .

"Men are being destroyed." By what? At this point reviewer and author prefer to leave ample play for the reader's imagination. The reader can fully satisfy his imagination by reading the statistics on factory accidents or by reading the party journals to see how the brave new society is being purified of all dismal, melancholic saboteurs like Volodya.

Here we have a fine assortment of the ingredients for a thoroughly modern love novel, a continuation of Jurenito's adventures. We have the intellectual atmosphere (the impact of a harsh era), the new eternal meaning: the collective mind's jeering at "ennui" and "Byronism," and the new inner conflict as well, though this is barely touched on—in the following passage:

One may wish at times [the reviewer concludes regretfully] that the novelist would give us a more intimate picture of the reorganization of a many-faceted psychological world. For example, he might have avoided racing so swiftly through the subject of Grunya's transformation from the daughter of a kulak to a self-confident comrade.

Alas, there is not time enough left for the fulfillment of such wishes! The mechanism of the state rolls on inexorably. During a single night shift Grunya, the kulak's daughter, matures under the neon moon into a self-confident comrade. She lies on the bed of the mighty forge while the members of the community embrace the foundries. For the true bride is the shining, tenderly oiled machine. Her thighs are pistons, her womb is a tank and her lust is velocity.

When the pregnant Grunya has an attack of dizziness and everything turns black before her eyes, she is given a camphor injection. But when the motor of the machine halts, the whole community of faith who serve it fall on their knees. . . .

The Spirit of the Library has disappeared.

I don't know where he has hidden: whether behind Auguste Comte's *Positivist Catechism* or behind Friedrich Nietzsche's Dionysiac, megalomaniac *Ecce Homo!* or behind Professors Haeckel and Ostwald's *Monistic Sunday Sermons* on evolution.

In the course of considering all these timely, "people's" abstractions, my heart has sunk into my boots. I feel a queasiness around the chest from the noxious breath of the New Will. Or perhaps it is only because outside my window the old Viennese foehn is blowing, that underhanded Austrian wind that from time immemorial has parched the energies of Viennese poets and made them weary unto death. Or perhaps I am only suffering from the *mal du siècle.* . . . What I want most of all now is a cup of strong Turkish coffee, or a glass of sharp plum brandy—slivowitz—or the Viennese heart of gold of a *Gschpusi.* There is no word for that anywhere else in the world. In Prussia the idea is arithmetically expressed as *ein Verhaeltnis,* in Paris zoologically as *une poule,* but neither of these is the same thing as a *Gschpusi*—none other is "so false but sweet" at the same time. Certainly not a "self-confident bed comrade."

But the curfew hour for the coffeehouses is long past, the last *Gschpusi* have long since vanished from the streets, to be replaced by Spartan, male vice that seeks *Anschluss* with the German totality. The *Gschpusi* still exist only as phantoms in Arthur Schnitzler's *Hands Around* (*Reigen*) and in Johann Strauss operettas—that music which rattles and clinks and whimpers in so macabre a fashion, like an "atonal" Ravel waltz.

When I began this history of my father's library I turned to the books, and it is with books that I must continue. Perhaps it is no better than drinking oneself into a stupor and thus procuring artificially the enjoyments that the present has denied us; but it is certainly no worse. The devil! Isn't there something in modern literature, something somewhere, that will rejuvenate the heart, that breathes an air of pure sensual pleasure?

What about James Joyce's *Ulysses?*

The trouble is that you need a literary atlas (cf. Leslie L. Lewis, *Framework of Ulysses*) to find your way around that phonetic labyrinth. And without a pilgrimage to his priestess, Sylvia Beach, in the Shakespeare & Co. Bookshop on the Rue de Tournon, and without a set of the *Encyclopaedia Britannica,* you cannot get into the mythological, pathological, hallucinatory bordello run by the massive madame Bella Cohen (Circe to the esoteric steady customers) and her "affect-epileptic, cyclophrenic, schizoid" girls, Zoe, Kitty and Lydia Douce. Moreover, all of them are afflicted with a suspicious verbosity. And who would want to kiss a mouth that performs linguistic feats with every endearment?

The Lost Library

In passing I doff my hat respectfully to Thomas Mann's *Magic Mountain*, where the Davos sanatorium houses a Venus whose picture is the X-ray print of her tuberculous cavities.

And then I try out D. H. Lawrence's (unexpurgated) *Lady Chatterley*. Every detail he touches on is bluntly named, but often the effect is as coy, as mannered, as in those pornographic works of the Victorian Gay Nineties that were imported into Europe from England, slanted for a foppishly obscene imagination.

All in all, the situation in contemporary erotic writing is wretched. Instead of rejoicing in marble amplitudes, poesy revels in steel and concrete. Not the lark but the radio being turned on in the morning startle Romeo and Juliet in their bed. And the Grand Courtesan of our times swaggers shamelessly on political platforms, exposing her lust for power to the assembled rabble.

But do you think yourself safe from the devil of vice when you hold your orgies and your Black Masses in the solidarity of mass meetings? Do you persuade yourselves that Beelzebub in the guise of a tractor cannot assail your prim class innocence? What an illusion! He tempts you with a voluptuous automaton whose streamlined buttocks curve plastically under the cellophane wrapper, and when he exposes technology's rear to you, you kiss it willingly.

The ejaculation takes place in the cerebrum. That is all there is to the contemporary way of saving time and effort.

"But there's the trouble," wrote D. H. Lawrence to a friend; he was far wealthier in ideas in his letters than in his books.

Men have most of them got their sex in their heads nowadays, and nowhere else. They start all their deeper

234

reactions in their heads, and work themselves from the top downwards, which of course brings disgust, because you're only having yourself all the time; no matter what other individual you take as a *machine-à-plaisir*, you're only taking yourself all the time.

Perhaps it will help to win indulgence from sins to repeat two lines of Pure Poetry:

Eines ist, die Geliebte zu singen. Ein anderes, wehe,
Jenen verborgenen schuldigen Fluss-Gott des Blutes . . .
(It is one thing to sing the beloved. Another, alas,
That hidden guilty river-god of the blood . . .)

Which is to be found in the third of the Duino Elegies of that creator of magical sounds, Rainer Maria Rilke.

Apage, Satanas!

Chapter XII

Side Trip to Prague—To the Golem and the Robots—Of the Endless Progress of the Soul through all Courts of Appeal.

IT SEEMS to be high time to start making plans for flight again.

For here in Vienna we are sitting in the cafés and in our libraries as on a powder barrel—that is the appropriate expression for the old-fashioned danger which threatens us in an age when the whole planet can be blown up.

If the barrel was to explode, the next logical goal was Prague—the second capital of Austrian literature and, after Paris, the second principal gathering place of the exiled German intellectuals.

Prague had always been a Holy City—sacred in the beginning to all Slovenians from the Urals to the Baltic, who prayed to their one *Bog;* later under the Hapsburgs the sanctuary of Jewish wonder-rabbis such as Rabbi Jehuda, the mathematician and colleague of the exiled Danish astronomer and viewer of God, Tycho Brahe. Prague was a semi-Asiatic fairground for dogma-overthrowing reformers, lyrical pantheists in the tradition of Jakob Boehme, and blaspheming Voltaireans. It was the cradle of necromantic personalities and swarmed with highly gifted diabolists. It was full of sectarians: Taborites, Kalixtiners, Hussites—whence its tradition of Irredentist, devout heroism which always ended in defeat, its gluttonous consumption of sausages, hams and pickled and smoked foods, as well as its long procession of martyrs. The line of martyrs begins with Prague's two Johns: St. John Nepomuk, who rose to life again out of the waters of the Moldau; and later John Hus, resurrected from the fires of the Holy Inquisition to finish fighting the dogmatic controversy over transsubstantiation. (The same controversy has been carried on by almost all Prague writers.)

In Prague in the fifteenth century the High Rabbi Löw reconstructed the magical and technical monster, the golem, and made it his servant by extracting from its mouth the Shem (the word: God). And in our time Karel Čapek followed the same procedures in devising his comedy *R.U.R.* (Rossum's Universal Robots), his utopia of a world organization of protoplasmic, animate industrial slaves. (It is no longer utopian; it is here.)

Prague had been the starting point from which the inferno of the Thirty Years' War spread, and from Prague the good soldier Schweik had marched off into the inferno of the First World War. Schweik was the Don Quixote and Sancho Panza rolled into one of the Czech Cervantes, Jaroslav Hasek. With his diabolically clever simplicity Schweik had disarmed the entire general staff of the Royal and Imperial Austro-Hungarian Monarchy. He had exposed the Hapsburg monarchy to the deathblow of ridicule. Whereupon the revered old insurgent and professor of Slavism, Thomas Garrigue Masaryk, took over the presidency of the Czechoslovak Republic like one of Plato's philosophers. And the Republic paid Hasek off by conferring on him the celebrity of a court jester.

Prague, a city hostile to the German language out of

a long history of bad experiences, was the birthplace
of the Symbolist Rainer Maria Rilke, who like Angelus
Silesius, the theosophic poet of the baroque age, feared
for what would happen to God when he no longer was.
It was the birthplace also of the "cosmophile," Franz
Werfel, that "spiritual, intellectual, sensitive, impetuous,
imaginative, receptive, compassionate, wholly musical
person"—to quote his own words. It was also the native
city of the humorist, satanist and yoga adept, Gustav
Meyrink, a writer in the tradition of E. T. A. Hoffmann,
Edgar Allan Poe and Villiers de l'Isle Adam.

Another who was born and who died in Prague was the
Talmudic clerk of the seraphim-and-gehenna bureaucracy,
Franz Kafka.

But in spite of the numerous very important persons
who inhabited the city, Prague remained occult because,
as the theosophists say, it lay in an astral plane.

Anno Domini 1919, when I was passing through
Prague, the walls in the suburbs were plastered with
election posters for Jaroslav Hasek's "party of moderate
progress within the limits of police regulations."

A fellow writer who was something of a celebrity in
Prague showed me the architectural and literary sights.
On the Karlsbrücke, in front of the headless figure of
St. Nepomuk, he deferentially greeted a lean sleepwalker
who absently returned his greeting while his feverish
eyes seemed to be looking into another world. As we
passed on, my guide explained to me in the past tense:
"That *was* Kafka."

And in a café room on the Wenzelplatz full of dark-red
plush I was introduced to Pan Johann Nepomuk Brzk,

doctor of metempsychosis, who was the author of the encyclopedia *BCDF-VWXYZ.* It was written in color-blind script for future readers whose language would consist only of toneless gray consonants, for they would no longer be able to distinguish the colors of the vowels, for which Arthur Rimbaud had created his scale.

"Future literature," Doctor Brzk taught, "will be a poetry of vowelless noises such as already exist in the insect world, where these are the sole means of communication in locust migrations and ant invasions."

As a precaution against this eventuality, I took a beginner's course in metempsychosis with Doctor Brzk. Under his direction I made an experiment, and for the sake of illustration I here insert part of an account of that attempt at metempsychosis which I published around 1920 in a Berlin magazine, *Der Blutige Ernst:*

REMARKS ON A LOCUST

You there, sitting reading this book—yes, you who are so self-assured, as if things couldn't possibly have turned out differently—has it never occurred to you what a matter of chance it is that your soul is occupying a human body? You think that must be so, that that was your destiny. You think you are one with your husk. Your soul has set up house in it as if it were for an eternity and not just for the pitiful term of a human life.

Your soul is one with your body—and yet it is not one.

At night it spreads out its wings and flies, with the ocean of the beyond beneath it, flies unhindered through cold, dripping darkness, uttering brutish cries, toward the horizon. There, beyond regions of ice, lurks the Evil Eye, the enchanter, the great abyss toward which it plunges. . . .

Irresistibly . . .

And night after night . . .

Until one day the accident happens and it does not return.

Serpents, especially basilisks, have this power, and also human beings, it is said. And perhaps you yourself have experienced it once, beholding the hypnosis of the abyss in an eye. Before such an eye you crawl on all fours, bark and wag your tail.

And the night after, your soul flies out again, and returns like an obedient dog.

But you can fall even lower.

More than sleep, is not death the Evil Eye with the glance that transforms all? Is not death in truth the great eye that reshapes and recreates, that holds you fixed from conception until your dying day, that bombards you with infinitesimal particles of force all your life, every night, like a conscientious hypnotist working on his subject. Does not death repeat the experiment of putting you to sleep again and again, until at last it succeeds? Does not death try out in dreams your proclivities for metamorphosis, in order to suggest to you in your last sleep the suitable form for your next life?

Far, eons far away, the reality of your humanness lies behind you now.

You are something wholly modern, wholly new. . . .

An insect, for example. . . .

The specimen which I had studied for my "Romantic Zoology" was a grasshopper which I identified as a deceased censor of the Berlin police. I had come across the creature in Doctor Brzk's tiny garden—the doctor lived in a one-story gabled house on "Alchemists' Street." Doctor Brzk had an extensive library of technical literature, which included of course the classics in his field: Apuleius's *The Golden Ass*; Geyler von Kaisersberg's *Emeis* (which deals with human ants); books on the siticines (or singers to the dead) who were transformed into birds, of whom Rabelais tells; on the epidemics of lycanthropy in the Baltic countries in the sixteenth century and in France in the seventeenth; and so down to the moderns: Anatole France's *Penguin Island,* in which the penguins baptized by mistake become good Christians and later Frenchmen; and to contemporary Prague writing on metamorphosis: Gustav Meyrink's gorillas who behaved like soldiers after being injected with "herdoglobin"; Franz Kafka's *Metamorphosis,* and Dr. Ernst Weiss's *Beasts in Chains* (*Tiere in Ketten*).

Doctor Brzk's ideas were very close to those of Gustav Theodor Fechner, the German philosopher and psychophysicist of the nineteenth century. He liked to introduce his lectures on metempsychosis with Fechner's illuminating statement:

All the areas of consciousness of man and beast can be distinguished within the area of the world-consciousness only to the degree that the material processes which sustain the consciousness of man and beasts are distinguishable from the surrounding, general process beyond a certain limit; otherwise they merge into the general consciousness of the world spirit, and although they still contribute to raising that consciousness on the whole, they are not themselves distinguishably raised above the whole.

Above all he was concerned with Fechner's law of "memory afterimage"—that is, the living aftervision which is awakened in us by a habitual sense stimulus (say, the sound of a clock that has just struck), or by the fleeting sight of a passing acquaintance whom we do not for the moment recognize. Under this heading Doctor

Brzk included the entire realm of art. For, he said, what
we term artistic imagination is in fact the memory afterimage of countless earlier realities which are released to
us by the present reality, that is by our present life. What
pleases us in our reading, for example, even in an unpleas-
ant work that is filled with horrors, is our meeting again
with familiar figures out of our pasts. But it is not only
the subject matter, the story, that gives us pleasure by
awakening memories of former existences. We are also
reminded by the prosody and the sound of rhymes of
languages which we have spoken in God only knows what
previous lives, or perhaps even on other planets or stars.
Our aesthetics with its apparently undefinable laws of
beauty is a relic of a cosmic ethics, an astral morality,
whose three conditions of existence we obeyed in every
state. These three conditions are: attraction (or love),
distraction (or the urge to do things), and weariness (or
death).

To illustrate this point, Doctor Brzk would read a
small black volume published in the *Buecherei Der Juengste
Tag,* Kurt Wolff Verlag, 1917. "The work of a friend
of mine," he would say, "with whom I have shared many
an existence, although I have not seen him again since
my last rebirth . . . " The book was Franz Kafka's
Metamorphosis. . . .

A Jewish traveling salesman, Gregor Samsa, awakes
one morning in his bed to find himself transformed into
a monstrous insect. Hitherto his place in Creation had
been that of a conscientious salesman. Suddenly he finds
himself assigned to the order of coleoptera (beetles);
and to test him as Job was tested, Jehovah's finger has
flicked him over on his back. The question is whether

without aid—the aid of his physical father or the boss of his firm—he can manage to stand once more before God on his three pairs of legs. There was no chance for him to pass the test; it was as hopeless as all the other "trials" pending in Kafka's courts.

"We take our second example," Doctor Brzk said, turning to me, "from an author whom you are bound to meet: Doctor Ernst Weiss. He was formerly a surgeon in the Poor Hospital. In the line of his professional duties he was occupied with the bodies of anonymous persons who were brought in either in a state of narcotic coma or on the threshold of death—human beings, in short, whose previous life here on earth was of only morphological interest.

"At one time Resident Physician Weiss had to operate on a prostitute, a murderess who had been shot by the Prague vice squad. She died under the knife. As a humane, artistic and conscientious surgeon, he carried out an autopsy, and in the course of it discovered that an essential part of her organism was missing. He sent a medical account of the case to the proper legal authorities, and in the course of writing it discovered his talents as a novelist.

"In bringing his findings to life with the artifices of art, in reconstructing the vicious circle of breathing, digestion, sexual functions and activity of the brain, he recaptured the departed impulses. The cadaver rose again and became the whore Olga, the heroine of the novel *Tiere in Ketten*. Once more she practiced prostitution, lured the male game of the Prague back alleys, extracted their last kreuzer from them, until for a second time she was laid low.

"But Weiss was not content with this realistic ending. An aesculapian disciple of the Expressionist school, he supplied a sequel:

"Captured in the madness of the last hours, Olga, the human being transformed from a beast, died. Nahar came to life, the beast transformed from a human being. Olga, the raging, murderous, pain-wracked prostitute who was shot running from the police, was transformed into the pliant, golden-downed shape of a tiger kitten that had just been born on a tropical island. . . ."

Nahar (*Tiere in Ketten, Part Two*) goes through the full circle of her next, animal karma: her mating with a royal Bengal tiger; the snarling tenderness of the marriage of predatory beasts; her anxieties over her young and her terror during a hunt, a jungle "police raid" employing elephants; and finally her end in chains once more and her death in a cage.

Doctor Brzk had spoken truly. For soon afterward I met Doctor Ernst Weiss for the first time. And I saw him now and again thereafter as he passed through his karma as a writer whose voice was audible only in the stillness of a tropical night. For he was as unsociable as a jungle beast, and watched over his supple, catlike actress Sanzara as jealously as a royal tiger. Their union resulted, not in a child, but in a book by her, *Das Verlorene Kind* (*The Lost Child*); she was to die childless in Germany, in one of the dictatorship's many cages.

Harried far away from her, wounded by the hunt, Ernst Weiss crawled into an exile's cave in Paris. But during the gloomy, blacked-out nights when Paris was besieged and the thunder of the antiaircraft cannon echoed hollowly, he became almost sociable, and night after night he would steal over to our darkened hotel garret where we waited together for the All Clear siren. But when the shouts of the battle drew near and the enemy's tanks broke through the gates of Paris, Weiss prescribed himself a fatal dose of sleeping powder and set out on his transmigration.

It is only very rarely, as the political novelist and adventurer André Malraux said in the passage we have quoted, that man can endure his fate, his *condition humaine*. "It is always necessary for men to intoxicate themselves."

"Only very few human beings," the great Talmudist Rabbi Isaac Lurja has taught, "are spared transmigration into an animal, a plant or a mineral. . . ."

And: "*Omnes angeli, boni et mali, ex virtute naturali habent potestatem transmutandi corpora nostra*," says Thomas Aquinas. (All the angels, both the good and the bad, by their natural virtue have the power to transmute our bodies.)

Thus doubly warned, I chose Prague as the next refuge for myself and my books. "Save the books first," the Czech patron saint of libraries, Saint Wiborada, had called out to the hesitant abbot of St. Gall when the Magyars attacked the monastery. But, as will be seen, it was already too late and I was unable to save my books. However, the human destiny and the astral lives of the above-mentioned Prague magicians demand a brief postscript in so old-fashioned a literary memoir as this.

The "High Rabbi Löw," to begin with him, the Faust of Prague, as he was called (died 1609), stripped his mechanical wonder, the golem, of its magic powers when the robot was about to desecrate the Sabbath and smash all things made by human hands. The relics of the golem were preserved in the Prague Altneuschul Synagogue, and three hundred years later the story was dramatized by Leivick, a Russian rabbi and social revolutionary. The play is still part of the repertory of the Hebrew theater Habima-Haivrith.

Franz Kafka kept account books of all his nocturnal journeys via the fevers of tuberculosis to the Swedenborgian, Hoffmannesque and Strindbergian infernos. He put his experiences down in the enigmatic style of charades to mystify his father. Undiscovered by the world, at the age of forty he slipped unassumingly into his grave. But about twenty years after his death he was translated into foreign languages and became one of the most-often-quoted literary phenomena in the Paris *monde,* London high life and at American cocktail parties.

Karel Čapek, the friend of the Czech philosopher-president Thomas Masaryk, killed himself when his nation, in the bloom of its youth, suffered the first attack of the White Plague—the disease of dictatorship which he had predicted in one of his wittiest comedies. That first bout came from Germany. The second bout, imported from Russia, crippled his compatriots for good, reducing them to R.U.R.'s (Russia's Universal Robots). With the peril to me and my books in Vienna growing more and more pressing, I rushed off a letter to Doctor Brzk, asking for his help. It came back marked "addressee unknown."

Franz Werfel, the author of *Spiegelmensch* and *Embezzled Heaven,* I met again in the unhappy year of the French collapse, 1940. We were both among the millions fleeing toward the Mediterranean coast. I came across him in a street in Lourdes, on the northern slope of the Pyrenees. The famous grotto had been closed off with boards and was abandoned by all the world. Here Werfel threw himself on the mercy of the inspired provincial girl, Mademoiselle Soubirous, the young Saint Bernadette. In his sore oppression, with the army of the Antichrist at his heels, he begged her forgiveness for all the literary sins of his youth, for his wrongheaded belief in her former slanderer, Émile Zola, and for his Bolshevist heresies. And she appeared to him three times: she saved him from the Devil's hosts and transported him across the seas to America. She placed his novel, *The Song of Bernadette*, on the best-seller lists all over the world; and she showered him with the fabulous California wealth from the motion picture factories of Hollywood, which filmed the book. And then, after he had finished the last line of his principal work, his typically Praguesque astrological utopia of a rebirth of the earth, *Star of the Unborn*, she stopped his heart and called him to herself. . . .

Rainer Maria Rilke died in 1926 in his phantom castle in southern Switzerland—of leukemia, the disease given him by the "hidden guilty river-god of the blood."

But that's another story.

Chapter XIII

The Tempest in the Inkpot—The Luciferian
Fall of the Library—The Legend of the Holy
Drinker—And the Dry Spring.

"RIDING. RIDING. Riding. Through the day. Through
the night. Through the day . . ."

Inevitably, like a music box that plays Handel's *Har-
monious Blacksmith* whenever the lid is lifted—I can
never start out on a journey without hearing in my head
the first beats of *The Song of the Love and Death of
Cornet Christopher Rilke,* which Rainer Maria sang for
his ancestor who fought in the Thirty Years' War.

"*Reiten. Reiten. Reiten. Durch den Tag. Durch die
Nacht. Durch den Tag.*"

In the bygone times of peace before the First World
War, this prose romance of Rilke's was as popular as
a soldier's song. In fact, had he never written anything
but that Mozartian military "song," in spite of his Slavic-
French "blood mixture" he would have been accepted into
the Valhalla of Teutonic poetry.

"Riding. Riding. Riding. Through the day. Through
the night. Through the day . . ."

But, damn it, I have forgotten how it goes on. Of
course I could find out immediately by going to the library,
for there is a copy of it in the precious linen binding—

like flowered underwear—of the Insel-Buecherei. Next to it stand Rilke's adaptations of his spiritual foster-brothers, André Gide and Paul Valéry.

And inevitably, whenever I think of Rilke, I see him on the steps of the leaning, dark-stained Hôtel Foyot on the corner of the Rue de Tournon in the Latin Quarter of Paris, going down the steps to this same cadence of *Cornet*. I see him exhausted, resting under the potted palms in the glassed-in foyer of this hotel, the onetime lodgings of the Bourbon aristocracy. And I see him as I accompanied him every day on his morning walk through the Jardin du Luxembourg. Floating an inch or so above the gravel, he would pause in front of every statue of a queen and comment, waving his lorgnette, on what he called "this petrified *chronique scandaleuse.*"

During his last stay in Paris—the city where once he had slaved as an ill-paid and ill-treated secretary for the sculptor Auguste Rodin—he was set up on a pedestal and worshiped by the society ladies of the Faubourg St. Germain. He was sick unto death then, paler and more porous than weatherworn sandstone. And as soon as the disintegration of his blood killed him, each of these ladies —especially the auburn-haired ones—boasted of having received a billet-doux from him, and rejoiced that at least she had afforded him the highest bliss earth has to offer.

As a matter of fact, his letters were always in the style of billets-doux—even the following one which was written to me. It refers to an outcry that resulted from Rilke's last love affair, his too intimate relationship with the French language. A sprinkling of Czecho-German literary hicks were mortally offended.

My Dear Herr Mehring:
The highly superfluous and theoretical affair in which
you so spontaneously lent me assistance is going on, and
spreading, on the same premises. A Swiss friend has
just sent me these clippings, two (attacking me) from
German Bohemia, as far as I can make out, and the
third sensible one from the *Prager Presse,* which calls
the others to order. . . . *Quelle tempête dans l'encrier!*
I am making haste to send you these clippings so that
you will be familiar with all the material and, as far as
possible, can obtain perspective on the whole attempt to
exploit me for the purpose of raising a fuss. . . .

With gratitude,
Cordially yours,
RILKE

At the moment I was lying in bed with a severe case
of grippe, and was therefore in a fine mood for polemics.
Temperatures above 101, moreover, raise your poetic
reactions to a pitch of which you were otherwise capable
only in childhood.

The previous week Rilke had come to my hotel room
(on the Rue de Vaugirard, near his hotel), had sat down
beside my bed and confided to me:

"Some time ago I translated one of my poems into
French, half for the fun of it. But suddenly I felt the
French language as an entirely new instrument—as
though I had never written anything before. I wrote this
one directly in French. Would you like to hear it?"

And in a Prague singsong, rather than in French
intonation, he recited:

Chemins qui ne mènent nulle part
Entre deux prés
De leur but détournés . . .

Sleepy and in a haze of aspirin as I was, I could not help smiling. Not at the verses, but at a picture that leaped into my memory: of Rilke wandering vaguely along a deliberately roundabout way to our *petit déjeuner* in the Crèmerie de Médicis (the scene of Strindberg's "comedy" of an artist, *There are Crimes and Crimes*). One always grins, rather stupidly and shamefacedly, at the sight of someone in the grip of an adolescent infatuation. I did not suspect at the time how serious his state was.

The next time Rilke came in flushed with anger, in spite of his advancing leukemia. He had a bundle of newspapers under his arm.

"Read this! On account of a few *études* in a foreign language they are defaming me in my mother tongue. Just read this! Perhaps you will be kind enough to answer them properly for me. . . ."

I leafed through the newspapers—shabbily printed slanders repeated in stereotype fashion in a Sudeten German argot that was as uncouth and ugly as its hypocritical nationalistic indignation over the "cultural miscegenation practiced in Paris by a poet who calls himself German, with the language of the hereditary foe."

The stuff seemed to me not to deserve any kind of answer. "A highly superfluous and theoretical affair . . . *Alors!*"

Not in my most cynical moments of pessimism did I suspect how serious this matter was. I never dreamed that such guttersnipe jargon would some day become the official German language, through the medium of *Mein Kampf*.

But Rilke was beside himself. He was as furious as a lover whose sweetheart has been molested by a group of stupid boors. He stormed, and I grinned over this tempest in the inkpot. Was it possible for a Rilke to get worked up over this sort of thing—Rilke, whom the aristocrat poetess, Anna Comtesse de Noailles, had locked in her *"coeur innombrable"* and to whom Gide and his circle paid court?

I never suspected how desperate the situation already was for all of us, nor that all the curses of Pandora's box would soon rise up out of the inkpots of literary thugs and journalists who drew their revolvers whenever they heard the word culture. I could not foresee inhumanity that would make mock of all fictions, a betrayal of the intellectuals that would stink to high Olympus, the ferocious pogroms against all creative minds, and a new Spanish Inquisition so terrible that even such orthodox Catholics as the moralist François Mauriac and Huysmans' disciple Bernanos (*Les Grands Cimetières Sous la Lune*) would quail before it—the gigantic cemeteries under the moon crammed full of the victims who had first been burned alive. I could not foresee extermination camps on a scale beyond the wildest dreams of a Rienzi, a Cromwell, a Robespierre. A gruesome study of what was to come is Franz Kafka's *The Penal Colony*. Kafka's desk job had brought him into close contact with the heads of administrative infernos, from which he had deduced their plans.

Future students of the origin and spread of our various intellectual pestilences should also look into a significant literary document entitled *Journey to the End of the Night* (Céline), a desperate, Rabelaisian outpouring of fury in a colossal monologue. The book is the cry of the underdog degenerating into poetry. The author, that Proust of the gutter, was a doctor in an insane asylum;

like so many professional psychiatrists and contemporary satirists, he infected his own psyche with madness, lost his grip on himself and succumbed to mass psychosis. He specialized in the "concentration-camp sicence and gas-chamber experiments" by which so many of his own countrymen and fellow writers were murdered.

On his "journey to the end of the night" his talent went to smash, and with the loss of that he lost all sense of shame. He sought refuge with the barbarians, and he defended his weakness like the hero in the *Mysterier* of his greater fellow worshiper of power, the Viking Knut Hamsun: "A great writer is a man who is not ashamed, who does not blush over the humbug of his profession. . . ."

May literary history have mercy on these lost souls!

"Riding. Riding. Riding. Through the day. Through the night. Through the day." Why do I go on saying that compulsively and all in one breath as soon as I start on a journey? Why do I torment myself trying to remember how it goes on? Riding. Riding. Riding. It gallops through my head with its trochees and anapests.

A red-haired hag hobbles, leaning on a cane, across Montparnasse and into the Café du Dôme.

"*Un ancien amour de Rilke,*" somebody at an adjoining table murmurs. The person across the table from him crosses his forefinger and middle finger against the Evil Eye. And the hag mounts her cane and rides over the roofs with a bundle of "*souvenirs à Rilke*" to the offices of the *Nouvelle Revue Française* in the Rue Sébastien-Bottin.

Rilke's room at the Hôtel Foyot was later inhabited

by the Austrian novelist Joseph Roth. Roth resembled Rilke in the musical quality of his style, the beauty of his handwriting and in his tendency toward religious enthusiasms. He too had a walrus mustache, but since his wife—a person of unnerving gentleness—had passed away into the darkness of dementia praecox, Roth's face had become the swollen, Silenus mask of the alcoholic.

All day long he drank and wrote in the *bistro* across the street. At sunset the parishioners of his exile thronged around him: faithful old revolutionaries, German writers whose books had been burned, actors and actresses expelled from their theaters, former cabinet ministers, former professors, former army men. And their number steadily mounted; there came what might be called the neophytes of exile: Hapsburg legitimists, Catholic clergymen from South Germany and from the Basque country, volunteers on the way to join the Spanish popular front. They were quarrelsome and worn out by disputes, vain and embittered, zealous and jealous. There were the Ahasueruses and the Beau Brummels of exile, the howling dervishes and the swindlers, the heroes and the Munchhausens, the wives and mistresses whose loyalty outshone all the misery, mendicant friars who begged for visas, and no-man's-land vagabonds. Their tribulations over food, passports and love, their eschatological and political inner conflicts—everything that concerned them they confessed to the writer, to whom this whole life on earth was nothing but a temporary exile from eternity. And he listened to them all night long, a keen-eared, drunken father confessor.

Through the day. Through the night. Through the day . . .

The Lost Library

The devil take it, I must look up the book and find out how that goes on.

But where is the library?

The devil has taken it. . . .

The devil came for it in Vienna on the eve of the Sabbath, March 12, 1938. And everywhere in the city, at the Hofburg and on the Ring, at the Cafés Central, Herrenhof and Rebhuhn, wherever I tried to cut my way through and get back to the library, the streets were black with the devil's minions, howling, obscene, reptilian creatures rearing up on their hind legs, spitting the devil's slogans and roaring: Heil, Satan!

All you good spirits of the nineteenth century, stand by me. And God have mercy on all you freethinkers. Woe, woe, woe to us all who are your readers. The pandemonium of your romanticists, the scum of your naturalists, Dostoevsky's Raskolnikovs, Ibsen's inherited ghosts, Strindberg's Infernos and Huysmans' diabolists, Melville's Leviathans and Conrad's typhoon and Kipling's whole jungle have been let loose. A whole literature has got out of control and will no longer obey the sorcerer's apprentices. . . .

"God protect Austria!"

With these words the last chancellor of the Christian Austrian *Staendestaat* ended his last radio broadcast before he stepped aside for the Antichrist.

Two telephone conversations decided my fate and that of my books.

A fellow writer whom I called up in panic shouted back over the telephone: "Vienna is lost. The Czech border's blocked. Run for it."

Then I called up my landlord, who said, "You had better

not come home again. You have had visitors and they have already taken your books with them."

Never had I possessed my library so literally, so physically, as at that moment when I lost it. Never, not for decades, had I read it so thoroughly as I did right then, after the lightning had struck it. I ran through the books from A to Z. Never had I longed for it so intensely as then when I was leaving it in the lurch. Never had I felt that seductive power of its intellectual charms, its grace of form, as then when I was leaving it in an express train without turning back to look at it, or at this city of Sodom and Gomorrah where innocent readers like myself were being humiliated, butchered, dragged away from their desks, their libraries, their cafés and their beds into slavery.

That journey—via Salzburg, the now-sunken festival city of Mozart and the Reinhardt-Hofmannsthal *Welttheater*—to the end of a night was lighted up by the headlights of the motorized German Wehrmacht, and by the campfires of the new religious war. And in the overcrowded car, among writers of books, students of books, bibliophiles, I chanted in the singsong rhythm of the rattling train *The Song of the Love and Death of Cornet Christopher Rilke.* So that ever since then the first notes of the song have been inevitably connected in my mind with the loss of the library, the tumult of Heils in front of St. Stephen's Cathedral, the sulphur-and-pitch stench of the victory torches, the passport examinations at every station of this way of the cross, an infernal six-hour arrest at the Austro-Swiss border, and the Strindbergian back door of the customs office through which I escaped as if in a dream play to continue my flight back to Paris.

The Lost Library

As always early in the morning in Paris, columns of meat and vegetable carts blocked the streets leading from the Gare de l'Est through the central markets. As on every morning, black cats hung around the garbage pails on the church square at the Sorbonne. In the secondhand bookshop under the arcades of the Théâtre de l'Odéon the first browsers were already sniffling around, dressed in the gray ulsters of the unattached scholar. On the corner of the Rue de Vaugirard and the Rue de Tournon, however, construction workers were busy tearing down the sagging Hôtel Foyot!

In the *bistro* across the street Joseph Roth sat in his corner, writing and drinking, drinking and writing:

AT REST IN THE FACE OF DESTRUCTION

Opposite the *bistro* where I sit all day long an old building is being torn down, a hotel where I stayed for sixteen years, except for the period of my travels. The night before last there was still a wall standing, the back wall, waiting for its last hour. The other three walls, transformed into rubble, were already lying in the area which was half enclosed by a fence. The area seems remarkably small to me in comparison with the large hotel that once stood there. It always seems as if an empty space should look larger than one occupied by a building. But probably the sixteen years, now that they are over, seem so precious to me, so filled with gems of experience, that I cannot understand how they could all be tumbled together in so narrow a space. And because the hotel is now as shattered as the years which I spent in it, in memory the hotel seems larger to me than it actually must have been.

On the one wall I can still recognize the wallpaper of my room, a sky-blue, gold-veined paper. As I watch, a swinging platform is drawn up along the wall, two workmen standing on it. With picks and sledge hammers they pound away at the wallpaper, at my wall. And then, when the wall is stunned and brittle, the men tie ropes around it. The platform with the workmen descends. The ends of the rope hang down on the two edges of the wall. Each of the men pulls at the rope, and with a clatter the wall collapses. A dense white cloud of plaster and mortar hides the scene. Out of the dust cloud, like mighty millers whose business is grinding stones, step the two men, covered with plaster dust. They come across toward me, as they do several times every day. The younger man jerks a thumb over his shoulder and says, "Now it's gone—your wallpaper." I invite them both to have a drink with me, as though they had just finished building a wall for me. They joke about the wallpaper, the walls, my precious years. These workers are demolishers; tearing down things is their profession, and they are never employed on building. And that is quite right, they say. Each man to his trade. This fellow's the king of demolishers, the younger man says. The older man smiles. The two destroyers are in fine fettle, and so am I.

Afterward I sit facing the empty lot where the building was, and I hear the hours trickling away. You lose one home after the other, I say to myself. Here I sit with my pilgrim's staff in hand. My feet are sore, my heart weary, my eyes dry. Misery sits beside me and grows larger and tenderer every moment. The pain remains; it becomes so tremendous that it is kindly; terror roars at you and can no longer frighten you. And that is the worst of it; that is what leaves you inconsolable.

Joseph Roth sat in the Bistro de la Poste, an old man at forty-four. His painful, swollen feet could barely carry him to the neighborhood bars, or on Sundays to Mass— the times that he was not sleeping off a drunk. An unbaptized convert, he could not free himself from his Judaism. A bred-in-the-bone reactionary, he jeered like a Jacobin. A ruthlessly malicious hermit, he paid court to every female like an Austro-Hungarian army lieutenant—which he had never been. The more crazily drunk he became, the more lucid he was. And in the hermitage of his exile he was sought out by laymen of every school and by priests of every creed—by apostates, by heretics, by the unfrocked—and all saw to it that he did not go without drinks.

Every new predatory expedition in Europe increased his congregation of the spiritually impoverished. The fugitives fled to him as, with Vienna, then Prague, then Spain, the outer bastions against barbarism collapsed: the gigantic demolition work in which there were workmen pulling the rope at both ends.

While all the values of the West staggered, while the Judeo-Christian morality and the Hellenic aesthetics of the Occident reeled, only the staggering drunkard kept his balance. Like a sailor on board the *bâteau ivre*, the Drunken Ship, he adjusted to the wild waves.

Roth had entered the Order of Drunkards in order to escape the temptations of sobriety. Since language had been hollowed out down to the last verbal scrapings, the written word seemed to him literally the last support there was. In order to plumb its depths, he guzzled every kind of alcohol—select Bourgogne and Bordeaux wines, rum and beer, benedictines and Fernet Branca—and every variety of philosophy: Maimonides and Thomas Aquinas, Spinoza, Marx and Bergson.

And so every evening those who doubted their popes in the Vatican, the Kremlin and Valhalla made pilgrimages to his cave in the Bistro de la Poste. And he catechized them all on their mortal sins of style, while he completed his own *Legend of the Holy Drinker*—the parable of a Polish vagrant who dies of delirium tremens and goes to his God in the sacristy of the Chapelle St. Marie-des-Batignolles in Paris, at the altar of his patron saint, the writer Theresa of Avila.

And after putting the final exclamation mark to the sentence, "God grant all of us drinkers so easy and sweet a death!" Joseph Roth collapsed in the Bistro de la Poste like a section of crumbling wall, and died of delirium tremens three days later in the hospital. At his funeral before the walls of Paris, a gentleman in frock coat laid down a wreath with a black-and-yellow ribbon: in the name of His Catholic Majesty, Otto von Hapsburg. A priest, without his surplice, spoke a brief prayer. Jews said Kaddish. A writer, in the name of a group of Moscow-oriented literati, added a wreath with a red ribbon and the words: "To our comrade." A band of widowed sinners wept for their unique lover.

Each of us, with the deepest conviction, mourned the irreplaceable loss of so equivocal a character in these times of unequivocal characterlessness. Each of us mourned the unforgettable saint of the healing spring of alcohol in the Latin Quarter. Each of us mourned the disputations that were being buried here. And each, without condescending even to glance out of the corner of his eye at his nearest opponent, went his way, leaning on the pilgrim's staff of his metaphors. Each hurried off to be about his business, his obligations, his destiny, to continue the "flight without end"—as Roth had entitled an early novel of his.

The Lost Library

For afterward there was no rest for us Westerners, no time for meditation.

After the expulsion of the heretics, the seers and the Jews—the only ones who knew the magic words—the golem raged unhindered. For then there was nobody left who was able to tear the key cipher from its iron mouth. It desecrated the Sabbath by historic acts of violence; it demolished the hotels that hindered progress, tore off the roofs of private life, toppled over the coffee-houses, trampled under forests, meadows and pastures, the sanctuaries of creative individualism, and destroyed all the ties of love and friendship. A sheerly utilitarian fiend, it had no soul to inhibit its actions. It was guaranteed to be free of the short circuits that an individual will is subject to. It automatically regulated social welfare by the least common denominator of the masses, chemically purified the enjoyment of living, provided sewage outlets for the secretions and excretions of the unconscious, destroyed the breeding places of sensuality and sterilized the morasses of art and philosophy, exterminating all metaphysical germs.

A technological creation, the product of human hands, it grudged man everything he created in dreams.

Above all it hunted down books that dealt with pleasure and the sufferings of individuals—things outside itself, in other words. And it was especially bent on wiping out private libraries, which otherwise escape censorship.

And when the Spirit of the Nineteenth Century creeps back to earth by night, a restless ghost, driven by his hunger for reading, knowledge and culture, he finds nothing left of his library but a heap of splintered shelves, crumpled volumes with the bindings torn off, dirtied, half-charred proofsheets, tattered remnants of literary and scientific magazines, letters from publishers, complaints from writers, unfinished manuscripts, photographs, love letters, broken dishes, smashed vases, shaving brushes, cigarette butts, broken records of Scarlatti, Bach, Debussy and Flamenco dances, spilled ink and red wine— all the sweepings that a New Order produces. And to one side, as though in an access of extra rage and fear, the imprint of a golem's boot ground into a Hebrew Bible.

And as the Spirit looks around with the sightless eyes of inner vision, which pierces through time and space, he sees his collection of books among trophies of victory in the cellars of the secret police, below the chambers where the victims of the New Order are tortured. Here an erotic cultural curiosity from his "poison cupboard" is held in the trotters of a grunting torturer's assistant; there a bibliophilic rarity with risqué copper engravings dangles from the nervous fingers of a smirking high official of the Reich Chamber of Culture; there an incunabulum, or one of the Elzevir prints, or a Rabelais illustrated by Doré, or a first edition of Swinburne's *Poems and Ballads,* resides on the rare-book shelves of an "Aryan" dealer in pogrom loot. Heinrich Heine's ritual murder tale, *The Rabbi of Bacharach,* is in the "Institute for Criminal Research into Jewish Crimes." And *Don Quixote,* in a tattered, tear-stained, paper-backed volume of Reclam's 20-pfennig *Universalbibliothek* lies hidden under the rotten straw in a penal colony barrack.

All this the Spirit of the Library looks on, speechless. So, he thinks, people are still reading—and alas, still writing. For it does not escape his spectral gaze that one of the inmates of the concentration camp is keeping a diary—secretly, of course, in order not to be caught by the camp guards. The man's name gives him pause, because the Spirit knows him as a Polar explorer, a writer and a philanthropist for whom he had always had the greatest respect: Nansen.

But this is not Fridtjof. It is his son, Odd Nansen. Imprisoned by the Germans as a Norwegian hostage, he warms himself in the Arctic cold of the dictatorship by keeping a record for himself and his fellow sufferers.

Dante's hell could not be more horrible. There were almost a thousand Jews—Jews, that is to say, they were once human beings; now they were living skeletons, brutalized by hunger. . . .

It was commonplace for someone to seize upon a corpse in order to have something dry to lie down on. . . .

And amid all this activity loud-speakers barked, whined, screeched vulgar operatic hits, chorales, military marches, reports or victories, propaganda . . . Bach . . . Beethoven, Schubert, Schumann . . .

"Midnight, midnight, the middle ages!" the Spirit moans. And not knowing what else to say, he dissolves into the void of not-knowing.

But when did this damnable midnight of the West actually begin: in the nineteenth century of our enlightened fathers, or in our twentieth century of parricidal sons, self-blinded Oedipuses? I asked a theoretical physicist, a Nobel prize winner, this question—and received the following answer:

At noon the night begins, at midnight the day. Mankind is eternally swung back and forth between these opposites, but there is a third way, free of opposites, the way of peace, of understanding, of TAO. This abstraction means to the Taoists what Christ means to the Christians—the way of salvation. The opposition between salvation *ex opere operantis* in the East, *ex opere operato* in Christianity, will probably always remain unresolvable.

"I do not know whose son he is: without past, without future," the Tao Teh Ching begins. . . .

If I understand that rightly, life—any life, and so my own, for example—has just as much and just as little meaning as any book, as any creation of nature or the imagination that does not know whose spiritual child it is, a changeling composed of premises and counterpremises, dicta and contradictions, theses and antitheses, born in a mother tongue from which it cannot be translated without harm, raised in a paternal library so that, once expelled, it will never feel at home again, unless it finds somewhere in the outside world a sweetheart who can understand its longings and its passions even without words.

But if the changeling cannot arouse love in another, cannot awaken the nymph Echo, it will fall in love with itself like Narcissus, will be drowned in the pool that reflects its own image, or in the artesian well from which all book learning springs, or it will perish of hunger and thirst as it traverses the way of salvation through the Sahara of humanity. For it will be helpless, and no living creatures will be able to understand its cries for help.

As it is written in the *I-Ging,* the Buddhist guide to the wastelands through which the soul must pass:

"The mud at the bottom of the spring is not drunk. The beasts do not continue to come to a dry spring."

Epilogue
on a New England Farm

THROUGHOUT my exile I had carried around with me the idea of writing the autobiography of a literature, or to put it more precisely, the story of a library to which I was intimately related. In my youth such a library was as much part of the household of a progressive European as the crystal chandeliers, the landscapes on the walls, the Pre-Raphaelite allegorical nudes, the Japanese prints, the pianino and the Persian rugs, the gaslight, the feather mattress on the marital bed, and the champagne in the "special cupboard."

The idea was old, but the decision to write the book came to me on a New England farm whose remoteness made me remember step by step what I had read, forget what I had lost; whose roughhewn integrity recalled me to myself. All my aimless agitation, the aftereffects of Europe, vanished into the blue mist above the waves of hills that rose up to either side of the Housatonic. Every evening fiery summer sunsets in the greenish-black ravine of the near-by enchanted forest overlaid more and more the afterimage of the bloody sky above the burning city of Orléans when bombs destroyed the last bridge a few moments after we had crossed it. Once I had thought I would never forget the horribly grinning buck teeth of the police chief of Perpignan who had caught me preparing to escape across the Franco-Spanish frontier and had locked me up in an underground cell. Now that memory arose from my unconscious only as a vague association when I saw the alarming jaws of the snapping turtles in the farm pond. The name of the tyrant which had echoed from every radio and every headline and had pursued me from country to country, from dream to dream, all the way across the ocean to the Antilles and the American continent, now occupied my imagination less than the melodious evening call of the whippoorwill which incessantly repeated its own name.

In this rural environment I would also have recovered from the loss of my library, had I not again been led into temptation. But the farmer at whose place I was boarding had intimidated me by his gruffness at our first meeting, when he called for me in his car at the village railroad station—and then later, in his clapboarded colonial house, had completely baffled me by his reproductions of Picassos and Braques, his collection of records extending from Vivaldi to Stravinsky, and above all by a library containing Hindu and Chinese philosophy, the Greeks, English literature from Chaucer to D. H. Lawrence, and those dangerous, insidious Americans (Poe, Melville, Ambrose Bierce, O'Neill, Thomas Wolfe, Faulkner).

He was a reddish-blond-haired fellow of Scottish descent. To some extent the contradiction between his rough exterior and his private interests could be explained by his marriage to a sensitive girl whom he had met when he was living in New York.

He advertised in the newspaper for summer boarders ("writers preferred") and hired men ("race, religion, previous experience unimportant; Thoreauists, pacifists and lovers of Beethoven welcome"). He himself, in fact, might well have been the protagonist of a Tolstoyan parable: a peasant's son who had gone back to the bosom of nature, whose adolescent thirst had remained unsatisfied in the city, and who was now doing penance for earlier sins by monogamy, pacifism, vegetarianism and tilling the soil.

But to describe the harpoonlike sharpness of his blue eyes and the bluntness of his fatalism, the narrative style of a Melville, a Stevenson or a Joseph Conrad would have been more appropriate (although, or perhaps because, he could not stand these very writers).

He was as self-righteous and obstinate as an Ahab, as intolerant as Ibsen's country pastor in his creed of God's goodness. And as soon as we reached the point during our midnight disputes—for by day he plowed his tobacco fields and I tilled my typewriter—he would interrupt me in the middle of a sentence, tramp over to his bookcase and proceed to crush me and everyone else present by reading aloud for hours.

His chief and only thesis was: "God is love!"

And he spoke the phrase so ferociously, so challengingly, that the devoutest believer would have been provoked into contradicting him.

No argument could touch him. It was no use demonstrating that the Incarnation of eternity and infinity should not be assigned human attributes, which involved temporal and spatial limitations; nor to refer to recent European history for examples of the opposite, nor to suggest that it was beyond human strength for men enduring incendiary bombs, gas chambers and death in freight cars to summon up the faith, love or hope which our friend demanded of them.

No matter what the provocation, he nevertheless cursed

every impulse of hatred, any active resistance to the men of violence. For evildoers, like the carriers of a disease, were a scourge of God, instruments of divine goodness; they made possible salvation through suffering for a metaphysical guilt that was subject to no statute of limitations.

"For a guilt incurred when?" I asked.

He took a book from the shelf and read:

There is a terrible distance between the newborn infant and the five-year-old child, an abyss between the embryo and the newborn. . . . But from non-existence to the embryo it is no longer an abyss, but the unsearchable.

"Hm. By whom is that, anyway?"

"Tolstoy!"

"Then you think that when a baby is crippled by, say, poliomyelitis, or strangled by a warrior of the master race who is drunk with victory, it is probably being punished for an embryonic or otherwise unsearchable crime?" At this point his three-year-old child spilled a cup of boiling hot coffee over my trousers. "I thought that in your hierarchy all children were angels of God."

He instantly opened another book:

There cannot be complete extinction of evil, not even in heaven, for nothing that has ever been an essential component of the human spirit can ever again be extinguished. Spirits—yes, even the angels no doubt—therefore took their abused organs of generation, in which evil remained latent, even into heaven. From time to time they are permitted to experience their sins in the flesh once more, but not without profit to themselves;

for by such changes in the condition of their blessedness they are constantly admonished to make progress. And so the renewal of man, which began on earth, continues through all eternity.

"Thanks all the same," I said, "but I don't have that much time in my life."

"The educational implications seem to me all wrong too," his wife said, pensively caressing her naughty youngster. "Who wrote that?"

"Swedenborg!" he replied, throwing down the name like a glove.

Even without books he and I continually misunderstood each other, although we were not so far apart on basic principles. Our fundamental misunderstandings stemmed from varying usages of expressions like horror, terror and misery.

My host had been divinely punished in life by rejection, near-starvation and humiliation just as much as I, the European, had been; but he had never suffered the absolute punishment that infallible dictatorships can inflict. Instead, pursued by ill luck, he had become involved in the stupid struggle for existence in a time of economic depression whose effects were as incalculable as this New England climate, where intense heat could suddenly give way to a furious, icy hailstorm.

Like the American pioneers he was in a constant state of alarm over the redskin tricks of the weather and the changeableness of his fellow countrymen. From childhood on he had learned to evade each of his Calvinist father's storms of temper, and in the slums to steer clear of the sudden attacks of youthful gangs. Still little more than a boy, he had lost the sweetest illusions of youth to a tavern tart as cosmetically angelic as a Hollywood star and as sophistical as a script writer—in circumstances that would have made the toughest Zolaist blush. In occupational versatility he far outdid me, the European: he had been a dishwasher, an undertaker's assistant, a musician in an itinerant jazz band. He had driven over the highways with his wife and child, through the purgatories of Faulknerian filth, through the monotony of Main Streets, "so lost, so naked and so lonely—wandering forever"—such as only one of Thomas Wolfe's Americans could endure. He had been an overseer of cotton pickers in Alabama and the publisher of *avant-garde* books (for conscientious objectors to military service and for sexual-Symbolist poets) which bankrupted him. Now he was a tobacco farmer in New England, laboring under a crushing mortgage.

But: God is love! was the moral he drew from all his personal experiences.

"Before we moved here," he narrated, in so printable a style that it sounded as if he were reading aloud, "we had rented a bungalow with two acres of land on a farm that belonged to a general's widow from Boston. There was a drought that summer such as had not been experienced for twenty-three years; there was no drinking water within a radius of nineteen miles except for the well near the main house. I wanted to fetch water for my family, but the old woman sat in the rocking chair on her porch, and when I came with the pail she raised the rifle she was holding, took aim and fired twice at me and once at little Bill, my oldest boy. She missed us by a hair. All of us almost perished of thirst. She was a wicked woman, but as I learned later on she profoundly deserved pity. She suffered from terrible frustrations—all her life she had longed for a husband who understood good books, fine paintings and classical music; and she imagined that she was surrounded by enemies and by creditors who demanded payment for the blood her late husband, the general, had spilled. . . . He had confessed his guilts to her on his deathbed. You see, grace comes to the hardest-hearted tyrant sooner or later, and he is warned by fear: Look into yourself and pour out your heart. . . . It is only we who do not hear and see that. . . . But you see, God is love!"

"Such profoundly-to-be-pitied characters ought to be lovingly isolated in asylums," I suggested, "before they become so terrified by their fears that they liquidate all grace, and out of frustration kill off all talent."

"Talent!" he barked at me. "What the devil has talent to do with grace?"

"Oh, please, dear, don't get excited," his wife admonished him.

Without waiting for my answer, he pulled a book from his shelves and read aloud without pause for periods or paragraphs the story of the Black Monk.

A Russian student of "psychology" plans colossal achievements, epoch-making masterpieces, in order to solve the universal riddles of humanity, and especially of Russian man and of the nineteenth century. But—I was sleepy and only half listening—he accomplishes nothing. Exhausted by studying, alcohol and nicotine, he returns to the estate he has inherited from his father and marries a childhood sweetheart. Running his father-in-law's orchard, he might have recovered; but unfortunately the Black Monk appears to him. The Black Monk is the phantom of utopia who traffics only with prominent personages, a Buddha, a Mohammed, a Shakespeare. The monk drives him out of his mind and literally talks him to death with lectures on "Eternal Truth" and the inescapable obligation of genius to promote the good of humanity. . . . In short, the tale of an unfortunate madman. But as G. K. Chesterton once put it: "There was something about him that is the making of every Bolshevist; something I have felt in every Russian I ever met. I can only say that when he walked out of the door one felt he might just as well have walked out of the window. He was not a Communist; but he was a Utopian, and his Utopia was far, far madder than any Communism."

"Well, what do you say to that?" my host demanded as peremptorily as the Black Monk.

"Very interesting," I said, shaking myself to wake up. "By the way, who wrote that?"

"Chekhov. Well, what do you say?"

"I . . . just a moment, I must think it over . . . I . . . it seems to me that this unsuccessful student's claim that a talkative Black Monk appeared to him and preached eternal truth is . . . well . . . I think Chekhov left out his proof, as so often happens in stories of illuminati and geniuses. I don't see——"

"Because you're blind," my host interrupted me. "The student saw the Black Monk, didn't he? That means he had a vision. . . ."

"A rather confused one."

"That doesn't matter. The vision assured him of the fact that he had genius, even though he couldn't make a concrete demonstration of it."

The Lost Library

"In other words, that he had no talent. All mediocrities legitimize their lack of talent with some such Black Monk; the meanest creatures make a dogma of virtue out of their intellectual poverty. They are the leaders who show the way to the Promised Land by God's grace and their own— Pharaoh, Moses and the Messiah all wrapped up into one, assassins who carry out the covenants of the Old and New Testaments, infallible lawgivers swearing by everything that's holy to them and by the indubitable truth of their vision of some Black Monk. He has authorized them to love humanity, the race, the nation, without mercy. Oh, yes, they're the Eternal Truth all right. That means, revealed mediocrity personified. And they can prove it in black and white by the signature of the Black Monk on their innocent white souls. And . . ."

But at this point my host glared at me, finished off his drink, went into the dark living room, switched on the phonograph and put on Mozart's *Eine Kleine Nachtmusik*.

Outside the August sun lifted the mist that overhung the valley, but toward noon the sky suddenly filled with ashen gray clouds; a furious hailstorm lashed the slopes of the hills and the rolling fields. When it was over, my host's tobacco fields were ruined—alone among all the tobacco farms in the surrounding region, as though a mean Providence had intended to strike him alone.

The evening of this black day—it happened to be a Friday the thirteenth—we sat in glum silence around the oak table. Even the children and the gaunt hound were gloomy and quiet. The farmer, bewhiskered like a sailor after his ship has weathered a typhoon, clumped over to the bookshelves, threw himself into an armchair and read silently for a long time.

"Yes, here it is," he said at last, and because the prevailing mood was one of frustrated vexation, he made his voice gentle, in order to compel our attention.

And the Promised One spoke:
You have a right only to the work, but not to the fruits. . . . Be neither tempted by the fruits of your action, nor give yourself up to inaction.

Look upon success and failure as the same; be steadfast in yoga and do your duty. For yoga is equanimity.

Pitiable indeed are those who labor for the sake of success. Whose mind is not excited by misfortune and who does not crave the pleasures of the senses, who is free from all ties, from fear as well as vexation, is truly a holy man and consistently wise.

But he who is concerned with the pleasures of sense becomes dependent upon them.

Out of dependence comes craving, and craving engenders vexation.

Vexation engenders self-deception; self-deception causes loss of memory; judgment is destroyed, and the loss of judgment (that is, the ability to distinguish between true and false) destroys the man.

"From the Bhagavad-Gita," he explained didactically, and then he clapped the book irritably shut and frowned so that his brow became as wrinkled as that of an angry old woman.

"I must put the children to bed," his wife said. "And don't forget you have to go to town to see the insurance company tomorrow morning, and before that you must fill out the hail-insurance form."

"Suffering," he said. "That is what counts. That is the only truth; it is what ennobles man and raises him above the animals. His ability to reason and his artistic gifts are presents from God. Love is for God, suffering for man." He stared at the kitchen chair where his wife had been sitting. "I judge all writers by their ability to achieve suffering. It means nothing to me how well a writer writes or how brilliant his inspirations are if the blooms and fruits of his writing are more important to him than the trials and torments of his failures; if he does not console me by his insight into the vanity of his work, and by the fact that he too has suffered and knows that God loves him whose whole harvest he has taken as a sacrificial offering. If we did not have sin to renounce, how could we receive grace? . . . And if you do not want to express your sufferings so that God may hear you, why are you writing at all?" he suddenly turned to me and interrogated me with vexation in his voice.

"Well, if you want an impromptu answer—naturally there are any number of motives for writing. Desire for success—claiming the fruits—is the first one that occurs to me. Our birth is our first success. And to enjoy life, to satisfy our cravings, is what impels us. To take the example closest to hand, for what purpose did my parents beget me? Because—forgive me if I resort to literary language—they liked the bodily pleasure. And at the same time they desired the fruit of it—the child. Any child, of course, but a child of theirs, to increase their joy and to perpetuate it. That was the purpose—but unfortunately things turned out differently from what they expected. Because my mother was a musician, she probably wanted to have a Mozart. Because my father was an "enlight-

275

ened," polemic writer, he wanted a kind of Zola for a son. The result was myself, a writer with musical sentiments and fierce resentments, as poor as Mozart and exiled like Zola. I have become what my parents wanted me to be, but not at all the way they wanted it. And to correct this error I have taken to the pen as others take to the sword, or to cash registers or lawbooks or science, theology or philosophy. The word has become what its begetter, its author, wanted it to be, but not the way he wanted it. Therefore he is eternally trying to correct it. His corrections are our eternal suffering, his improvements our eternal misfortune. One version, the eighth (though why it happened to be the eighth I don't know), which he published in Sanskrit under the pseudonym of Krishna, alias Vishnu, is the Bhagavad-Gita. But since he was apparently dissatisfied with the success of this work, he added a decalogue and a testament as an appendix, and when those too were a colossal flop he altered the story in favor of his incarnated son who allegorically did penance on the cross for all our offenses. Since the beginnings, since, that is, within the memory of man, things have only become worse after every attempt to improve the Creation. The individual at best can only correct himself, unless he is put through a merciless process of correction by the Almighty, and is simply erased. Self-correction is the most anyone can attempt, and the second best is to embellish the world, to entertain it, to comprehend its sufferings and divert it from them. There is the purpose. When I write I take note of all the corrections: tortures, mutilations and final extinction. I take note of them, laughing until I am weeping with laughter. I recognize that it must all be endured, but whether it has a meaning—no, I wouldn't vouch for that."

My host paced nervously around the table, took a book at random from the mantelpiece and read:

"If one's wise," he said at last, "one doesn't ask whether it makes any sense. One does one's work and leaves the problem of evil to one's metabolism. That makes sense all right. . . .

"Because it's not oneself," said Sebastian. "Not human, not a part of the cosmic order. That's why animals have no metaphysical worries. Being identical with their physiology, they know there's a cosmic order. Whereas human beings identify themselves with money-making, say, or drinking, or politics, or literature. None of which has anything to do with the cosmic order. So naturally they find that nothing makes sense. . . ."

"Are you or aren't you paying attention?" my host asked.

"I beg your pardon?" I said. My attention had wandered to the dog, who was lying asleep at my feet, all four feet twitching, uttering fierce growls; apparently he was troubled by wild dreams and metaphysical worries.

"Yes, oh, yes . . . Who wrote that anyway?" I asked cautiously.

"Aldous Huxley. From his novel, *Time Must Have a Stop.*"

"May I borrow it? Huxley strikes me as a typical personality of our era, in the same way that Martin du Gard's Jean Barois was typical of the Third French Republic—a true offspring of the nineteenth century, of *raison* and *clarté,* an anticlerical intellectual, a socialist of the school

277

of Jaurès. In the end he turns to the Catholic faith for his soul's peace. That type of European is extinct now. Huxley, the descendant of the great Darwinist biologist Thomas Henry Huxley, has been a model pupil in all the schools and has graduated from all of them: materialism, psychoanalysis, the metaphysics of modern science, genetics, and lately Buddhism, Yogaism and even spiritualism. . . . Even the title of the novel attracts me."

"It's from Shakespeare—*Henry IV,*" my host said, with an undertone of discomfiture.

But thought's the slave of life, and life time's fool;
And time, that takes survey of all the world,
Must have a stop. . . .

"The last words of Hotspur when he is dying after his fight with the prince."

"Yes, 'there is no end to Shakespeare,' " I said. I too had the feeling that there was a third person in the kitchen, or behind the curtain (or was it a moth?). " 'There is no end to Shakespeare' is the title Goethe gave to an essay on the poet. Shakespeare, he wrote, ought to be performed word for word, even if both the actors and the audience perished in the process. Yes, that is what Shakespeare's power is like; even when he goes in for the crudest histrionics, for blood and thunder, he has such a dramatic hold on you that you can't get away. And what is even more fantastic is the dynamics of his language. Every verse in his monologues sounds like the last words of a dying man. 'To be or not to be'—that is always the question with him, the inescapable question. When he talks about life, Shakespeare does not speculate like a philosopher on an abstract *élan vital* or on the logic of the psychic

278

processes. Thought's the slave of life. . . . So conscience doth make cowards of us all. . . . He is not concerned with the meaning of existence; he does not construct any reasonable pattern for reality from which governments, church and state can then derive their own divine rights and their divine infallibility and their divine privilege of reforming the world. What worries him is what dreams may come. . . . Because we are thinking creatures, slaves of our existences who need commandments, laws, regulations, who have to be able to shift responsibility to some superior, be it the nation, the race or a God, we have installed an Almighty. Because we think, we live in constant fear of a father of all things, who is war. Religious war, struggle for survival, class struggle, competition, the battle of the sexes, then the conflicts of the family, then the struggle of the heirs—we would long ago have annihilated our intellect itself in a Pyrrhic victory, would long since have become a race of technological ants (the only zoological collective group we know that fights wars), if we had not been able individually to escape into the imagination. For the imagination is a realm where thoughts and feelings are free and equal, where every ego, no matter how insignificant, is one with the supreme personality, with the Self— the Sanskrit Atman, if I understand the meaning of that term correctly. In the imagination alone is the harmony of good and evil, of love and of sin, of beauty and ugliness, of voluptuous dream and nightmare. That realm, the realm of art, was—I use the past tense deliberately—was to us Europeans what, I suppose, the realm of Yoga discipline has been to the Hindu. That is, it involved unceasing exercise, a self-imposed training of the self, labor

without reward, without any prospect of attaining theological worldly dignities. Its only goal was to attain to
pure contemplation. To the Hindu that meant to empty
oneself entirely of images. To the Occidental: to fill his
emptiness with images . . . In both cases the guide was
intuition, or, as we call it in animals generally, instinct.
For the 'lower orders' also have their artists, like the bees,
the wasps, the spiders and the songbirds. In the economy
of nature the songbirds strike one as almost sheerly ornamental, as tragicomically superfluous as poets in human
society. But let us not underestimate them. One of the
boldest explorers of this world, Savinien Cyrano de Bergerac, who on one of his expeditions to the *'Etats du Soleil'*
ran afoul of the dictatorship of the songbirds, speaks of
one cruel method of execution practiced in that country.
The condemned man was tied to a somber cypress—it must
have looked like one of those painted by Van Gogh—and
exposed to a regiment of the country's melancholy musicians who filled his ears and soul with mournful melodies
until he died of melancholy. . . . So let us pray—I mean
to say, write—to conclude my speech, since by now I've
drunk up all the gin. Time must have a stop . . . Amen.
Prosit!"

"I guess it's time to go to bed," my host said, glancing
at the empty bottle. "I have an awful lot to do tomorrow
and can't sit up talking about literature. . . ."

I spent a restless night.

My bed rolled, lurched and dipped. A hurricane shook
the house, and the portentous howl of it reminded me of
that gust of wind which had shattered a plane tree on the

Champs Elysées and crushed to death a friend of mine, the young writer Ödön von Horváth—five years after he had successfully escaped into exile. In his hotel room, one floor below my own, stood two glasses of red wine, half filled, for him and for the woman we both loved. Next to the glasses lay the manuscript of a novel he had just begun, entitled:

A POET EMIGRATES TO AMERICA

And the last lines he had written, the ink of them still fresh, read:

Yesterday the storm was even fiercer. In the night the nets were ripped, and one sloop did not return. Perhaps it will reappear a year hence with black sails, a phantom without a soul skimming over the water.

The morning edition of *Figaro* reported:

A storm which descended upon Paris last night caused several deaths. In the Champs Elysées it toppled a plane tree. Seven persons underneath the tree were not injured, but one, a Hungarian, was killed. . . .
The same gust of wind overturned a fishing sloop in the Channel. All men aboard were drowned. Early this morning the boat, unmanned, beached on our coast. . . .

The uncanny part of it was that this item of local news was so complete, in fact was wholly in the same style and, as it were, written in the same breath as the author's inspiration—as though it had sprung from the same impulse, the same imagination. It was almost as if some other writer had completed in a few words the briefest of all novels, finishing the theme of *A Poet Emigrates to America,* so that now nothing was lacking but the subtitle: "Or, the Irony of Fate."

It was as though the author who wrote the news item were identical with the author who formed the subject of the item, as though my friend Horváth were describing his own end post mortem, just as the hero did in an earlier work of his, the novel in monologue, *A Child of Our Time.* That novel begins:

> I am a soldier.
> And I am glad to be a soldier.
> Mornings, when the hoarfrost covers the meadows, or evenings when the mist comes out of the woods, when the grain billows and the scythe flashes, whether it is raining or snowing or the sun beams gaily, whether it is day or night, again and again I feel the joy of standing in line with my fellows.
> Now my life suddenly has meaning again! I had already given up to despair. . . . The world was so hopeless and the future so dead. I had already buried the future. But now I have it again, it has been resurrected from the grave, and I shall never let it go again.

So the soldier begins his soldier's life, the life of a child of our time, a fool of our time, and he ends that life by freezing to death on a bench, and beyond his own death, beyond his end, as crudely earnest as ever, he delivers his report.

The storm howled, and suddenly the door to my bedroom was wrenched open and my host strode in. He planted himself in front of my bed, pinned me with one well-aimed harpoon look, and said mildly, "I have a short-

short story I want to read to you. Its title is: 'The Lost Library.' I hope you don't mind. . . ."

"Oh, let me sleep, please," I wanted to say, but I could not utter a sound. I tried to raise my hand to write a protest in the air, but my arm would not move.

And, holding nothing in his hands, he read:

I am the Black Monk. I am your dream of Europe, which you cannot escape. Yes, I am. Be still. Don't contradict. I know what you want to say—that I am not black and wear no cowl, and that in general I correspond no more to my description than Terror corresponds to yours.

I am the archetype, who doesn't look like what he really is, but rather looks to each man the way he really imagines him. I am the legend which I myself have told about myself. Metaphorically by fire and sword, and officially by censorship and forced labor, I have eliminated all other descriptions of myself. I have done this for so long that all who have really seen me have described me only as I would have them do, and everyone else has copied from them, so that at last out of millions of plagiarisms I have become an original, out of millions of legends a fact. I have in fact become the Eternal Truth.

Now no one can put me out of his mind any longer. For I exist in a book, in the library of the nineteenth century. I am as real as anything that is printed. I am —fifty-fifty. One half research and the other half dogma—in other words, a double half-truth, which signifies a brutal phantom reality. For only the half-truths can be made real, made black on white. . . .

Blacker than the Black Plague, than the blackest superstition, the blackest despotism, the blackest future, I am the Black Man, the children's bogey, *la bête noire* of the Enlightenment. I am the masked hangman of your freedom, the torturer of your libido, the Messiah

283

of your technological miracles—and I shall decapitate your intellect. I am the author of all tragedies and martyrologies, of all the divine, human and diabolic comedies that you will ever write. In them I repeat myself and copy myself until I am bored to death.

Out of paper thou art and to paper thou shalt return —to birth and death notices, to items of local news and historic slogans, to bank notes, statistics, passports, police files, death sentences, to rags and to grass—until after the last correction is made you stand in the book of books, printed in a single line: "God is love!"

A joke of world history.

He stopped speaking as the Black Monk, and suddenly addressed me as my American host. "When you came here to board," he said, "you claimed you were a writer and that you were writing a book—a book about books. But maybe you're just a common swindler. Maybe tomorrow when you wake up you'll find you have nothing but a piece of blank white paper. Or possibly you will not wake up again at all; possibly you have never existed at all. Possibly you are a work of fiction trying to get yourself published as nonfiction—poetry pretending to be truth. Possibly you're no different from your whole library."

At this moment I pulled myself up out of sleep with all my might, but he was already at the threshold. With a crash that shook the floor, he slammed the book behind him, so that the earth trembled.

THE END

Index

Index

Index

Index

Index

Notes

P. 15:
dulce et decorum est. . . .
"It is sweet and fitting to die for one's country."

P. 16:
midinettes: shopgirls
Justum et temace. . . .
The man of firm and righteous will,
No rabble, clamorous for the wrong,
No tyrant's brow, whose frown may kill,
Can shake the strength that makes him strong . . .
(translation by John Conington)

P. 20:
Weh im Kerker noch. . . .
Ah, me! this dungeon still . . .
Hemmed in by many a toppling heap
Of books worm-eaten, gray with dust,
Which to the vaulted ceiling creep,
Against the smoky paper thrust, . . .
Ancestral lumber, stuffed and packed . . .
(translation by Bayard Taylor)

P. 30:
rien ne l'arrêtera: nothing can stop it!

P. 36:
raison d'état: reason of state; national interest

P. 43:
jeunesse dorée: gilded youth; rich and fashionable young people
rastaquouère: social intruder, especially foreign
A nous deux, maintenant!: "It's between the two of us now!"

P. 44:
romans feuilletons: journalistic novels

P. 51:
école de Médan: Zola's home was at Médan

P. 54:
Inter faeces et urinam nascimur: We are born between feces and urine.

Notes

P. 75:
Alles Vergaengliche. . . .
Everything transient
Is but a parable;
What is insufficient,
Here comes to pass.

P. 76:
coup de théâtre: sudden dramatic turn of events in a play

P. 88:
honnêtes gens: honest people
coiffure pleureuse: literally, "mourner's hairstyle;" an idiom for a hairstyle with ringlets.

P. 93:
l'implacable enfant: literally, "implacable child," but here to mean "flirt."

P. 94:
Fais ce que vouldras!: Do what you will!
Écrasez l'Infâme: Crush the infamous.
On y danse: There we dance, from a French children's song.
le Caveau: the cave
La Ballade de la Mauvaise Réputation: "The Ballad of the Bad Reputation."
pauvre Lélian—ce cochon de Verlaine: Poor Lelian—that pig Verlaine.

P. 97:
Au Lecteur. . . .
To the Reader
He would willingly make rubble of the earth
And swallow up the world in a yawn;
This is Boredom which with ready tears
Dreams of hangings as he smokes his hookah.
You know him, reader, this delicate monster.
De la vaporisation. . . .
Of the vaporization and centralization of the Self. That is everything.

P. 99:
Exilé sur le sol. . . .
Exiled on the ground amid hooting crowds

Notes

He cannot walk because of his great wings.

P. 101

Plus vague et plus....
More vague and more soluble in the air
With nothing in it heavy or fixed ...
II
It must also be that you do not go about
Choosing your words without some carelessness:
Nothing dearer than the shadowy song
Where Indecision and Precision are joined.
IX
Let your verse be the happy adventure,
Afloat on the restless morning wind,
Which goes about smelling of mint and thyme...
And all the rest is literature.

P. 108

jupon: petticoat
Il faut être absolument moderne: One must be absolutely modern.
Des châteaux batis....
From châteaux built of bone comes mysterious music.

P. 109

poules de luxe: high-class prostitutes

P. 112

défauts: faults or defects

P. 114

Damné par l'arc-en-ciel: Damned by the rainbow
Fileur éternel des immobilités....
Eternal spinner of the blue immobilities
I yearn for Europe with its ancient parapets.
Pourquoi Christ ne m'aide-t-il pas....
Why does Christ not come to my aid by giving my soul nobility and
liberty. Alas, the Gospel is passé ...

P. 130

Il n'y a ici, comme partout, qu'um problème mécanique!: There is here, as
everywhere, a mechanical problem!

Notes

P. 131
Guerra sola igiene del mondo: War, the only hygiene of the world.
La guerre divine . . . l'effusion du sang: une vertu expiatoire: Divine war .
. . the effusion of blood is a true expiation.
Je songe à une guerre, de droit. . . .
I dream of a war, of right or of force, of logic quite unforeseen. . . . It
is as simple as a musical phrase.

P. 133
À Travers L'Europe. . . .
Across Europe
Rotsoge
Your scarlet face your biplane becoming a hydroplane
Your round house where a sour herring swims
I need the eyelid key . . .
I searched the roads a long while
So many eyes are shut at the edge of the roads . . .
Open open open open open
Look, but really look
The old man washes his beet in the basin . . .
And you you show me a terrifying shade of blue . . .
But your hair is in the trolley
All across Europe in tiny multicolored lights . . .
Un méteque: French derogatory term for foreigners from the south,
from Greek "metic."
d'une logique bien imprévue: logic of the unanticipated

P. 138
Et Vigny, plus secret. . . .
And Vigny, more secretive, retreated before noon as if to his ivory tower. . .

P. 140
ce magasin de toutes les choses utiles: the storehouse of all useful things

P. 146
arbiter elegantiarum: authority in matters of taste

P. 147
poèmes simultanés: poetry to be read aloud by multiple voices simulta-
neously

Notes

P. 152
eo ipso: by that very fact

P. 171
Madame Bovary, c'est moi: I am Madame Bovary.
JE est un autre: I is another.

P. 172
Heurige Wein: current year's wine

P. 191
Un nouveau mal de siècle: A new sickness of the century.
La délectation morose. . . .
The morose pleasure, the masochism, the anxiety . . .

P. 192
Certe, il viendra le rude et fatal châtiment: Certainly, hard and fatal punishment will come.
Monumentum aere perennius: a monument more lasting than bronze

P. 193
levée en masse: mass military conscription

P. 200
A-E-I-O-U: a symbolic device of the Hapsburg emperors that has various interpretations, including "Austria will be the last [nation] in the world," or "Austria will endure forever."
A noir, E blank, . . .
Black A, white E, red I, green U, blue O: vowels,
I shall recount someday your mysterious origins.

P. 203
Vanitas, vanitatum vanitas: vanity of vanities
thanatos: death
Tu auras le pix Goncourt: You will have the Goncourt prize! The *Prix Goncourt* is awarded to the "best and most imaginative prose work of the year."

P. 204
caudillo: strongman
Comme un animal fort qui. . . .
Like a strong animal that oversees her prey—

Notes

P. 214
acte gratuit de liberté: free act of liberty

P. 215
Fils à papa, toi–même: The son of the father, even you.

P. 217
Je prends mon bien où je le trouve: I take my own property where I find it.

P. 218
Vous pouvez disposer: You may sit.

P. 219
Weltschmerz: world-weariness, or romantic sadness
Weltanschauung: worldview
mal au coeur: heartache

P. 227:
L'esprit seul peut tout changer: Spirit alone can change everything.

P. 232:
ein Verhaeltnis: a ratio or proportion

P. 235:
Apage, Satanas: Begone, Satan!

P. 250:
Quelle tempête dans l'encrier!: What a storm in ink!
Chemins qui ne mènent. . . .
Paths that lead nowhere
Between two meadows
Diverted from their goal. . . .
(from the *Quatrains Valaisans* by Rainer Marie Rilke)

P. 252:
coeur innombrable: numberless heart; also, the title of Noailles's first collection of poetry.

P. 264:
ex opere operantis: from the action of the doer
ex opere operato: from the work done